JOSEPHUS
AND THE JEWS

THE RELIGION AND HISTORY OF
THE JEWS AS EXPLAINED BY
FLAVIUS JOSEPHUS

BY

F. J. FOAKES JACKSON, D.D.

FELLOW OF JESUS COLLEGE CAMBRIDGE
AND BRIGGS GRADUATE PROFESSOR OF CHRISTIAN INSTITUTIONS
IN THE UNION THEOLOGICAL SEMINARY
NEW YORK

BAKER BOOK HOUSE
Grand Rapids, Michigan

ALEXANDRO NAIRNE

SACRAE THEOLOGIAE PROFESSORI REGIO

OLIM DISCIPULO NUNC AUTEM QUANTO MAGIS,

CETERISQUE MEIS DISCIPULIS,

PER ORBEM TERRARUM DISPERSIS,

HOC OPUSCULUM

NON SINE VERECUNDIA IAM SENEX

D.D.D.

A.D. IV ID. AUG. MCMXXX

Paperback edition issued
by Baker Book House Company

ISBN: 0-8010-5069-3

First published 1930

PHOTOLITHOPRINTED BY CUSHING - MALLOY, INC.
ANN ARBOR, MICHIGAN, UNITED STATES OF AMERICA
1977

INTRODUCTION
TO PAPERBACK EDITION

Josephus remains an enigma. He admired his country-men who would die rather than face enslavement by the Romans, yet he abandoned the cause of Jewish freedom to save his own life. Josephus was an intensely practical man. He was interested in antiquity, particularly the antiquities of his own people. From the Jewish point of view he sold out to the Romans. He found a comfortable, and probably satisfying, life explaining the Jewish community, its history and institutions, to the Romans. He spoke with appreciation of the stricter Jewish sects, although they would not find in him the piety they demanded.

F. J. Foakes Jackson's book was published in 1930. It is quite recent as these studies go, but in the Middle East and in Biblical studies the decades since 1930 have brought great change. The basic information of the book is still valid. Some of the nuances will be updated.

Foakes Jackson knew Zionism as a political movement looking toward the establishment of a Jewish state in Palestine. He saw the modern Zionists in terms of the ancient Zealots. Josephus, as an advocate of peace with Rome, was thus placed in an anti-Zionist stance. Judaism must be "a divinely appointed rule of life," not a "scheme of worldly domination" (xv).

It is understandable that Josephus did not become a hero of later Judaism. Josephus, Foakes Jackson, and many others have wrestled with the problem of defining a Jew. Is a Jew simply a member of a religious denomination? If so, why speak of a state with political boundaries, forms of government, coinage, and armies? A good Jew, such as Josephus, would be content to live in a Roman state.

Others in Josephus' time, as well as today, view the Jew as part of a people—an ethnic entity—with all the desires and rights of self-determination held by any other ethnic group. The debate goes on.

About the time of the establishment of the Jewish state (1948) archaeologists and Biblical scholars were hearing about a series of amazing discoveries made near the northwest corner of the Dead Sea. The discoveries became known as the Dead Sea Scrolls and were attributed to a community of Essenes which flourished during the first century before Christ and the first century of the Christian era. The latter part of this period was contemporary with Josephus. We can read the books from the library of an Essene community even as we read Josephus' description of the Essenes.

Similarly we can now read the detailed discussion of the fall of Masada in the text of Josephus, and examine in detail the excavated site. Josephus is vindicated as a good historian. Archaeology helps us to fill in details, but the basic outlines are still valid. Josephus gives us information concerning the sects (he calls them "philosophies") of the Judaism of his day, which basically coincides with New Testament descriptions of various Jewish sects.

Foakes Jackson provides a useful outline of major subjects treated in Josephus' writings. True, Josephus emerges as a man of expediency rather than a man of real faith and conviction. Still he is an able writer and an eye-witness to the events immediately preceding the fall of Jerusalem (A.D. 70), and an interesting commentator on the attitude of one segment of Judaism toward the Jewish Scriptures. His chief task was to explain the Jewish mind to the Roman mind. In that he succeeded.

Since F. J. Foakes Jackson subscribed to the more liberal trends of theology, some readers may discover in this volume that his view of the inspiration of Scripture was less than adequate. Nonetheless, his contribution in clarifying the works of Josephus remains valuable unto all Bible students.

Charles E. Pfeiffer

CONTENTS

PART I

LIFE AND FAITH OF FLAVIUS JOSEPHUS

CONTENTS

CONTENTS

PART III

Independence of the Jews

PAGE

CHAPTER VI.—The High Priests as Warrior Princes . 95

Obscurity of the Jews in Palestine—The sons of Tobias—Hyrcanus, the son of Joseph—The Jews as tax farmers for Egypt—Palestine annexed by the Seleucids of Syria—Antiochus Epiphanes—Revolt of the Maccabees—Dying speech of Mattathias—Religious aspect of the revolt—Early victories of Judas—Dedication of the Temple—Judas in Eastern and Northern Palestine—Not all Jews attached to Judas—Antiochus V, Eupator—The Syrian kings recognise the Jewish religion—Defeat of Nicanor and death of Judas—Jonathan—Battles of Judas the Maccabee—Embassy to Rome—Desperate condition of the patriots after Judas' death—Disintegration of the Syrian monarchy—The *Acra* taken by Simon—Prosperity under Simon—Embassies to Sparta and Rome—Antiochus VII and John Hyrcanus—Further successes of Hyrcanus—Pharisees and Sadducees—Aristobulus I, Philhellene—Alexander Jannaeus.

CHAPTER VII.—The Fall of the Asmonaeans and the Rise of the Herods 121

Rivalry of the sons of Alexander Jannaeus—Power of Rome in the East—Pompey—The rivals appeal to Pompey—The family of Antipater consistently pro-Roman—Pompey besieges Jerusalem—Pompey's Jewish policy—Gabinius—The Idumaean influence in Jewish affairs—Antipater—Herod the Great—Brigandage—The Parthian invasion—Herod proclaimed king—Herod marries Mariamne—Herod and Augustus—Splendour of Herod's reign—Herod's domestic troubles—Herod and the sons of Mariamne.

PART IV

The Roman Yoke

CHAPTER VIII.—The Descendants of Herod . . . 139
(Archelaus—Antipas—and Agrippa I)

The Herodian family—Importance of the descendants of Mariamne. (See map and table annexed)—Herod's fortune—Jewish riots against Archelaus—Herod's family plead the cause of Antipas before Augustus—Speech of Antipater, son of Salome—Nicolaus defends Archelaus—Petition of the Jews—Partition of Herod's dominion among his sons—Archelaus in Judaea—Antipas as tetrarch of Galilee—Antipas marries Herodias—Antipas in the Gospels and in Josephus—Antipas and the Parthians—Antipas and Jesus—War with Aretas—Deposition of Antipas—Fortunes of Herod Agrippa—Early life of Herod Agrippa—Herod Agrippa returns to

PART V

AFTER THE FALL OF JERUSALEM

CONTENTS

PAGE

CHAPTER XVI.—JOSEPHUS AND THE NEW TESTAMENT . . 259

Did ' Luke ' borrow from Josephus ?—The Enrolment—Rebellion of Judas of Galilee—Theudas—Was there a rebellion under Judas of Galilee ?—Chronological notice of the Baptist—Josephus and the political divisions of Palestine—Lysanias of Abilene—Annas and Caiaphas—Herod the tetrarch and the death of the Baptist—Herod Agrippa I—The Egyptian and the *sicarii*—Acts does not seem to owe information to Josephus.

APPENDICES

NOTE.—The quotations from Dr. H. St. J. Thackeray's translation in the Loeb Library are used by kind permission of the editors and of the publishers (London: Messrs. Heinemann; New York: G. P. Putnam's Sons).

INTRODUCTION

WHY JOSEPHUS DESERVES ATTENTION

Object of this book.—The works of Flavius Josephus have long been widely circulated, and in most devout families used to be regarded as hardly less indispensable than the Bible itself. Yet it is perhaps permissible to say of them that, though they are widely known and freely quoted, yet upon the whole they have been rarely read intelligently. But, although Josephus is frequently entertaining, it is no easy task to construct a consistent history out of his voluminous literary output. For this reason, among others, he has, on the one hand, been treated with undeserved contempt ; whilst, on the other, many have accepted his statements with somewhat unreasonable credulity. This book is an endeavour to supply a key to the study of an author who, with all his defects, is not only a remarkable man and an historian of exceptional value, but is personally worthy of study as a character of almost unique psychological interest.

Unique value of Josephus' writings.—The life of Josephus was both long and varied. Born in A.D. 37, the year that Caius (Caligula) was proclaimed emperor, he probably survived till the early days of the reign of Trajan (A.D. 98–117). Brought up in exclusively Jewish circles, priestly, legal, and ascetic, he was in youth untouched by Greek culture. Yet after his active civil and military life was over, and he was fully thirty years old, he first applied himself to a literary career, and produced two considerable histories in the Greek language. Pro-Roman in sympathy, he wrote an excellent apology for the religion of his own people, a work full of curious learning and containing really eloquent passages. Educated as a rabbi in the legal subtleties of the Schools, he made Judaism at least intelligible to the cultured Gentiles of his time, and showed that the history of its adherents was deserving of attention. Because Josephus was a Jew and wrote about the affairs of his nation, it has too often been assumed that he may be neglected by the secular historian. Yet his descriptions of Roman armies, their siege operations, triumphs, and the like, throw much light on the military affairs of his age ; and but for him we should never have known how Caligula was put to death, or Claudius was recognised as Emperor. It is indeed difficult to imagine how much we should have lost had the works of Josephus perished. Without him the remarkable family of the Herods would be practically unknown ; how Jerusalem was destroyed by Titus, despite his famous arch in Rome, would be a matter for conjecture ; and with the exception of the story of the earlier Maccabees the history of the Jews from the close of the Old Testament to the coming of Jesus would be a blank. Nay more, the New Testament itself would be filled with names and allusions to events to which the reader could have no possible clue. Further, even when a Jew attempts to relate what happened to his nation in the first centuries of the Christian era, the only contemporary literature available for his purpose is to be found in Josephus, the Gospels, and the Acts of the Apostles.

Neglect by the Jews.—Yet, strange to say, the Jews actually allowed all Josephus had written to fall into oblivion. This may be in part accounted for by the fact that this historian is conspicuously deficient in patriotism in so far as the national aspirations are concerned, despite his admiration for the law of Moses, and his defence of the antiquity of the people of Israel, who, as their Scriptures prove, enjoyed the protection of God from the first. But this explanation does not account for the Jewish neglect of the entire national literature outside the Old Testament, all of which would have perished but for the preservation of some by the Christian Church.

Value of Josephus for the criticism of the sources of the New Testament.—No one interested in the study of the methods of ancient historians, or even of the sources of the record of facts in Scripture, can dispense with Josephus. In the New Testament, especially, scholars recognise a variety of sources for the Gospels and Acts. As their predecessors had done in regard to the Old Testament, they have realised that earlier documents were employed to produce the Hebrew and Christian books as we now have them. But what these sources were is purely a matter for conjecture; and symbols have been invented to express what each one is supposed to have been. Ingenious and even scientific as much source-criticism has undoubtedly proved, it is after all hypothetical, as it is possible only to hazard a guess as to what documents were used, and to imagine the method adopted by the writers or redactors in producing the present books of the Old and New Testaments. But Josephus gives us hints both as to his methods and as to his sources of information.

Josephus' account of his work as an historian.—He informs us that he wrote his first draft of the 'War' either in Hebrew or Aramaic for the use of the Jews in the East, and that Vespasian and Titus encouraged him to prepare a Greek version for Hellenic readers. He confesses that he made a thorough study of Greek literature, and paid attention to its syntax and rules of composition as a preparation for his task. During his stay in Rome the emperors gave him ample leisure for his undertaking, and some ten years after the fall of Jerusalem the 'War' appeared in Greek. One would expect that a work of this kind, produced by an Oriental who must have thought in the language of his youth, would show traces of its origin by numerous Aramaic if not Hebraic modes of expression. On the contrary, the seven books of the 'War' are written in excellent Greek. We are not, therefore, surprised when Josephus incidentally tells us that he made use of the assistance of others in order to render his Greek acceptable to cultured readers; Dr. Thackeray has pointed out how in the composition of the history different collaborators were employed. May it not be permissible to enquire whether some books of the New Testament have been subjected to similar literary revision, and, though Hebraic in origin, have been Graecised almost beyond recognition? The Epistle of James, for example, reads in English like an Old Testament prophecy, and in Greek like a well-written *diatribe*.

Josephus rewrote parts of his narrative.—The 'Life,' as compared with the 'War,' as also the 'Antiquities,' furnish examples of the way in which Josephus rewrote his narrative after a lapse of years, and made alterations, either because he was not satisfied with what he had previously said, or on account of the criticism of his friends and the misrepresentation of his foes. Thus, in the 'Life' he evidently tries to correct some of the impressions which the story of his proceedings in Galilee had made upon those in authority in Rome. For some less obvious reason he has represented Herod the Great in the 'Antiquities' as a less heroic figure than in the earlier 'War.' But, whilst we detect signs of revision in most early writers but can only conjecture what they had originally presented, in Josephus we have before us what he first published, and the subsequent modifications of his judgment.

Sources used by Josephus.—We have several examples of Josephus using sources with which we are acquainted. The most notable, of course, is the way in which he wrote the history of Israel with the Bible before him, and the use he made of 1 Maccabees, the later part of which was either unknown to him, or deliberately disregarded. Like all who have to write about events before their own time, Josephus must have used early authorities; and although most of these are lost, we still can learn something by his method of adapting those which are still extant. As to the New Testament, with the possible exception of Luke's use of Marcan sources, we have no definite guide, and much can be conjectured from what Josephus has done.

'Zionism' in the days of Josephus.—One modern problem comes to our mind in the study of Josephus, namely, that of the Jewish claim to predominance in Palestine now known as 'Zionism.' In the days of Ezra and Nehemiah, Judah was the home of successive colonies of returned exiles, who rebuilt Jerusalem and its temple, and restored their ancestral law in an amended form. At first an obscure and almost unnoticed community, persecution ultimately made the Jews a formidable band of warriors burning with religious fanaticism. Within two generations they established a priestly monarchy which overspread the territory ruled over by David, and became a dominant power in Palestine, increasing daily as the Syrian Greek empire hastened to decay. When the Romans came, they introduced the stern discipline of an alien race. In the interests of peace and order the Greek and Syrian cities, which the priest-kings had annexed, were given independence, and the Jews confined to their own territories. For a time, however, Judaism once more became rich and powerful, but under a king whom the people detested, partly because he was of alien birth, and also because he was a nominee and a servant of the hated Romans. The question then arose, whether the Jews ought to submit patiently to the yoke of Rome or rise in rebellion, and by God's help regain their political independence. Josephus was one of a powerful minority who believed that God was opposed to all schemes of worldly domination for his nation, whose duty was to observe the Law and submit to the world order, as supported by the supremacy of Rome. To him Judaism, as a divinely appointed rule of life, seemed inconsistent with national aggrandisement ; and though for a time he fought, as he says, valiantly for his people, he was glad to surrender to Rome, and desirous that his countrymen should do likewise. Much of his history is an exposure of what is now called militant Zionism ; and in his opinion a Jewish patriot was little better than a bandit. To judge by some utterances in recent times, the spirit to which Josephus was so firmly opposed is not altogether dead ; and his history, if unpalatable to some Jews, should at least be carefully studied by all.

Josephus not yet a dead author.—In a word, Josephus is not a dead author, but is still alive with a message for this generation. His character cannot command the admiration of any reader, whether he be Jew or Gentile, but this is no reason why he should be neglected. He is our only authority for a long and important period of human history; and though it is customary to disparage his abilities, the more one studies him, the more remarkable they appear to have been. His patriotism may have been exceedingly cold, his religion mechanical rather than spiritual, he may have profited unscrupulously by the labours of others, and be guilty of serious inaccuracies. Nevertheless, he should be carefully studied before he is condemned, or refused his place as the great historian of Judaism, and an invaluable contributor to our knowledge of antiquity. For a Gentile to write about Josephus requires some courage, but the present writer hopes that if he has nothing extenuated, he has at least set down nought in malice.

PART I

LIFE AND FAITH OF FLAVIUS JOSEPHUS

CHAPTER I

THE LIFE OF JOSEPHUS

Four works by Josephus.—Josephus has left four separate works which posterity has preserved. The two earlier are major efforts, the 'War of the Jews' and the 'Antiquities.' At the end of his life he produced two minor treatises, an autobiography, known as his 'Life,' and two books in defence of Judaism, popularly designated 'Against Apion.'[1]

The 'Life' and 'Against Apion' compared.—Dr. St. John Thackeray in his excellent edition and translation of our author, which is appearing in the Loeb series, has done wisely in devoting his first volume to the 'Life' and 'Against Apion,' because they are the best introduction to a proper understanding of Josephus. His judgment of the relative merits of these pamphlets—for they are little more—is sound, though open to criticism in one respect.

> 'The two treatises,' says Dr. Thackeray, 'form a strange contrast ; we see our author at his worst and at his best. . . . In style, arrangement and treatment they are so different that one would hardly suppose them to be contemporary productions from the same pen.'[2]

This is a perfectly just estimate of the relative merits of the 'Life' and the books 'Against Apion.' The 'Life'

---

[1] Strictly speaking, only the second book should bear this title. Book I. consists of a proof of the antiquity of the Jewish nation.
[2] Loeb Classical Library, *Josephus*, vol. i. p. xiii. Dr. Thackeray points out that Richard Laqueur in his *Der jüdische Historiker Flavius Josephus* (Giessen, 1920) has developed a theory that the main part of the *Life* was anterior to the composition of the Greek edition of the *War*.

is not an autobiography at all, the greater part being a rather lame justification of the conduct of the author in Galilee during some six critical months at the beginning of the Jewish war in A.D. 66 and 67. The style is crude ; as a literary production the ' Life ' is scarcely above contempt. Nor is the argument convincing. After perusing it, one cannot help wondering whether Justus of Tiberias, the rival historian, to whom it is a reply, was not right in his estimate of Josephus, who appears by his own confession to have taken no little credit to himself for a course of action hardly to be described as straightforward.

When we turn to the ' Apion ' we are in a different atmosphere. The arrangement of the argument is good, the style that of a well-read and learned man. Josephus' enthusiasm for his nation and its religion is evident ; and the treatise takes a high place among apologies for any faith. The question naturally arises whether the two documents can be the work of the same man. That this is so admits of little doubt in the minds of competent critics ; and, if this judgment be correct, it shows how precarious it is to pronounce that style is a sure test of difference of authorship.[1]

If, in the opinion of the critic and the scholar, the ' Apion ' is an admirable production, the ' Life,' with all its defects, is of far greater value to the historian. Every apology in the course of time becomes obsolete and out of date, but the story of the experience of an individual, however crudely and inaccurately told, is of importance for the light it throws on the character both of the writer and of the circumstances of his age. In this spirit it appears permissible to approach the subject of Josephus' so-called ' Life.'

---

[1] The resemblance of the language of Josephus to that of the New Testament throughout the *Life* is remarkable. In this section alone, besides the word προκόπτειν, we find ἀκριβέστερόν τι γνῶναι (*cf.* Acts xxiii. 15, 20 ; xxiv. 22) ; αὐτομάτως φυομένη (*cf.* Mark iv. 28) ; πολιτεύεσθαι in the sense of ' manner of living ' (*cf.* Acts xxiii. 1 ; Phil. i. 27). It seems that the difference in style between the *Life* and the other writings of Josephus can be accounted for by the fact that, whereas he employed elsewhere the assistance of scholars, here he writes in the Greek he was accustomed to hear and speak.

Josephus' position in later life.—Our author, as he was approaching old age, could with justice congratulate himself on having secured a very comfortable situation. He was in high favour with the imperial household, had wealthy patrons, and had won a recognised position as a man of letters. Moreover, he was living a life of dignified leisure as an historian of his own time, luxuriously lodged in a mansion in Rome, with access to copious libraries and official documents. In addition to all this he enjoyed the privileges of a Roman citizen, and the comfort of an assured income. But as a Jew his position had been secured by incurring the undying hatred of his countrymen, many of whom, not without reason, regarded him as a traitor to his people. True, he had supported the national faith valiantly with his pen, but at the price of having in his youth surrendered his sword to the enemies of the nation. This was never forgotten by those who had fought for Israel, and Justus of Tiberias, who had been his rival when hostilities broke out in Galilee, wrote a reply to Josephus' account of the war, in which our author must have been represented as a time-server, faithful neither to Israel nor to Rome, ready to betray either to serve his own interests.

Subjects treated in the ' Life.'—In the ' Life ' Josephus attempts to explain his actions in Galilee, and to justify his conduct throughout the interval between the retreat of Cestius Gallus, the governor of Syria, from Jerusalem in November of A.D. 66, and the arrival of Vespasian and his son Titus at Antioch to conduct the war in the spring of A.D. 67. The book in some editions is divided into 430 sections. Of these, the first 16 relate the early career of the writer, sections 17–406 are devoted to events in Galilee before the arrival of Vespasian, and 407–421 to the rest of the Jewish war. The last nine sections relate the subsequent life of Josephus till A.D. 100, when Herod Agrippa II. died.

Ancestry and early life of Josephus.—Josephus is careful to inform his readers that he came of a very illustrious priestly family and belonged to the first of the twenty-four sacerdotal courses. ' On my mother's side,' he adds, 'I am of royal race, since she was a daughter of Jonathan, the first of the Asmonaeans to rule over Israel in the capacity of High Priest.'

With such a pedigree, preserved in the public records, Josephus felt he had a sufficient answer for those who sought to impugn his noble ancestry.[1]

The intelligence of this high-born youth was worthy of his race. By the time he was fourteen he was so renowned for his learning that the chief priests and leading rabbis used to consult him on difficult points of the Law.[2] At the age of sixteen he studied under Pharisaic, Sadducean, and Essene masters, and attached himself particularly to an ascetic named Bannus, who had retired to the wilderness, 'wearing only such clothing as trees provided, eating only what grew of its own accord, and bathing by day and night in cold water to preserve his purity.' At the age of nineteen Josephus decided finally to adopt the manner of life prescribed by the Pharisees.

Visit to Rome.—When he was twenty-six Josephus was entrusted by the authorities at Jerusalem with an important embassy to Rome, charged with the task of obtaining liberty for some priests whom Felix had sent to Nero, doubtless on some charge of treason. On the way his ship, containing six hundred in all, foundered in the Adriatic; and, in the words of our historian, 'they swam all night,' until eighty, including Josephus himself, were rescued by a Cyrenian vessel and landed safely at Dicaearchia, or Puteoli, near Naples, as Paul

---

[1] *Life* c. 1 (3–5). The pedigree of Josephus is given :

    (1) Simon Psellus, contemporary of Hyrcanus I. (High Priest 135–106 B.C.)

    (2) Matthias, known as the son of Ephaeus, who married d. of Jonathan (High Priest 153–144 B.C.).

    (3) Matthias Curtus, b. 135 B.C., first year of Hyrcanus.

    (4) Joseph, b. 70 B.C., ninth year of Alexandra.

    (5) Matthias, b. 6 A.D., tenth year of Archelaus,

    (6) Josephus, b. 37 A.D., first year of Caius (Caligula).

[2] The education of Josephus reminds us of what Luke records of Jesus, and of what Paul says of his own training. The progress of all three is described by the word προκόπτειν (Luke ii. 52 ; Gal. i. 14). It is characteristic of the vanity of Josephus that, whereas Luke makes Jesus sit in the Temple as a disciple in His 13th year (Luke ii. 42–46), the rabbis consult Josephus when he is about 14.

had done after his shipwreck a few years before.[1] At Rome Josephus evidently became well known and made important friends, as was seen later when he surrendered himself to Vespasian after the capture of Jotapata in Galilee. The famous Jewish actor Aliturus introduced him to Poppaea Sabina, the wife of Nero, who gave him valuable presents and obtained the liberation of the priests, of whom Josephus says that fear of defilement had made them while in Rome refuse all food except figs and nuts.[2] Josephus was in Rome about A.D. 64 ; but he says nothing about the fire, which may have occurred in July, after he had left the city.

Return to Jerusalem.—On his return to Jerusalem Josephus found that hostilities were commencing and war with Rome was inevitable. The hot-heads in the city were resolved to drive things to extremities, though, as he declares, he risked his life to avert the catastrophe. The retreat of Cestius Gallus from Jerusalem and the discomfiture of his army in the pass of Bethhoron brought matters to a crisis, for the Greeks and Syrians had openly attacked the Jews and put many of them to death in such places as Scythopolis in Galilee, and Damascus, in consequence of which the Jews prepared to fight.[3]

Discrepancies in the ' Life ' and the ' War.'—The narrative in the ' Life,' in which Josephus tells of his difficulties in Galilee, abounds in details which would be quite uninteresting were it not for the personal element which is introduced. What actually occurred is not easy to discover, since Josephus gives a very different version in the ' War,' which he wrote to glorify his own valour

---

[1] *Life*, c. 3 (15–16). *Cf.* St. Paul's shipwreck, Acts xxvii.–xxviii. For Josephus *swimming* all night, *cf.* 2 Cor. xi. 25, where Paul says : ' Thrice I suffered shipwreck, a night and a day have I been in the deep.'

[2] *Life*, c. 3 (14). This abstinence may be compared with that of Daniel and his companions (Dan. i. 8–16), and is analogous to the abstinence practised by those described by Paul as living on vegetables, because of their scrupulous faith (Rom. xiv. 2).

[3] *Life*, cc. 4–6 (17–27). The outbreak of the war in Jerusalem is given at length in *War*, ii. 15–17 (309–456). This includes the great speech of Herod Agrippa II. in which he dissuaded the Jews from provoking the hostility of Rome, ii. 16 (345–401).

and the military prowess displayed by Vespasian and Titus in defeating him. The object of the 'Life,' on the other hand, is to show that at heart he was always well disposed to the Romans and desired peace above all things.

Josephus in Galilee. — According to the 'War' Josephus was sent to Galilee in a military capacity. Foreseeing that Galilee would bear the brunt of the invasion of Palestine, he fortified the villages which were most capable of bearing a siege. He organised magistracy throughout the country, and spared no effort to secure the good will of the people. But his great work consisted in disciplining the army in Roman fashion, and he soon found himself at the head of 60,000 infantry, 350 cavalry, and 4500 mercenaries. In the last named, and in a picked bodyguard of 600 men, he placed especial confidence. Josephus then tells us concisely, what he relates more fully in the 'Life,' of the opposition he met with at the hands of his inveterate enemy, John of Gischala.[1] But in the 'Life' Josephus is sent to Galilee with two other priests, Joazar and Judas, with instructions to induce the disaffected (πονηρούς) to disarm, and to hand their weapons over to more experienced soldiers who would be more prepared to resist the anticipated advance of the Romans.[2]

Factions in Galilee.—The task of the delegates was hopeless, for Galilee was seething with faction. There was the party of Herod Agrippa II., opposed to engaging in war with Rome. There was the moderate section of the Jews, headed by Josephus, who desired peace if possible, and if war were inevitable, a resistance to Rome in which national differences would yield to the necessity of presenting a solid front to the enemy. Lastly, there were the extremists, or brigands (λῃσταί) as Josephus terms them, who desired at once to engage in war not only with the Romans but with the other Jewish parties. Josephus was the special object of their resentment and, as the sequel will show, this was not altogether without justification.

[1] *War*, ii. 20–21 (556 ff.).   [2] *Life*, c. 7 (28 ff.).

Local jealousies also played their part in exciting the three factions against one another. The three great cities of Galilee each represented one of the parties. Sepphoris was on the side of the Romans[1] ; Gabara seems to have been neutral[2] ; Tiberias espoused the cause of John of Gischala and the extremists, its strongest passion being envy of its rival Sepphoris.[3] Josephus represents himself as popular with the major part of the inhabitants of Galilee ; the only city which he found he could implicitly trust was Tarichaeae.

Hostility to Josephus.—The chief and the most unscrupulous of the personal enemies of Josephus was John of Gischala, who, as a local chieftain, claimed the allegiance of the people of Galilee against the representative of the priesthood of Jerusalem. It would appear that John's patriotism was accompanied by an aptitude for making money, as he is said to have realised a fortune by securing a monopoly in the sale of oil. Josephus did what he could to allay the resentment of so formidable an antagonist. He gave way to John in the matter of gathering a supply of corn in view of the threatened invasion and allowed him to fortify his native Gischala. Though there is no allusion in the 'War' either to Pistus of Tiberias or to his unscrupulous son Justus, we learn from the 'Life' that they were hostile to Josephus from the first. Nor was Josephus much better supported by his priestly colleagues, who were more occupied in collecting their dues than in preparing for the war, and were by no means above taking bribes from the authorities in Galilee. It would be tedious to detail at length the story of Josephus' experiences in Galilee as found in the 'Life' ; a few incidents related by our author suffice to give a clearer idea of the condition of Galilee in the months preceding the arrival of Vespasian.

Herod's palace in Tiberias.—When Herod Antipas built Tiberias he is said to have incurred much opposition from the strict Jews, who refused to live in the city because he had chosen a site which had been largely used as a burial ground. He was consequently compelled

---

[1] *Life*, c. 8 (31) ; c. 65 (346).   [2] *Life*, c. 25 (123).
[3] *Life*, c. 17 (87).

to settle the lowest of the people as tenants in the fine houses he had erected.[1] But when Josephus came to Galilee the city had become a centre of fiercely orthodox Judaism, and the fact that it had occupied the site of a cemetery seems to have been forgotten. It still contained an object of offence in Herod's palace, which had probably been erected by Greek artists, since it contained figures of animals. This the priests of Jerusalem had ordered Josephus to destroy, though the more moderate party in the city, to whom he had attached himself, were at first unwilling to co-operate. Whilst they were debating, the extremists under Jesus, son of Sapphias, who was the leader of the boatmen and the disorderly element, burned the palace, after pillaging it of all its valuables, and proceeded to murder the Greek residents in the city. In the meantime, Josephus, who had gone to Upper Galilee, hastened back to Tiberias and rescued what he could recover from the plunder of the palace in order to restore it if possible to its owner, Agrippa II. Here we see that Josephus is doing his best to convince his readers that, far from sympathising with the insurgents, he was doing all he could to further the interests of his subsequent patron, Herod Agrippa.

The bandits of Dabaritta.—The solicitude of Josephus for the interests of Agrippa was displayed when some young men of Dabaritta attacked the wife of Ptolemy, one of the *procurators* (stewards) of the property of that monarch. She was travelling under the protection of a troop of cavalry across ' the Great Plain,' when her cavalcade was assaulted and she had to flee for her life. The brigands brought the spoil to Josephus at Tarichaeae, who declared that he would sell it and devote the proceeds to the repair of the walls of Jerusalem. Disappointed of their booty, the men of Dabaritta went round the country declaring that Josephus was a traitor who meant to betray Galilee to the Romans. Josephus admits that his intention was to restore their stolen

---

[1] *Antiq.* xviii. 3 (36). Is it permissible to suppose that Josephus, in penning this description of their origin, was actuated by his resentment at his treatment by the inhabitants of Tiberias ?

property to Ptolemy and his wife, but there is little doubt that his chief anxiety was to provide for every contingency and to secure the support of Agrippa, if things went ill with the nationalists.[1]

Josephus persuades the Tarichaeans.—But even in friendly Tarichaeae the duplicity of Josephus had exposed him to popular resentment. Jesus the son of Sapphias went into the hippodrome there with a copy of the Law of Moses in his hands, and exhorted the people to punish the traitor. Josephus clothed himself in black, with his sword suspended from his neck, and fell on his face in tears before the people. He told them: ' If I have done anything worthy of death, I do not refuse to die.'[2] The money he had taken from the robbers would not be given to the Romans, nor to Herod, nor would it be sent to Jerusalem ; but the people of Tarichaeae could spend it on fortifying the town. This brought the Tarichaeans over to his side, but Tiberias remained hostile to Josephus and besought aid from Agrippa. At last, by various devices, or, to use our author's favourite word, ' stratagems,' Tiberias was for the time subdued, and the cities of Galilee were fortified against the expected invasion.

Attempt to have Josephus recalled.—The next move on the part of the enemies of Josephus was to induce the authorities in Jerusalem to recall him. The instigator was John of Gischala, furious at the success of his rival as a popular leader in Galilee. An embassy was sent to the High Priest, Ananus, consisting of John's brother Simon,[3] Jonathan, the son of Sisenna, and about a hundred armed men. They secured the support at Jerusalem of Simon the son of Gamaliel, a Pharisee of illustrious birth, who had the reputation of being able to retrieve a losing cause by his wise advocacy. Simon, however, found it no easy matter to persuade Ananus

---

[1] *Life*, c. 26 (126 ff.).
[2] *Life*, c. 29 (141–142). There is a striking similarity between the language of Josephus on this occasion and that of St. Paul before Festus, Acts xxv. 11 : " if . . . I have committed anything worthy of death, I refuse not (οὐ παραιτοῦμαι) to die.'
[3] *Life*, cc. 38–40 (189–203).

to recall Josephus, but where eloquence failed, bribery succeeded, and a deputation was sent to prejudice the Galilaeans against Josephus. It consisted of three Pharisees, Jonathan, Ananias, Jozar, and a young man of high priestly descent named Simon. These secured the support of a Galilaean named Jesus, who was commander of a force of six hundred soldiers (*hoplites*).

Josephus' dream.—Josephus was saved from yielding to depression by a dream, in which he saw someone standing by the bed and telling him to sorrow no longer but to expect greatness and prosperity, for his present and future trials would only increase his coming felicity. When he presented himself to the people he was further encouraged by their earnest protestations of loyalty, and he proceeds to relate the arrival of the deputation in Galilee, the plots against him, and his own 'stratagems.' The authorities of Jerusalem acted towards Josephus much as they had towards St. Paul, when they endeavoured to persuade Festus to send him to be tried at Jerusalem in order that they might kill him on his journey thither.[1]

The enemies of Josephus desire a conference.—Here is an account of the delivery of the first letter of Jonathan, the chief of the envoys, inviting Josephus to a professedly friendly conference :

'It was the second hour of the night, and I was dining with my friends and the chief men of Galilee (τῶν τῆς Γαλιλαίας πρώτων, cf. Mark vi. 21). My servant announcing the arrival of a Jewish horseman, this fellow, being called in by my orders, gave me no salute whatever, but reached out the letter and said : "The party who have come from Jerusalem have sent you this. Write your reply immediately as I am in a hurry to return to them." My guests were astonished at the soldier's audacity. I for my part invited him to sit down and join us at supper. He declined. I kept the letter in my hands as I had received it, and conversed with my friends on other subjects. Not long after I rose, and, dismissing the others, directed four only of my

[1] *Life*, cc. 42–44 (208–219) ; *cf.* Acts xxv. 3.

closest friends to stay, and ordered my servants to set on wine. Then, when no one was looking, I unfolded the letter, took in at a glance the writer's design and sealed it up again. Holding it in my hands as though I had not yet read it, I ordered twenty drachmas to be presented to the soldier for travelling expenses. He accepted the money and thanked me for it. Noting this cupidity as the surest means of gulling him, I said: " If you will consent to drink with us, you shall receive a drachma for every cup." He readily assented; and, in order to win more money, indulged so freely in the wine that he became intoxicated, and unable to keep his secrets any longer to himself. He told me, without being asked, of the plot that had been hatched, and how I had been sentenced to death by his employers.' [1]

The above is a revelation of the baseness of the intriguers as well as of the diplomacy of Josephus. Josephus relates at some length all the ramifications of the plot against him ; and how, though strongly supported by the people of Galilee, he did his best to avoid causing a civil war. The centre of the storm was Tiberias, and constant debates were held in the Prayer-house (προσευχή) of the city, which seems to have been not only a synagogue but the most suitable place for a public meeting. Once more Josephus had to take refuge among his faithful friends at Tarichaeae, where he received the news that the priests at Jerusalem had confirmed his appointment. A long section of the ' Life ' is an answer to the strictures of Justus, contrasting his ignoble conduct with the honourable behaviour of Josephus. [2]

Vespasian arrives in Galilee.—But now Vespasian and his army were in Galilee, and on the 18th of June, A.D. 67, had invested Jotapata, a place which Josephus had made the strongest fortress of Galilee, and where he was in command.

Defence of Jotapata.—As the defence of Jotapata, related in the ' War ' but not in the ' Life,' is the great

---

[1] *Life*, c. 44 (220–225), Thackeray's translation.
[2] *Life*, c. 65 (336–367).

military event in our author's life, and is told by himself with no sparing of self-approval, it may be justly regarded as an invaluable description of a contemporary siege as well as a most instructive study of the psychology of the writer. One is amazed how a man who has no small opinion of his courage and is constantly commending his own magnanimity could relate without shame so much to his own discredit. No one can doubt the ability and resourcefulness of Josephus in peace, and he was probably a brave leader when fighting was necessary, but no one could be more devoid of any sense of shame when the opportunity of saving his own life occurred.

Jotapata was built on a cliff, precipitous on every side except the north. This Josephus had taken every precaution to fortify so as to prevent the enemy from occupying the ridge which commanded it. So surrounded was the town by hills that it was invisible to the traveller till he came close to it. Vespasian placed his camp on the northern hill, nearly a mile from the walls, whence he could overlook the city, and might hope to overawe the garrison by the sight of his formidable army. The two first assaults were repelled, and the siege began in earnest. Earthworks were erected despite the desperate efforts of the Jews to prevent them, and the artillery engines, numbering one hundred and sixty, were set to work. Showers of missiles were discharged from the catapults, and huge stones drove the defenders from the walls.[1] But Josephus was equal to every emergency. He disguised his soldiers as animals, and sent them through a deep gully to obtain supplies. When the water was nearly exhausted, he drove the Romans to despair by hanging out wet clothes as if there were an abundant supply in the city. He led sallying parties to burn the works erected by the besiegers. In fact, he declares that he did all that a brave and skilful captain could to save the place. Then, as he artlessly informs us, he thought it time to save himself. He called together

[1] *War*, iii. For the description of the advance of a Roman army see c. 6 (115–126); of Jotapata, c. 7 (158–160); of the artillery engines, c. 7 (166–168).

the leaders in the city and explained that, if they were destined to perish it would do them little good if he was killed. On the contrary, Vespasian, when he heard that so important a general as Josephus had fled, would probably abandon the siege. Indeed, Vespasian's real motive in thus obstinately pressing the attack on so insignificant a place as Jotapata, was to destroy its experienced commander. Finally, Josephus declared that he was not trying to save himself by leaving Jotapata, but only hoped to secure help from outside by mustering a force to relieve the city. Strange as it may appear, the besieged would not listen to these plausible arguments, but hinted that they would take care that he did not desert his post.[1] Seeing that escape was impossible, he exclaimed: ' Now all hope of deliverance is past, let us renew the fight, for it is an honourable thing to sacrifice life for glory, and to do some noble exploit which posterity will not forget, before we die.' For about a fortnight more the fighting continued, and on July 20, A.D. 67, Jotapata was taken. The incredible number of 40,000 are said to have perished in the siege of what had previously been a small and almost unnoticed village.[1]

' By some divine providence,' Josephus succeeded in stealing away from the enemy, and by way of a deep pit entered a cavern where forty other distinguished (τῶν ἐπισήμων) men had taken refuge. These fugitives had a good supply of provisions and had hopes of escape, if they could but hold out till the vigilance of the enemy had somewhat abated, but a captive woman betrayed the hiding-place, and three officers, among them Nicanor, an old friend of Josephus, were sent to beg him in flattering terms to surrender.

Josephus resolves to save his own life.—Josephus now summoned his religion, such as it was, to aid him. He remembered that as a priest he could interpret the holy books, and know the meaning of dreams and divine the ambiguous oracles of the Deity. He realised that in the visions of the night he had been told that the Jews

[1] *War*, c. 7 (337).

must perish and Vespasian become Emperor, and, fortified by these assurances, Josephus put up this remarkable prayer :

> ' Since Thou who didst create the people of the Jews hast seen good that it should sink into the dust ; since fortune is transferred to the Romans ; since Thou hast made choice of my spirit to announce the things that are to come, I voluntarily surrender to the Romans and consent to live. But I go to them not as a traitor but as Thy servant.'

Josephus has many merits as a writer ; if at times inaccurate, he is generally entertaining ; his character, if ignoble, is interesting as a study ; his vanity is frequently amusing ; but when he means to be pious he is frankly repulsive, and never more so than in this hypocritical prayer.

But the forty fugitives in the cave were no more deceived than the Deity ! They pointed their swords at him and threatened to kill him if he surrendered to the Romans. Yet, according to his own story, he maintained his calmness and began to treat the dilemma in which he found himself philosophically (φιλοσοφεῖν ἐπὶ τῆς ἀνάγκης). He declares that he made his companions a long, dreary speech on the crime of suicide,[1] to which his companions are supposed to have listened respectfully, if unconvinced. He then proposed that they should kill one another and cast lots who should slay his companion. Whether by good fortune or providence, Josephus drew the last number and was left alone with a companion whom he persuaded to come forth with him and trust to the mercy of the conquerors. Many of the Romans clamoured for his death, but Titus, pitying his youth—he was 30 years of age—interceded for him, and Vespasian decided to send him to Nero.

Josephus predicts that Vespasian will rule the world.— Thereupon Josephus played his strongest card. He asked for a private interview with Vespasian and Titus, and said that through him God had promised them the

---

[1] Suicide was not considered a crime in rabbinic Judaism.

empire. Finally, he boldly addressed the Roman general in these words :

> ' Vespasian, no doubt you think that you have in Josephus taken no more than a prisoner ; but it is not so ; for I come to announce that great things are in store for you. For were I not God's messenger, I know that, according to Jewish custom, generals should not survive defeat. Are you going to send me to Nero ? For what purpose ? Nero will die ; others will succeed him for awhile, but in the end it is you, Vespasian, and this your son, who will be the Caesar and the supreme ruler. Keep me in the strictest bonds ; for you are to be the master of land and sea, and of all the race of man.'

A bold prediction for Josephus to utter, or for Vespasian to listen to, but Josephus evidently staked all on the Roman general's superstitious confidence in his star. Vespasian, at the suggestion of Titus, spared the prophet, and the fortune of Josephus was made. His knowledge of Jewish affairs, his unquestionable ability, and doubtless his agreeable manners won the favour of his patrons. From a prisoner of war he became a free man, riding beside Titus as his adviser, and in the end he was given all the highly prized privileges of a Roman citizen. Honours and wealth were heaped upon him, and he soon found himself in a situation so advantageous that he could view the ruin of his country and the terrible punishment of its defenders from one of the most comfortable seats in the theatre of the world. Whether his conscience disturbed his complacency we have no means of knowing.[1]

Josephus and the favours he received in Rome.— Josephus became the constant companion of Titus during his campaign in Palestine, and accompanied him in triumph to Rome. There he was given apartments in

---

[1] The siege of Jotapata is only just mentioned in the *Life*, but is related at great length in the Third Book of the *War*, cc. 7–8 (132–408). The narrative is throughout dramatic, and the military details are of great value. For the present purpose the importance lies in the psychology of the historian.

the Emperor's private house, Roman citizenship, and a pension. Many Jews accused him of treason to his Roman masters, but all were punished. Titus continued the favours of his father, and even the suspicious Domitian added to the honours bestowed by his father and brother by making Josephus' property in Judaea free of taxes. He found a constant benefactress in the Emperor's wife, Domitia. Herod Agrippa wrote no fewer than sixty-two letters about the histories, two of which, addressed to ' his dearest Josephus,' are quoted in the ' Life.' [1] A rich man named Epaphroditus acted as a faithful and liberal patron.[2]

Such was Josephus. No hero, nor a man of sensitive honour ; but, whilst we cannot admire his character, and are at liberty to question his merits as an historian, it is impossible to deny the greatness of the debt posterity owes him for having given an invaluable record of events which, but for him, would have been buried in oblivion.

---

[1] C. 65 (364–366).   [2] *Life*, c. 76 (430).

CHAPTER II

The Religion of Josephus (the 'Apion')

Josephus as an apologist.—If Josephus displays himself in a bad light in his very frank description of his actions in his so-called 'Life,' his character appears very favourably in his two books popularly known as 'Against Apion.' [1] The 'Life' leaves us with the impression that he was a Jew completely devoid of patriotism, but the 'Apion' must be the work of a man who was an enthusiastic admirer of the religion of Israel. Before one attempts to account for this apparent discrepancy it is desirable to have a clear notion of the apology for Judaism which Josephus composed.

The Roman showed no natural antipathy to the Jewish spirit; and the Spartan, whose virtues were rather those of Rome than of Greece, was the Jew's hereditary ally. [2] In the second book of the Maccabees, the instigator of the persecution of the Jews selected by Antiochus Epiphanes was 'an old man of Athens'; [3] and whether this reading is the correct one or not it expresses a truth. Athens, which represents culture, art, philosophy, freedom of thought, versatility, in a word all the wisdom and attraction of the world, stands and must ever stand as the antithesis of Jerusalem with its austere morality, its inartistic religion, and its unchanging reverence for what appears to the world to be

[1] The proper title of the book is *On the Antiquity of the Jews*. Only the second book is addressed to Apion. What we commonly call the *Antiquities* is properly the *Archaeology*. ἀρχαιολογία in Greek = ancient history.

[2] 1 Macc. xii. 5–23. The Lacedaemonians and the Jews were both believed to be descended from Abraham. *Antiq.* xii. 4 (225 ff.) and xiii. 5 (164 ff.).

[3] 2 Macc. vi. 1. The Vulgate has 'an old man of Antioch.'

an arid legal code ; and Josephus was fully justified, when he undertook the defence of his religion, in recognising the Greek spirit as its greatest enemy. The Romans had, it is true, treated his nation with barbarity, but had, on the whole, respected its religion. The attacks of Latin writers are often coarse and ignorant ; but the Greeks assailed Judaism with the more dangerous weapons of criticism and disparagement. There is something quite modern in the arguments advanced in the first book of the ' Apion ' and also in the method of reply adopted by Josephus.

Silence of Greeks concerning the Jews.—The ' Antiquities ' had raised a perfect storm among the scholars of the day, because it claimed that the Jews had a history extending over five thousand years.[1] The learned asserted that such a pretension was preposterous, and had nothing to support it. Why, they asked, had no Greek writer of respectable antiquity ever so much as mentioned the Jews ? The answer of Josephus is that the Greeks are a comparatively modern people. They admit that the records of the Egyptians, Chaldaeans and Phoenicians are far older than theirs. As to their literature, it cannot go further back than Homer, who must have written after the Trojan war. But did he write at all ? ' Many say he did not leave his poetry in literary form, but only scattered songs, which were collected later ; and the form in which they now appear, with many inconsistent statements, is a proof of this.' The Greeks themselves are sceptical about the antiquity of the books attributed to Pythagoras and Thales. As to the Greek writers of history, their chief object seems to be to prove that their predecessors were all wrong. Even Thucydides, for all his supposed accuracy, has been criticised by some ; and everybody condemns Herodotus. The reason is plain : The Greeks kept no public records. The consequence of this is that their historians aimed at style rather than truth ; had Josephus written to-day, he would have applied to their works the most damning of all epithets, ' unscientific.'[2]

---

[1] *Antiq.* Preface (13); *Apion*, i. 1 (1).   [2] *Apion*, i. 1-4 (1-22).

Greeks kept no records like the Babylonians and the Jews.—Everyone, however, says Josephus, knows how carefully the Babylonians kept their records, as well as the Egyptians and Phoenicians, and the Jews did the same through their priests whose pedigrees were most carefully preserved. He then goes on to speak of the twenty-two books of their Scripture which go down to the days of Artaxerxes, 432 B.C.,[1] and adds :

> ' From Artaxerxes to our own time the complete history has been written, but has not been deemed worthy of equal authority with the earlier records because of the failure of the exact succession of the prophets.' [2]

Josephus goes on to explain how he came to write his book on the ' Jewish War ' and the ' Antiquities,' and proceeds to sketch the plan of his argument. I. He explains the silence of the Greek historians about the Jews ; II. He cites the witness of other nations : (A) Egyptian, (B) Phoenician, (C) Chaldaean, (D) Greek. III. He refutes the calumnies of the opponents of the Jews. This elaborate task occupies four-fifths of the first book, and is less interesting to us as an apology than as a library of extracts from many otherwise unknown authors.

Why the Greeks ignored the Jews.—I. Josephus gives an ingenious and, upon the whole, convincing reason for the silence of the ancient Greek authors in regard to the early history of the Hebrews. He naturally assumes the accuracy of the impression conveyed in the biblical account of the settlement in Palestine, that Israel, having received the entire legal system of the Pentateuch, was settled in the Promised Land with

---

[1] The canon of Josephus is (a) the five books of Moses, (b) thirteen books from Moses to Artaxerxes, (c) four books of hymns and moral precepts. The number, twenty-two, was adopted by the Christians, Melito, Origen and Jerome, and this evidently corresponds to the letters of the Hebrew alphabet. *Apion*, i. 8 (40–41).

[2] Thackeray's translation. His rendering of πίστις by ' credit' is scarcely satisfactory, if credit = credibility. Josephus seems to imply that the early books are ' inspired ' in a different sense from the later records.

the object of becoming a community existing solely for
the purpose of living the life prescribed for it by God.

> ' Ours,' he says, ' is not a maritime country, and
> neither commerce, nor the intercourse it promotes
> with the outside world, has any attraction for us.
> Our cities are built inland, remote from the sea, and
> we devote ourselves to the cultivation of the pro-
> ductive country with which we are blessed.   Above
> all, we pride ourselves upon the education of our
> children, and regard as the most essential task the
> observance of our laws and the pious practices based
> thereupon, which we have inherited,' etc.[1]
> ' Surely then, it should no longer excite surprise
> that our nation, so remote from the sea, and so
> deliberately living its own life, should likewise have
> remained largely unknown and offered no occasion
> to historians to mention it.' [2]

Here we have the clue to the popular view of the
Jews, from the return from captivity to the days of
Antiochus Epiphanes, namely, that they were not a
nation but a church, or, to use the language of the time,
' a sect ' of philosophers.   For this reason there is no
real Jewish history during this long period.   This
provided the Greeks with a plausible excuse for saying
that the Jews were a new people, who had sprung into
being without any historical background.   Thus, certain
perverse modern criticism was anticipated in the first
century of our era.   But, in the age of Josephus, the
Oriental records of a remote antiquity were lost, only
to be recovered in our own day ; and thus the apologist
had for his sole argument the presumed genuineness
of the Mosaic law, and of all the prophetical writings of
the Old Testament.

Manetho's history of Egypt.—II. (A) The only testimony from Egypt which Josephus adduces is that
of Manetho, a priest who lived under the first two
Ptolemies at the beginning of the third century B.C.
He wrote a history of Egypt, the second book of which
is here quoted, in which he tells the story of the Shepherd-

---

[1] *Apion*, i. 12 (60) (Thackeray's translation).
[2] *Ibid.* i. 12 (68).

kings, who were, he says, called Hyksos. These were
finally driven into their city of Avaris (perhaps Pelusium),
on the eastern branch of the Nile, by a king named
Misphragmouthosis. His son Thoummosis besieged
Avaris and allowed the shepherds to march out of Egypt,
which they did, and founded Jerusalem. Later on
Josephus relates how a priest of Heliopolis, called
Osarsiph, taught the shepherds to insult the gods and
sacred animals of Egypt, and gave them a code of laws,
changing his name from Osarsiph to Moses.

But for Josephus, Manetho would be unknown to us,
though his testimony was extensively used in later days
by Julius Africanus, the Christian chronographer, who is
quoted by Eusebius in his ' Preparation for the Gospel '
and in his ' Chronology,' and much later by the Byzantine
George Syncellus (ninth century). Authors like Tacitus,
Pliny, etc., who lived later than Josephus, have allusions
to Egyptian history, but the use made by Josephus of
Manetho, an author never mentioned by any earlier
writer, is a proof alike of his erudition and of his anxiety
to get at his sources. [1]

Phoenician testimony.—(B) The historical evidence,
taken from Phoenician sources, is from the Tyrian
archives, among which, as Josephus avers, have survived some of the letters which passed between Solomon
and Hiram. The Temple of Jerusalem was built 143
years and eight months before Carthage was founded.
Josephus also quotes an historian, named Dius, otherwise
unknown, and Menander of Ephesus, who is, so far as I
am aware, unnoticed by any earlier writer.[2]

The Babylonian Berosus.—(C) Berosus is Josephus'
authority for Chaldaea. Here again we have another
writer, who, but for our author, would to all appearance
have entirely perished. Yet without Berosus we should
never have known about the Babylonian legends of
Xisuthrus and the Flood, and of the Ark resting on the
mountains of Armenia. It is only in quite recent times
that his testimony has been confirmed by the discovery

---

[1] *Apion*, i. 14–16 (73–105) ; see also *Apion*, i. 26 (238 ff.).
[2] *Ibid.* i. 17 (106–115) ; see also *Antiq.*, viii. 2 (50–54).

of the cuneiform literature, of which the contemporaries of Josephus were as ignorant as they were of the Egyptian hieroglyphics, a remarkable fact considering that both writings were widely employed down to the days of the Seleucids of Syria, and the Egyptian Ptolemies. Berosus is quoted concerning Nabopolassar and his son, Nebuchadrezzar, kings of Babylon, and the destruction of the Temple.[1]

Testimony of Greek writers.—(D) The testimonies from Greek writers are numerous, if not particularly weighty. Josephus mentions Pythagoras, or rather his disciple, Hermippus; Theophrastus; Herodotus, who speaks of the Syrians being circumcised, evidently meaning the Jews, since they were the only people in Palestine to submit to the rite[2]; Choerilus of Samos, in a poem on the Persian War (fifth century), in which there is a mention of the Solymian hills; and others. Of the two most important names one is Clearchus, the disciple of Aristotle, who makes his master tell a story about a man,

' a Jew of Coele-Syria. These people are descended from the Indian philosophers. The philosophers, they say, are in India called Calani; in Syria by the territorial name of the Jews; for the district which they inhabit is known as Judaea. Their city has a remarkably odd ($\pi\acute{a}\nu\upsilon$ $\sigma\kappa o\lambda\iota\acute{o}\nu$) name; they call it Hierusaleme. . . .'[3]

The other is Hecataeus of Abdera. There were two writers of this name, the earlier of Miletus, a contemporary of Herodotus and a geographer, and Hecataeus of Abdera, who lived under Alexander and the early *diadochi*. Josephus quotes largely from writings under this name. A fragment of the 40th Book of Diodorus Siculus, an historian who lived under Julius Caesar and Augustus, has an account of Moses from Hecataeus, but our earliest informant of this is Photius, Archbishop of Constantinople, who flourished about A.D. 860.[4]

[1] For Berosus see *Antiq.*, i. 3 (93).
[2] Other nations, Moabite, Edomite, etc., were circumcised, and the Philistines were distinguished by the epithet ' uncircumcised.'
[3] *Apion*, i. 22 (179) (Thackeray's translation).
[4] For the evidence of the Greek writers see Théodore Reinach, *Textes relative au Judaisme*, Paris (1895).

Manetho criticised.—III. The rest of the first book of the 'Apion' is occupied by an attempt to show how unreliable Manetho and his successors are in regard to the story of the Exodus. The criticisms of Josephus are both ingenious and acute, but are somewhat tedious to the modern reader, nor do they seriously assist us in deciding the question of the antiquity of the Hebrew nation and its records.

Josephus had no easy task.—The general impression left by the book is that Josephus and the Christian writers who used him had no easy task to prove that the Hebrew nation had the right to claim great antiquity, except on the authority of their Scriptures. But Josephus is correct as to what he says about the Greeks. As the Babylonian captivity and the destruction of Jerusalem took place in 586 B.C. there is little real continuous history of the Greek peoples before Judah ceased to be an independent kingdom. Samaria fell in 722 B.C., and scarcely any surviving Greek literature belongs to this period. In the days of Herodotus and the glorious outburst of literary activity in the fifth century B.C., the Jews were a very obscure sect, settled in Jerusalem around what was probably a scarcely restored Temple. Even the non-Greek writers whom Josephus quotes, Manetho and Berosus, related only what they thought would be of interest to the Hellenistic readers.[1] We must be grateful for what Josephus has preserved for us ; but, whilst we have to acknowledge that he has done what he could to make a case out of very scanty materials, he has shown little skill in dealing with them either as a critic or an antiquarian. At the same time, the so-called First Book of this treatise supplied the Christian apologists with a perfect armoury in defence of the Old Testament.

Jews unpopular after captivity.—Very different in point of interest is the second book, which is a reply to Apion, the most virulent opponent of Judaism. What is now known as anti-semitism existed long before

---

[1] Manetho probably lived in the early years of the third century B.C., in the days of the first two Ptolemies. Berosus is said to have written in the reign of Antiochus II. (*Theos*), 261–246 B.C.

Josephus in much the same form as it does to-day, though the name is misleading, since it is the Jewish race, and not the great Semitic family of nations, which has been the special object of resentment. There is little evidence in the Old Testament that the Israelites were more unpopular with their neighbours than any other of the races of Palestine, and we find constant notices in the Old Testament of alliances with Moab, Edom, Tyre, and even the Philistines. But, when the exiles came back from Babylon, all the inhabitants of Palestine seem to have been opposed to them. Nehemiah's enemies were Sanballat, the Horonite ; Tobiah, the Ammonite ; and Geshem, the Arabian. In fact, the Zionism of the fifth and sixth centuries before Christ, like that of the twentieth century of our era, met with strenuous opposition from the native races, who were determined that, if they could prevent it, the Jews should never again become a strong nation in what they claimed to be their own land. This enmity became ten-fold more bitter when Hellenistic civilisation was introduced by the Macedonian conquerors. Nor was the unpopularity of the Jew confined to Palestine. It was perhaps greatest in Alexandria, where there was a large settlement, whose wealth excited envy, and whose religion provoked the fury of a fanatical population. The first sign of the coming trouble of the great Jewish war was the riot in Alexandria in the days of Avilius Flaccus, the pro- curator, at the time of the accession of Caligula, A.D. 37.

Character of Apion.—The chief literary enemy of the Jews at this time was Apion. He may be described as an Alexandrian professor who flourished under Tiberius, known as μόχθος, the toiler, because he was a laborious commentator on Homer. Modesty was certainly not his forte, and he was so prone loudly to advertise that the sarcastic Emperor termed him ' the universal cymbal,' (*cymbalum mundi*). He had conceived a violent prejudice against the Jews, and, according to Josephus, was one of the Alexandrian delegation to Caligula which opposed the Jewish protest against the placing of the Emperor's statue in the Temple. Strangely, however, Philo, who was one of the Jewish representatives on that occasion, does not so much as mention Apion.

However, Apion's name in the mind of Josephus was representative of the anti-Semitism of the first century. His book has not survived, but at times when we read his arguments as reported by the Jewish apologist we rub our eyes and wonder if, instead of reading a book more than eighteen centuries old, we are not perusing the work of some fanatic bigot of our own day.

In the first place, it is full of the sort of perverted learning which is the plague of sober scholars at the present time ; when we read the introductory remarks of Josephus we feel they are applicable to certain of our contemporaries. These are our author's words concerning Apion, who is called by Dr. Thackeray ' an erudite but ostentatious writer ' :

> ' I am doubtful whether the remarks of Apion the grammarian [1] deserve serious refutation. For some of his statements are not original and most are purely buffoonery . . . and, to tell the truth, betray the gross ignorance of their author. Yet since most people are so foolish as to find greater attractions in such compositions than in works of a serious nature, and are charmed by abuse and impatient of praise, I think it incumbent upon me not to pass over without examination this author, who has written an indictment of us enough for a court of law. . . . His argument is difficult to summarise and his meaning to grasp,' etc. [2]

Josephus, after having thus characterised Apion's work and pretentious knowledge, criticises his version of the story of the Exodus, and then gives a specimen of his absurd erudition. Because the Egyptian word for the boils with which the Israelites were afflicted is *sabbo*, it is the original source of the Graecised Hebrew word *Sabbaton*. [3]

---

[1] γραμματικός does not mean a grammarian in the modern sense. I think Josephus had he written the English of to-day would have said ' Dr. or Professor Apion,' or perhaps ' Apion, Litt.D.'

[2] *Apion*, ii. 1 (2–6) (Thackeray's translation).

[3] *Ibid.* ii. 2 (21).

Jews accused of ritual murder.—We may pass over the attacks of Apion on the Jews' claim to Alexandrian citizenship, on their being the cause of much sedition, and on their refusal to worship the national gods. Important as these charges were at the time, they and their refutation are of little interest to us. We next come to an accusation which, ridiculous as it is, has continued through the ages, has been transferred from Jews to Christians, and then been employed by Christians against Jews, and has even in modern days been reiterated, not only by unlettered peasantry of backward countries, but by men of learning. Apion, on the authority of the Stoic philosopher, Poseidonius of Apameia, and Apollonius Molon, accuses Judaism of encouraging ritual murder.[1]

The jealous care with which the Jews excluded all but those of their own race from the Temple, and even all but priests from its most sacred recesses, must have given rise to a belief that they performed rites which had to be carefully concealed. In the same way the secrecy with which the early Christians celebrated their Eucharistic services, allowing none but baptised members to be present, made the heathen world suspicious that they had good reason for insisting on the privacy of their mysteries. As the Jews in later times kept the Passover to themselves, the surrounding Christians believed that the feast was attended by unholy ceremonies. In each instance there was an unwarranted suspicion that a human sacrifice was part of a worship so carefully hidden from the outside world. Thus, many a city in medieval Europe had its boy-saint, who had been martyred by the Jews; of Chaucer's 'Canterbury Tales,' one of the most beautifully told is that of the Prioresse about a little boy who was decoyed into the Jewish quarter and foully done to death. Not so long ago this absurd and wicked fiction caused a cruel persecution of the Jews in Eastern Europe, and in the defence of its leaders it was gravely argued that, at any

---

[1] *Apion*, ii. 8 (92 ff.). This part of the treatise has only been preserved in a Latin version.

rate in the days of the New Testament, the Jews were accustomed to sacrifice a man on the day of Atonement, and the writings of modern scholars were adduced in support of this view.[1]

Apion's authority informed him that, in the days of Antiochus Epiphanes, when Jerusalem was taken, the king entered the Temple and found in it a Greek prisoner who fell at his feet and prayed for deliverance. He had been lying on a couch before a table covered with every delicacy, but had just learned that he was being fed up in order to prove an acceptable human sacrifice.

> ' He heard of the unutterable law of the Jews for the sake of which he was being fed. The practice was being repeated at a fixed season. They would kidnap a Greek foreigner, fatten him up for a year, and then convey him to a wood where they slew him, sacrificed his body with their customary ritual, partook of his flesh, and while immolating the Greek, swore an oath of hostility to the Greeks.' [2]

Refutation of Apion's calumny.—Josephus answers this calumny by pointing out that Antiochus is never recorded to have taken this Greek captive to any of his cities in order to expose the cruelty of the Jews, though by so doing he would have gained great credit from the majority of his subjects and justified his barbarous treatment of the Jews. Further, the whole constitution of the Temple service rendered such an accusation as impossible as it was ridiculous. Apion knew the whole story to be a lie ; he had not even the excuse of uncritical credulity. Like his other stories of the worship of an ass's head, etc., this only proves that he was trying deliberately to incite the Greeks against the Jews.

We may hurriedly dismiss Apion's other criticisms of the Jews, though some are even now worth attention, and come to the conclusion of the Apology, which is in some respects among the best literary works of Josephus :

---

[1] See *Jewish Encyclopedia*, arts. ' Blood-Accusation ' and ' Polna Affair.' If I recollect aright, some anti-Semite scholars tried to prove, when the case was tried in Vienna, that the Jewish religion had encouraged ritual murder.

[2] *Apion*, ii. 8 (94, 95) (Thackeray's translation).

namely, his description of what the Jewish religion and
law really stand for. Here we have Josephus at his
best and we may let him speak for himself.

Josephus explains Judaism.—He naturally has a very
high idea of the noble character of Moses, whom he
represents as ' unlike all other rulers, seeking no personal
domination, but giving them laws,' in the belief that this
was the best means of displaying his own virtue and of
ensuring the lasting welfare of those who made him their
leader. With such noble aspirations and such a record
of successful achievements, he had good reason for
thinking that he had God for his guide and counsellor.

With this in view, Moses constituted Israel as a
theocracy (ὡς ἄν τις εἴποι βιασάμενος τὸν λόγον
θεοκρατίαν) [1] ' placing all authority in the hands of
God. To Him he persuaded all to look as the author
of all blessings, both those which are common to all
mankind and those they had won by prayer. . . . He
represented Him as One, uncreated (ἀγένητος = without
parentage like a heathen god) and unchangeable for all
eternity,' etc.[2] The strength of the system inculcated
by Moses is that he did not make religion one of the
many virtues, but rather summed up all virtues in religion.[3]

Perfection of the Law.—In one respect Josephus
agrees with St. Paul, that the Law if perfectly observed
is a sufficient guide to a life pleasing to God. The
Apostle fully acknowledges the holiness, goodness and
justice of the Law, only, as it is impossible for any man
to observe it in its entirety, it is necessary to look not
to the Law, which, though perfect, is impossible for man
to fulfil,[4] but to the saving power of Jesus, the ever
living Christ. Josephus commends the wisdom of Moses
as a lawgiver thus :

' He did not leave practical teaching in morals
voiceless ; nor did he allow the instruction of the
law to remain without effect. He left nothing,

---

[1] *Apion*, ii. 16 (164–167). The laws are attributed to the wisdom
of Moses rather than as dictated by God to the legislator.
[2] *Ibid.* ii. 16 (167) (see Thackeray's note), ' not born like the
Greek gods.'
[3] *Ibid.* ii. 16 (170).   [4] Rom. vii. 12 ff.

however trifling, to the capricious discretion of the individual. . . . Our leader made the Law our standard and rule, that we might live under (God) our father and ruler, and be guilty of no sin through wilful ignorance.' [1]

Jews all profess the same doctrines.—The advantage every Jew had over other men in being educated from childhood in the Law, and being constantly reminded of its contents, is that in Judaism all profess the same doctrine. Unlike the rest of mankind, the Jew saw nothing fine ' in breaking away from inherited customs,' nor was he ready to credit those who defied their ancestral law with being exceptionally clever.[2] This reverence gave the people their remarkable steadiness and cohesion. Life under the Law is contrasted with that of the heathen who had been captivated by the Mystery Religions :

> ' Can there be any more saintly government than ours ? Can God be more worthily honoured than by a scheme under which religion is the end and aim of the training of the entire community . . . and the whole administration of our state resembles some holy ceremony ? Practices, which under the name of mysteries and initiations can only be observed by the heathen for a few days, are maintained by us all our lives joyfully and with unfailing determination.' [3]

The superior morality and humanity of Judaism is sharply contrasted with the laxity and cruelty of the law and practice of other nations ; and Josephus lays stress on the fact that Judaism freely invites other men to share its privileges if only they will accept the conditions which its law imposes.

> ' The consideration given by our legislator to the equitable treatment of aliens also merits attention. It will be seen that he took the best of all possible

---

[1] *Apion*, ii. 16 (173–174) (Thackeray's translation, slightly altered).
[2] *Ibid.* ii. 20 (182–183) (Thackeray's translation).
[3] *Ibid.* ii. 22 (188–189) (Thackeray's translation

measures at once to secure our own customs from corruption, and to throw them open ungrudgingly to any who elect to share them. To all who desire to come and live under the same laws with us he gives a gracious welcome, holding that it is not family ties alone which contribute relationship, but agreement in the principles of conduct. On the other hand, it was not his pleasure that casual visitors should be admitted to the intimacies of our daily life.' [1]

Kindness to all, even animals, is strongly inculcated in the Law. According to Josephus, a Jew may not kill an animal which takes refuge in his house.[2]

Jewish observance practised by Gentiles.—Josephus points triumphantly to the fact that the principles of the Jews, which were adopted by some of the best Greek philosophers, prevailed among the heathen in all parts of the world. Everywhere the sabbath is kept, and the lighting of the lamps, and the food laws. In fact, when Apion and his friends condemn the Jews they also condemn many of their friends and countrymen.[3]

The treatise concludes with a panegyric on Judaism in these eloquent words :

' I would therefore boldly maintain that we have introduced to the rest of the world a very large number of very beautiful ideas. What greater beauty than inviolable piety ? What higher justice than obedience to the laws ? What is more beneficial than to be in harmony with one another, to be a prey neither to disunion in adversity, nor to arrogance and faction in prosperity ; in war to despise death, in peace to devote oneself to crafts or agriculture ; and to be convinced that everything in the whole universe is under the eye and direction of God ? Had these precepts been either committed to writing

[1] *Apion*, ii. 28 (209–210) (Thackeray's translation).
[2] *Ibid.* ii. 29 (213). He says this is in the Law ; but the term ' Moses says ' or the like is very freely used.
[3] *Ibid.* ii. 39 (279 ff.). This is an interesting testimony, written after the destruction of Jerusalem, of the widespread influence of Judaism on the world at large.

or more consistently observed by others before us, we should have owed them a debt of gratitude as their disciples. If, however, it is seen that no one observes them better than ourselves and that we were the first to discover them, then the Apions and Molons . . . may be left to their own confusion.' [1]

Josephus both a priest and a Pharisee.—Josephus has a genuine admiration for his ancestral religion, and his exposition of it confirms what he says in the ' Life,' that he was both a priest and a Pharisee. He is most careful to assure us that the preservation of the Law is in the hands of the priesthood, and he is equally insistent on such a Pharisaic doctrine as that of the resurrection and the future life, as well as on the humane purpose of the Mosaic legislation. But he has no sympathy whatever with those Pharisees who were disposed to side with the extreme patriots, whom he frequently calls ' robbers' or banditti ($\lambda\eta\sigma\tau\alpha\iota$). If we employ the language of the Gospels, which, after all, are our best contemporary authorities, we should describe Josephus as both a Pharisee and an Herodian ; his religion being Pharisaic, and his political views Herodian.

Ideals of Josephus.—He had no patriotism beyond a belief in the divine destiny of his people and the perfection of the law. entrusted to its care. Perhaps his ideal was that of Ezekiel : a priestly nation under a native prince, neither impatient of a foreign overlord nor ambitious of becoming an independent world power. When he had to fight for his country he did his best as a general, but he saw from the first not only the hopelessness but the wickedness of the attempt to defy the Roman world power and was not sorry to submit himself to it, feeling, one may charitably suppose, that he could serve his religion better by enduring the contempt of his countrymen and by persuading them to submit to the inevitable. In this he was but following the example of the prophets of the school of Jeremiah, who had recognised the wisdom of saving Jerusalem by accepting the yoke of Nebuchadrezzar.

---

[1] *Apion*, ii. 41 (293–295) (Thackeray's translation).

But no attempt to apologise for the conduct of Josephus can save him from the reproach of being a thoroughly selfish individual who was prepared to secure ease and comfort at the expense of his nation, and complacently to witness its ruin on the ground that it was a divine punishment. Naturally, the Jew, even if he admits that the judgment of Josephus was correct, regards his character with abhorrence ; whilst no Christian, though using his writings as a condemnation of the Jewish system, can honestly regard him with sincere admiration.

Herod Agrippa II on the Jews' religion.—In a long speech which our author puts into the mouth of Herod Agrippa II, who is represented as addressing his countrymen before the outbreak of the war with Rome, we have a clue to the view of Josephus regarding the nature of the Jewish policy and religion :

> ' The only resource left to you is to seek God's alliance. But this must belong to the Romans ; for they never could have obtained so wide an empire without His help. For consider, how hard it would be for you to observe the rules of your religion, even if you were at war with a less formidable foe. . . . How could you call for God's assistance whilst you were of your own accord refusing Him the worship which is His due ? ' [1]

Agrippa clearly means that war and the Law of Moses are incompatible because such rules as those about the Sabbath cannot be properly observed in a campaign or a siege. A modern man would probably advance a different motive, but his meaning would be the same : namely, that a religion based on a divine law was not intended for a warlike race. In fact, this idea of Moses having designed to found a peaceful community, not conforming itself to the standard of the world but content to be a holy nation unlike any other, and trusting solely to the Divine protection, reminds us of the prophet Samuel's indignation at the demand that he should give them a king ' to go before us and fight our battles.' Circumstances made it, to all appearance, no longer

[1] *War*, ii. (390–394).

possible for Israel to remain 'a holy nation, a royal priesthood, a peculiar people,' and God sanctioned the appointment of a king. But the disasters of the nation recorded in the 'Books of the Kingdoms,' culminating in the Babylonian captivity which followed the ruin of the Northern Tribes, proved that Samuel was right in his anticipation of disaster accompanying the rejection of Jehovah as King.[1]

Once more the Jews rose to power under the Asmonaeans, and became one of the nations, with a territory like that conquered by David and Solomon ; once more they rose in patriotic fury against the domination of a great world power, to meet with greater disaster. Like the Christian Church, its parent the Jewish nation was intended for a greater destiny than to lose itself in the strife and policy of the kingdoms of the earth. Josephus may have been right in advising submission to Rome, though his was a pacifism which cannot inspire respect.

[1] 1 Samuel viii. *passim.*

PART II
THE RELIGION OF THE JEWS

CHAPTER III

THE TEMPLE

The Temple not at first the only sanctuary in Israel.—
The Temple of Jerusalem was of such immense importance in the eyes of the Jewish people in the days of
Christ, that it is hard to realise that before the exile
there were other sanctuaries in Israel, and that the first
Temple till its destruction was used for the worship of
other gods beside Jehovah. Indeed, the restored Temple
and its worship were planned during the Exile, their
inspired designer being the prophet Ezekiel. Of the
ancient Temple of Solomon we know but little, and still
less of what went on in it, most of our information in the
Bible being coloured by the impression made on the writers
by what they saw in the second Temple.

Purification of the Temple by Josiah.—In the reign of
Josiah, the last of the pious kings of Judah, in the
seventh century B.C., we have a description of the purification of the Temple by him and his priests. The
state of affairs described in the second book of Kings is
hard to realise, especially if we have been taught to
believe that the Temple in the days of the kings of
Judah was the one monotheistic sanctuary of a righteous
God on earth. First we read that they brought out all
the instruments made for the worship of Baal, of the
sacred column (*asherah*), and of the stars. The priests
of the cults, who were called ' Chemarim,' were then
expelled, and the ministers of the foulest forms of Semitic
worship were driven out and their houses destroyed.
Moloch worship and the sacrifice of children were made
impossible by the defiling of Tophet, the valley where
they were practised ; and the horses and chariots, which

the kings of Judah had given to the sun, were taken away,
as well as the altars which Josiah's predecessors, Ahaz and
Manasseh, had placed in the courts of the Temple.   From
this we might judge that the Temple was no national sanctuary, but was treated by the king as his private property
and used for any sort of worship which took his fancy.[1]

Ezekiel's vision of idolatry in the Temple.—But even
the reformation of Josiah and the exhortations of such
prophets as Jeremiah made but little difference.   Just
before the final destruction of Jerusalem and the Temple
by Nebuchadrezzar, Ezekiel, then in captivity, had a
vision of what was happening in Jerusalem.   By the
altar gate stood the image which provoked God's jealousy.
In a secret chamber seventy men were burning incense to
the 'idols of the house of Israel,' portrayed on the
walls.   Elsewhere in the sanctuary women were weeping
for Tammuz, and twenty-five men were adoring the
rising sun.   Thus it appeared that nothing could eradi-
cate the idolatry inherent in the first Temple but its
destruction.[2]

Ezekiel's vision of a restored Temple.—This vision,
recorded in Ezekiel's eighth chapter, explains the conclusion of his prophecy (xl.–xlviii.), in which he
sketches a reformed Temple with a purified worship.
It is unnecessary to enter into details ; this Temple, for
example, could never have found a place on the limited
area available for its erection.   Nevertheless Ezekiel's
work profoundly modified the future worship of the
restored Temple, and, although what he had outlined
was never carried out, two reforms were adopted.   In
the first place, the priesthood was henceforward confined
to the house of Zadok.   ' The priests the Levites, the
sons of Zadok, that kept the charge of my sanctuary
when the children of Israel went astray from me, they
shall come near to minister unto me, etc.'[3]   And

---

[1] 2 Kings xxiii. 4–14 ; Stade, *Gesch. des Volkes Israel*, between
pp. 313–315, gives a plan of the buildings of Solomon, reproduced
by G. A. Smith, *Jerusalem*, ii. 59, which shows the Temple as part
of the royal residence.   It was as literally the 'chapel' of the kings
of Judah as the sanctuary of Bethel was of the kings of Israel ; see
Amos vii. 13.

[2] Ezekiel viii. 5–16.   [3] Ezekiel xliv. 15.

' No stranger, uncircumcised in heart and uncircumcised in flesh, shall enter into my sanctuary.'[1] Thus the sanctity of the new Temple was established, and the Jews henceforward regarded the slightest profanation in these respects with unspeakable horror. Any attempt to introduce an image of any kind into the Temple roused the people to frenzy. Strange to say, Josephus never so much as alludes to the suggested reforms of the prophet Ezekiel, nor does he mention his name. Another interesting point in Ezekiel's prophecy, which must demand further attention later, is that, although subsequently the High Priest became the head of the Jewish people throughout the world, Ezekiel never alludes to anyone fulfilling the duties which, according to the Law, that official alone could perform.

As a priest Josephus is deeply interested in the Temple, and his description of it is that of one who has actually seen it, and ministered in its courts. The New Testament alludes to parts of the building, and the Talmudic treatise *Middoth*, or ' Measurements,' though in written form later than that of our historian, is of great importance.

Ancient temples not built for congregational worship.— Before entering upon Josephus' description of the Temple, it is well to remember that an ancient sanctuary was not intended for what we should call congregational worship. This explains why comparatively so few of the old temples were taken over and made into Christian churches. The word *basilica*[2] shows that the idea of a Christian church was a law court, or place of assembly, whereas a temple was built on the principle that it was to be the shrine, or dwelling-place, of the God, into which none but His priests might enter. Outside in the open air in front of the shrine (ναός) stood the altar on which the victims were offered. A sacrificial altar in a covered building is wellnigh unthinkable. The tent sanctuary of Israel, known as the Tabernacle, carried out this idea, but, being designed

---

[1] Ezekiel xliv. 9.
[2] Used vaguely of any large room ; applied to a church means a royal room—like κυριακόν. See Cabrol, *D.A.C.* art. ' basilique.'

for transportation from place to place, it consisted of
no more than a shrine standing in the midst of an enclosure with an altar before it. A permanent temple,
however, though designed primarily for sacrifices in front
of a shrine, had other purposes to fulfil. Much space
was required for slaying and preparing even the daily
sacrifices, still more those on great festivals. Chambers
were needed within the outer precincts for the reception
of worshippers, as were storerooms in immediate proximity
to the shrine. In addition to this the Temple at
Jerusalem, in common with those elsewhere, was a
repository not only for its own wealth, but for much placed
there under the protection of the sanctity of a building
which was erected with a view to military strength. Consequently, when Solomon built his Temple the chief
requirements were a sanctuary, an altar, rooms for the
use of numerous sacrificing priesthood, a large court
for worshippers, a strongly protected treasury, and,
one must add, an adequate supply of water to cleanse
the place after the sacrifices and to carry away the blood
and refuse of the victims.

Foundations of the Temple.—The account of the
Temple as built by Solomon is found in the books of
Kings and Chronicles, but it is supplemented by Josephus
in one important particular : namely, the engineering
skill displayed in making the ground on which the building
stood level for the purpose. To judge from his language,
and possibly from that of Samuel and Chronicles, the
threshing floor of Araunah, the Jebusite, was on the
narrow top of a hill, suitable for a threshing floor or an
altar, but with room for little more than a comparatively
small shrine.[1] To make the necessary plateau required
a great amount of labour, and, though Josephus uses

[1] The site of Solomon's Temple was supposed to have been the
scene of Abraham's readiness to offer up Isaac in ' the land of Moriah '
(Gen. xxii. 2). In 2 Chron. iii. 1 the Temple is said to have been
' at Jerusalem in Mount Moriah, . . . in the threshing floor of Ornan
the Jebusite.' Moriah is only mentioned in these two places in our
Bible. Josephus (*Antiq.* vii. 13 (333)) says : ' Now it happened that
Abraham came and offered his son Isaac for a burnt offering in this
very place.' This is the Jewish, Christian and Mohammedan tradition ;
and to-day the so-called ' Dome of the Rock ' forms the centre of a
circular mosque.

language which is more vivid than credible, his purpose is to impress on the minds of his readers that Solomon undertook a very difficult task.

Of Solomon, after describing his buildings and offerings, Josephus says :

> ' He made that temple . . . such as exceeds all description in words ; nay, if I may so say, is hardly believed upon sight ; for when he had filled up great valleys with earth, which, on account of their immense depth, could not be looked on when you bended down to see them, without pain, and had elevated the ground four hundred cubits, he made it to be on a level with the top of the mountain on which the temple was built, and by this means the outmost temple, which was exposed to the air, was even with the temple itself.' [1]

The second Temple rebuilt by Herod the Great.— Of the Temple of Zerubbabel little is known, though in it the devotional worship of Israel was developed, and it was greatly enriched in the great days of the high priesthood, especially by the spoils taken by the warlike Asmonaean pontiffs. In and before the Macabbaean wars Jerusalem itself was frequently taken and retaken, but even at this time the Temple was a well-nigh impregnable fortress and the treasure house of the Jewish nation. Its wealth and splendour is alluded to by various writers and especially in the letter of Pseudo-Aristeas.[2] But what really interests us is the last of the temples in Jerusalem, the one built by Herod the Great. In demolishing the ancient Temple and entirely rebuilding it, Herod doubtless hoped to gain immortal fame and to conciliate his Jewish subjects.

In his description of Herod's undertaking, Josephus hints that one reason for rebuilding the Temple was the artificial character of the ground on which it stood.[3]

---

[1] *Antiq.* viii. 3 (97–98) (Whiston's translation). The concluding words in Greek are διὰ τοῦτο ὑπαίθριον ὃν τὸ ἔξωθεν ἱερὸν ἴσον ὑπῆρχε τῷ ναῷ, which I suppose means that ' the outer Court was on a level with the shrine.'

[2] *Antiq.* xii. 2 *passim*.

[3] *Ibid.* xv. 11 (380 ff.), but see Whiston's note.

Herod, therefore, took extraordinary care to make the foundation of the whole space enclosed by the Temple wall secure, and the vastness of the stones used in the building and its foundation was a subject of universal admiration. ' What stones ! ' said the astonished disciples of Jesus when they went up with Him to Jerusalem ; and Josephus says : ' Blocks of stone were used in the building measuring forty cubits.' [1]

Josephus, who actually saw and ministered in the Temple, has given in the ' War ' a careful description of its general appearance. Of its magnificence as a distant spectacle there can be no doubt :

> ' The exterior of the building wanted nothing that could astound mind or eye. For being covered on all sides with massive plates of gold, the sun was no sooner up than it radiated so fiery a flash that persons straining to look at it were compelled to avert their eyes as from the solar rays. To approaching strangers it appeared from a distance like a snow-clad mountain.' [2]

The historian's description of the Temple and its surroundings, though of great value, is like the biblical account of Solomon's foundation, or of Ezekiel's visionary temple, not always easy to follow. One is indeed inclined to regard the different attempts to reconstruct the edifice with some suspicion, and to wonder if any of them resemble the actual buildings. We all, however, know something of the appearance of the great square on which the Temple stood, although the level of the city has greatly changed since its destruction by Titus and the many overthrows it has experienced in the course of history. The sightseer standing on the Haram-es-Sherif is at least able to appreciate what both Josephus and the earlier Pseudo-Aristeas assert, namely, that the city had the appearance of a vast theatre, evidently

---

[1] *War*, v. 5 (189) ; Mark xiii. 1.

[2] *War*, v. 5 (222–223). This chapter of the *War* is occupied by a careful account of the Temple at the time of its destruction. The rabbinic description in the treatise *Middoth* is at least a generation later than that of Josephus. The two accounts differ slightly. See, however, the maps and plans and pictures in Sanday's *Sacred Sites of the Gospels*, made with the assistance of Paul Waterhouse.

as seen from the stage.   For the Temple hill is not the
highest in the city, the western part of which is in places
wellnigh a hundred feet above the Temple enclosure.

An imaginary visit to the Temple. The Porticos.—
We may imagine a visitor entering the precincts of
the Temple from the city, crossing a bridge over the
Valley of the Cheesemakers (*Tyropoeon*), now filled up, or
ascending from thence by steps.   He would find himself
in a large open court crowded with a busy throng of
people, bargaining with the money changers, and with
the merchants who sold the sacrificial victims.   On the
four sides of the court were porticos with spacious walks
between the pillars.   In these porticos might be seen
groups attracted by those teachers who happened to be
in Jerusalem.   At the north side of the Temple,[1] on the
flat roof of the porticos, the Roman soldiers acted as
sentries and watched the motley crowd of both Jews and
Gentiles in the open square ; for at any time a serious
riot might break out, as when Paul was attacked by the
mob, and it was proclaimed that he had profaned the
Temple.[2]   The house itself was surrounded by a low wall
called in the Mishna the *soreg*, on the stones of which were
inscriptions warning any Gentile who passed the boundary
that he did so in peril of his life.   The warning was in
Greek and Latin.[3]

What is called ' the House ' was not a covered
building but a series of courts divided by walls.   It
stood on a terrace approached by fourteen steps, leading
to a narrow terrace ; five steps more brought one to the
gates of the Temple.   The sacred building could be
approached by the steps on any side but the west.   The
gates were very magnificently covered with golden and
silver plates.   One gate, that outside the Sanctuary,
called in *Middoth* the Gate of Nicanor, which may
possibly have been the Beautiful Gate of Acts, was not

---

[1] John x. 23 ; Acts iii. 11 ; v. 12.
[2] Acts xxi. 28.   In *Antiq.* xx. 5 (108) a Roman soldier insulted
the Jews by an indecent act during a festival in the days of Cumanus
the procurator.
[3] One of the inscriptions was found by M. Clermont-Ganneau
in 1871, and is now in the Museum at Constantinople.   A photograph
of it appears in Deissmann, *Light from the Ancient East*.

plated with gold, but was made of Corinthian brass, and was far more costly than the others. After passing two gates, the first opening upon the court of the women, and the Nicanor Gate, the worshipper would come in sight of the altar. Beyond this was the sanctuary with its two chambers, the first containing the seven-branched candlestick, the table, and the altar of incense : beyond this the mysterious and empty Holy of Holies.

The golden vines and the great veil.—Two of the wonders of the Temple were the golden vines and the great veil of Babylonian tapestry, which was apparently over the façade of the Sanctuary itself. To quote the words of Josephus :

> ' But whereas the sanctuary within consisted of two separate chambers, the first building alone stood exposed to view, from top to bottom, towering to a height of ninety cubits (135 ft.), its length being fifty, and its breadth twenty. The gate opening into the building was, as I have said, completely overlaid with gold, as was the whole wall around it. It had moreover those golden vines, from which depended grape clusters as tall as a man ; . . . and it had golden doors fifty-five cubits high and sixteen broad. Before these hung a veil of equal length of Babylonian tapestry, with embroidery of blue and fine linen, of scarlet also and purple wrought with marvellous skill.' [1]

Josephus goes on to describe the mystical symbolism of the colours of the veil, the vestments of the High Priests, the jewels in the ephod, etc., giving to most a cosmic significance.

We learn from Josephus that for wealth and richness of adornment the Temple must have been unequalled

---

[1] *War*, v. 5 (209–212). The veil is particularly mentioned in Pseudo-Aristeas. Is it permissible to wonder if the veil which according to the synoptic Evangelists was rent was this vast curtain, and not the one over the doors of the Holy of Holies ? The portent would be more significant were the curtain which all worshippers could see the one alluded to in the Gospels, though it would not teach the spiritual lesson of the rending of the smaller veil. Although Dr. Easton in his *Commentary on St. Luke* says : ' The Temple veil hung in front of the Holy of Holies,' he rightly adds : ' Luke gives no hint of any symbolic meaning of this portent.'

in the world. For generations every Jew had contributed
his half shekel to its support, and all Jewish inhabitants
of Palestine had paid the tithe to the priesthood. Since
Antiochus Epiphanes, 160 B.C., with the doubtful exception of its spoliation by Crassus, its treasury had never
been plundered, and kings and potentates had been liberal
in their offerings. It says much for the moderation of
the Roman imperial government, that the worst offence
in this direction that Josephus can allege against it is
that Pilate once used its treasure for the benefit of
Jerusalem's water supply.[1]

THE HIGH PRIESTHOOD

The High Priest in the Pentateuch.—Our next task
must be to consider the story of the chief minister of the
Temple, the High Priest, as the ruler and finally the
king of the nation of the Jews till the rise of the Herods,
when the office, contrary to all the provisions of the
Mosaic Law, became purely a temporary appointment.
The attempt to construct a history of the High Priesthood
from what Josephus has recorded, if difficult, is certainly
instructive. It is remarkable how very rarely the
words ' High Priest ' occur in the Law. We find them
in Leviticus in reference to the ceremonies of mourning
for the dead, where ' he that is the high priest ' is forbidden
to practise them even for his father and mother. He is
further forbidden to marry a widow or any woman who
is not a virgin. The reason given is that he is the man
' upon whose head the anointing oil is poured, and that
is consecrated to put on the garments.' [2] The celebrant
on the Day of Atonement is not called ' the high priest,'
but ' Aaron.' [3] The other mention of the office is in
Numbers, where the law is declared that the unwitting
murderer is to remain in the city of refuge till the death
of ' the high priest.' [4] No one is named ' high priest '

---

[1] *Antiq.* xviii. 3 (60).   [2] Lev. xxi. 10 ff.
[3] Lev. xvi. 3 ff. The ceremony on this day was apparently the
only one which, according to the Law, Aaron or his successor (xvi. 32)
could alone perform.
[4] Numb. xxxv. 25, repeated in Josh. xx. 6.

ın the days of the Judges, Saul, David, or Solomon.
Eleazar, Phinehas, Eli, Ahiah, Ahimelech, Abiathar, and
even Zadok, are called priests.   Only two are styled High
Priests of the Temple at Jerusalem—Jehoiada in the days
of Joash, and Hilkiah in those of Josiah.[1]   In Ezekiel's
restored Temple there is no mention of a High Priest,
though, after the Return, his office was, in accordance
with the Priestly Code, indispensable.

The High Priest at the Return.—At the time of the
Return the High Priest comes into prominence, as
the second person in the Jewish state, Zerubbabel as
governor of Judah being more important than Joshua
the son of Josedech, and Nehemiah than Eliashib.[2]   Only
after the close of the Old Testament narrative do we find
that the High Priest has become the recognised head of
the Jewish people. We may, however, commence with
Eliashib, who is, in truth, in many ways, the first
representative of what may be termed the political
High Priesthood.   The doings of Eliashib and Nehemiah
in Jerusalem in the thirty-second year of ' Artaxerxes,
king of Babylon ' (433 B.C.), are related in the last chapter
of the book.

In the capacity of governor of Jerusalem, though not
a priest but an extremely religious Jew, Nehemiah played
the part of supreme ruler, not only in the city, but in the
Temple. He apparently decided who were to be recognised as its priests, ordered the observance of the Feast
of Tabernacles and, with the aid of ' Ezra the priest,'
promulgated the written law. His name is at the head
of the list of those who sealed the solemn covenant.   In
this and in all similar transactions the name of Eliashib
does not occur, the only mention of him being in connection
with the fortification of Jerusalem, where we read : ' Then
Eliashib the high priest rose up with his brethren the
priests, and they builded the sheep gate.'[3]   Perhaps

---

[1] Strictly speaking, Hilkiah is the only person called High Priest
before the Captivity (2 Kings xxii. 4); but although Jehoiada is
called both in 2 Kings and 2 Chronicles ' the priest,' in both books
it is implied that he bore the title (2 Kings xii. 10 ; 2 Chron. xxiv. 11).

[2] Haggai i. 1 ; in Zech. iii. 1 the High Priest figures as an accused
person.

[3] Neh. iii. 1.

for some years, we are not told how long, Nehemiah
was absent, and on his return he found that Eliashib was
in close alliance with the avowed enemies of the restorers
of the walls of the city. Tobiah the Ammonite had
actually been lodged in ' the courts of the house of
God,' and a grandson of the High Priest had married
the daughter of Sanballat, Nehemiah's most formidable
adversary. The party of laxity was evidently in the
ascendant during Nehemiah's absence ; and in Jerusalem
even the Sabbath was treated as an ordinary working
day. The orthodox governor took vigorous measures
to restore order, but it is evident that Eliashib had
been intriguing with the object of becoming the real
master of the Temple, and was opposed to Nehemiah's
policy of making the Jewish state into ' a church ' entirely
separated by its written law from the society of the rest
of Palestine. It may be that the publication of the
Law was distasteful to the priestly authorities, who
regarded the performance of the rites of the Temple as
the all important matter, and took little interest in
whether the people observed the Law or not.[1] The
secularity of the ruling priests from the days of Nehemiah
to the appearance of the Maccabees is remarkable, for
evidently Mattathias and his family at Modin did not
belong to the inner circle of the hierarchy at Jerusalem.
It may be permissible to see in Nehemiah the germs of
Pharisaism, and in Eliashib of the Sadducean doctrine
regarding the Law. To the first-named the Law was
for all Israel, whilst to the priests it was applicable chiefly
to the duties of their order.

Successors of Eliashib.—According to the book of
Nehemiah, Eliashib was succeeded by Joiada, Jonathan,
and Jaddua : but Josephus makes Jaddua the grandson
of Eliashib, the succession being Eliashib, John, Jaddua.[2]
Of John, who may be identified with the Jonathan of
Scripture, Josephus tells the following story, which in

[1] See Nehemiah xiii. 4 ff., 28 ; ii. 6 ff. ; viii. 13 ff. ; x. 1 ; xii. 1 ;
xiii. 6. The books of Ezra, Nehemiah, 1 Esdras (the Greek Ezra), and
the *Antiquities* of Josephus are so contradictory as to their statements
that it is hard to make a consistent historical narrative of the period.
[2] Neh. xii. 10 ; *Antiq.* xi. 7 (297 ff.).

itself sums up the priestly history for several generations. Bagoses, whom Josephus calls the general ($\sigma\tau\rho\alpha\tau\eta\gamma\acute{o}s$) of ' another Artaxerxes,' *i.e.* Mnemon (405–362), or Ochus (362–339), was, like Nehemiah, the Persian governor of Judaea. It is the tale oft repeated in the succeeding centuries of two brothers, rivals for the vacant high priesthood, the appointment to which was in the hands of the secular power. John had succeeded his father Eliashib in his office, from which Jesus his younger brother, with the support of Bagoses, tried to oust him. The two rivals quarrelled in the Temple and John slew Jesus. Thereupon Bagoses came to the Temple, and after sternly rebuking John, insisted on forcing an entrance. Josephus seems to imply, though his language is vague, that the Temple was closed for seven years as a punishment for this crime, or that a tax was imposed on every sacrifice.[1]

Jaddua and Manasseh.—Again, if we may trust Josephus, the rivalry of brothers was a cause of trouble. Jaddua, the son of the John above mentioned, had a brother called Manasseh, who apparently acted as his coadjutor in the priesthood. Darius Codomannus, the last Persian king, sent a Samaritan (Cuthaean) as satrap to Samaria, whose daughter Nicaso Manasseh married. Strange to say, the name of the new governor was Sanballat, the same as that of Nehemiah's enemy a century before. The people of Jerusalem objected to this illegal alliance between a man who apparently at times performed high priestly functions and a woman who was neither of Levitical nor even of Jewish birth, but was sprung from the hated Samaritans ; and Manasseh was driven out of Jerusalem. Thereupon Sanballat, to console his son-in-law, built the temple on Mount Gerizim and installed him as its priest.[2]

---

[1] *Antiq.* xi. 7 (297–301).

[2] *Ibid.* xi. 8 (304–312). It is very difficult to construct the story of the Jews from the Captivity to the Maccabees. Nehemiah returned to Jerusalem about 434 B.C., in the 32nd year of Artaxerxes, to find the Temple priesthood in close alliance with the non-Jews in Palestine. Eliashib, in fact, represents the party of mixed marriages and laxity, his grandson having married Sanballat's daughter. Josephus related a similar state of things a century later (331 B.C.).

Jaddua and his descendants.—Jaddua is famous as the High Priest who met Alexander the Great when he visited Jerusalem, and won the favour of the conqueror as he was advancing on his triumphant march to meet Darius at Arbela. From this time the Jewish state came under the rule of the Macedonians,[1] and ultimately became part of the dominions of the Ptolemies.

For aught we know, Jaddua may have been a religious reformer. He is the last High Priest mentioned in the Old Testament, and it is just possible that in his days the books of Chronicles were compiled. Anyhow, the services of the Temple began about this time to be characterised not only by magnificence, but by a spirit of reverence which greatly impressed all visitors, including Gentiles. Jaddua was succeeded by his son Onias,[2] and Onias by Simon called the Just, whose praises are celebrated in the fiftieth chapter of Ecclesiasticus, especially for the dignity with which he performed the ceremonial duties of the high priesthood. He was followed by his brother Eleazar, in the days of Ptolemy Philadelphus (283–257), under whose patronage the translation of the Law (the Septuagint) was made in Alexandria. The next High Priest was Eleazar's uncle Manasseh, who was succeeded by Onias II, the son of Simon the Just, each of whose three sons became High Priest in his turn. None of them was worthy of his father. Onias II was so parsimonious that he was only saved from war with Egypt by the acuteness of his nephew Joseph, who consented to become Ptolemy's relentless

There was then a Sanballat who was father-in-law to Eliashib's grandson, Manasseh. Josephus gives no real information about Judaea under the later Persian kings. We have evidence for Samaria being under someone named Sanballat in the Mond papyri (408 B.C.). Nothing, however, is clear, except that the higher ranks of the Jerusalem priesthood were so far from being strict Jews that they were ready to be friendly with those whom such as Nehemiah considered the enemies of true Judaism ; and this fact amply explains why the priests were eager to go over to Antiochus Epiphanes and the Syrians. I have consequently ventured to suggest that the promulgation of the Law was distasteful to the priestly caste, and popular with the deeply religious people of the land.

[1] *Antiq.* xi. 8 (329 ff.).
[2] For the different priests named Onias, see the article in the *Encyclopedia Biblica.*

agent in exacting tribute in Coele-Syria. By the time of the death of Onias II Palestine had become a province of Syria under the house of Seleucus, whose policy was as far as possible to bring the Jews under Hellenistic influences. Two brothers, as usual, rivals for the high priesthood, vied with one another for the favour of the Syrian monarch. Their Hebrew names were Jesus and Onias, which they exchanged for the Greek appellations of Jason and Menelaus.[1]

High Priesthood in 2 Maccabees.—We must now take leave of Josephus for awhile and make our authority the Second Book of the Maccabees, which it has been the custom of writers of Jewish history either to ignore or so to dovetail its narrative into those of 1 Maccabees and Josephus that a smooth and connected story is the result. But as regards the rivalry of Jason (Jesus) and Menelaus (Onias) the discrepancies in the two accounts are wellnigh irreconcilable ; the two brothers are not both descendants of Simon the Just, but Menelaus is said to have been the son of Simon, the Benjamite governor of the Temple, and therefore totally ineligible for the priesthood. Menelaus appears as the murderer of the righteous Onias III, whose death he procured by foul means when he came to Antioch.[2]

But whichever version is true, it seems evident that two brothers, rivals for the high priesthood, took Greek names, and not only consented to but petitioned for the Hellenisation of Jerusalem. By this time the sacerdotal aristocracy in Judah had become utterly

---

[1] In the French translation of Josephus' *Antiquities*, vol. iii. p. 82, Théodore Reinach gives the stemma of the High Priests from the Captivity to the accession of Antiochus Epiphanes. The last names are :

Simon the Just—his brother Eleazer of LXX fame in the days of Ptolemy Philadelphus.

Onias II.—whose sister married Tobias (see below, p. 96).

Onias III Jesus (Jason).   Onias IV (Menelaus).

Onias V—of the temple in Egypt.

This list, as the note says, literally ' swarms ' with improbabilities, but it is the only one we have.

[2] 2 Maccabees iv. *passim*.

indifferent to the Jewish religion, and were ready to encourage the nation to merge itself in the rest of mankind by adopting the prevailing Greek worship and manner of life. Finally, the victories of the Maccabeean brethren caused the Jews to recognise the necessity of transferring the high priesthood to this family, thereby setting up a completely new line of priestly rulers, in place of their godless if more legitimate predecessors. The old line of priests ministered at Leontopolis in Egypt, where Ptolemy Philometer (181–146) had granted Onias V, the son of Onias III, leave to build a Jewish temple.

The Asmonaean priests.—The ascendency of the Maccabees marked the triumph of the popular religion, namely of the Law as promulgated by Ezra, over a priesthood which was zealous neither for the Law nor for the nation. The new High Priests, because of their devotion to the Law and to the advancement of Israel, became leaders both in war and religion. Posterity spoke of Judas and even of his father Mattathias as High Priests ; and Judas seems to have acted at the rededication of the Temple in that capacity ; but Jonathan was the first of his race formally to assume the office, 160 B.C. From that time till the days of Herod (160–37 B.C.) the Asmonaean house held the high priesthood and the kingdom. Not, however, altogether without protest, for the Pharisees were constantly opposed to this complete secularisation of the high priestly office.[1] After the coming of the Romans and the accession of Herod, the High Priest no longer held the dignity his predecessors had enjoyed. The position was limited to a few great families, but the occupant only held his place for a brief period at the pleasure of the secular ruler. The priestly aristocracy became increasingly unpopular, even with those Jews who fanatically reverenced the Temple. It is noteworthy that of the forty-eight so-called High Priests from Jaddua to the destruction

---

[1] *Antiq.* xiii. 10 (289 ff.). The historian adds that such was the influence of the Pharisees with the people that even if they spoke against the king or the High Priest they would be believed.

of the Temple (330 B.C.–A.D. 70), hardly any would have been known to us even by name but for Josephus and the New Testament. There is a well-known passage in the Talmud in which the high priestly aristocracy is unsparingly denounced.[1]

THE SERVICES IN THE TEMPLE

The so-called Letter of Aristeas.—No one can study the ceremonial law in the Pentateuch without feeling that it consists almost entirely of ritual action of a kind with which he is entirely unfamiliar, and which would be extremely repulsive to him if he witnessed it. In the remarkable ' Letter of Aristeas,' a supposed courtier of Ptolemy Philadelphus, which belongs to about the beginning of the first century before Christ, Aristeas, as one of the envoys of the King of Egypt to Jerusalem, gives a description of the Temple. The writer was impressed by the wealth and splendour of its sanctuary, and greatly attracted by a magnificent curtain. He also speaks of the altar ; but his real interest is in the wonderful arrangements for carrying away the sacrificial blood by innumerable pipes overlaid with lead.

> ' They led me more than four furlongs out of the city, and at a certain place bade me stoop down and listen to the rushing noise of the meeting of the waters ; thus was the magnitude of the receptacles made evident to me.'

Aristeas was also struck by the fact that the manual work of the priests was tremendous. Some of them, he declares,

> ' bring the pieces of flesh for the burnt-offering, displaying extraordinary strength. For they grip with both hands the legs of calves, most of which weigh over two talents, and then with both hands and with wonderful dexterity fling the beast to a

---

[1] Peshaḥim 57a. Foakes Jackson and Lake's *Beginnings of Christianity*, vol. i. p. 33 *note*. See Appendix A.

considerable height, and never fail to plant it on the altar,' etc.[1]

It is true that Aristeas when he saw Eleazar officiating in the Temple was so moved that he says :

' The general aspect of these things produces awe and discomfiture insomuch that one thinks that one has passed into another sphere outside the world ; indeed, I confidently affirm that any man who witnesses the spectacle which I have described will experience an amazement and wonder indescribable, and will be profoundly moved in his mind at the sanctity attaching to every detail.'

But it is doubtful whether we, who unlike Aristeas (supposing him to have been a Greek and not a Jew) are totally unaccustomed to sacrificial worship, should not have regarded the Temple as a wonderfully beautiful building, but for all that as a gigantic slaughter-house. We should look on the proceedings with those mingled feelings of interest and disgust which a visit to see the wholesale killing of animals for a packing house inspires. And, had the whole ritual of the Temple consisted in animal sacrifices, it would have been difficult to differentiate it from any heathen shrine where victims were offered on a large scale.

The musical service and the Psalms.—There is, however, another side to the Temple worship which must have impressed every Jew who made his pilgrimage to Jerusalem, and may have appealed even to Gentiles, who might not enter the House itself. The Levites, who might not perform the priestly duties of offering sacrifice, had their place in the more beautiful portions of the service. For generations the greatest care had been taken to train men in music ; nor may it be forgotten that some at least of the Psalms, the best devotional poems in the world, were designed for the Temple.

The Temple in the New Testament.—It is unquestion-

---

[1] Thackeray's translation (S.P.C.K., London). Professor Kennett, in his *Old Testament Essays* (Cambridge, 1928), p. 88, notices the extreme exiguity of the dress of the priests when ministering in the Temple, which, considering their duties, need cause no surprise.

able that we have no written evidence for the Temple
and Synagogue worship in the time of Josephus comparable to that of the New Testament ; and it is further
remarkable that the author of the books in which
it is to be found is the one contributor to the Christian
Scriptures who traditionally was not of Jewish birth.
In the Gospel according to St. Luke we have one description of a service in the Temple and one of a synagogue
service, and in the Acts of another in a synagogue.[1]

The scene of worship in the Temple is found in the
account of the vision of the priest Zacharias when the
angel announced the birth of the Baptist. It reveals
the character of the devotions of priests and people in
the sanctuary and helps to explain the religious feelings
which inspired the worshippers. Further, all that is
told us is confirmed by the rabbinical tradition, which
was certainly committed to writing later than the
publication of the Third Gospel. The popular daily
service of the Temple appears to have been that of the
offering of the incense, when the priest entered the Holy
Place and the people remained in prayer without. In
the words of the Gospel :

> ' Now it came to pass, while he exercised the
> priest's office before God in the order of his course
> . . . his lot was to enter into the sanctuary ($\nu\alpha\delta\varsigma$)
> of the Lord to offer the incense. And the whole
> multitude of the people were praying outside at the
> hour of the incense. And there appeared unto him
> an angel of the Lord, standing on the right side of
> the altar of incense. And Zacharias was troubled
> when he saw him, and fear fell upon him . . . and
> the people were waiting for Zacharias, and they
> marvelled at his tarrying in the sanctuary ' (Luke i.
> 8-12 and 21).

The daily service in Middoth.—The service thus
described was repeated morning and evening every
day, and evidently the devout assembled in crowds to
witness it. The offering of the incense was the highest
privilege any priest could enjoy. It was decided by lot,
and, as there were literally thousands of priests, it could

---

[1] Luke i. 8–12 ; Luke iv. 16 ff. ; Acts xiii. 15 ff.

only fall to the same priest once in his whole life. Zacharias had to wait till old age before he obtained the precious lot, and consequently the angelic visit came to him at the supreme moment of his priestly career. When the time for the offering of the incense came a sort of gong, called *Migrephah*, was struck, and the sound was heard throughout the city. When the service was over the priests stood on the stairs and blessed the people. Every day of the week had its special Psalm. The prayers and songs were supplementary to the parts of the Temple service prescribed by the Law, which were almost entirely sacrificial. Our imaginary modern visitor, when he had accepted the offering of beasts as a necessary part of the Temple ritual, would have to acknowledge the beauty and appropriateness of the devotional worship of prayer and psalm. Nor must it be forgotten that the failings of the hierarchy of Israel were confined probably to a few powerful families, and that the general conduct of the worship was conducted with devotion, dignity, and decorum. So intent were the priests on their duties that, when Pompey's soldiers were massacring the people in the Temple, ' many of the priests, seeing the enemy advance sword in hand, calmly continued their ministrations and were killed as they poured out the libations and burned incense.'[1]

Destruction of the Temple inevitable.—The ruin of the Temple and the destruction of this sort of worship in Judaism were inevitable. The religion of the Jew in one form or another was destined to spread throughout the world, and had begun to do so when the Roman soldier fired the building on which so many hopes were centred, in which so many associations were deeply rooted. From a very early period in its history there had been those who had perceived that the Temple was a danger to the spirituality of the religion of Israel. Even at its dedication Solomon in his prayer is made to declare that the ' heaven of heavens ' cannot contain God—a solemn warning against localising His worship.[2] Just before the fall of the first Temple Jeremiah had warned the people that it was not inviolable, and that the religion of Israel was

---

[1] *War*, i. 7 (150).   [2] I Kings viii. 27 ; Acts vii. 49.

not bound up with its continuance. It was the same with the sacrificial system, which the earlier prophets had declared to be positively harmful, and which, if one may venture to hazard such a remark, could not have survived the first Temple but for the very positive commands of the Law. As it was, the express injunction not to sacrifice anywhere save where God had specially chosen to place his sanctuary was really fatal to habitual sacrificial worship, as only a limited proportion of the rapidly increasing Jewish population could live in or near enough to Jerusalem to be able to practise it. For some time after the Exile the sacrificial worship was considered so necessary to the worship of Israel that we hear of three Temples being built. Two were in Egypt, the first belonging to the Persian period at Yeb or Elephantine as the recently discovered Mond papyri have revealed, and another at Leontopolis, near Cairo, erected in the second century B.C. The third was the Samaritan temple on Mount Gerizim, built, according to Josephus, shortly before the coming of Alexander the Great to the East. But the non-sacrificial ritual of the synagogue soon became the distinguishing feature of Judaism, making its practice possible in every part of the world.

But if the fall of the Temple was a gain rather than a loss to humanity, the work that great sanctuary had accomplished had proved permanent. It contributed to the causes which made the ancient worship of Israel no longer local but national. It ended by destroying the prevalence of pagan ideas so inherent in the Chosen People, despite the efforts of lawgiver and prophets to counteract them. It gave the ancient traditional sacrificial customs a spiritual meaning which is still conserved in the language of to-day. Above all, it proved a bond of unity which prevented the tribes sprung from Levi, Judah and Benjamin from sharing the fate of the northern tribes to whom exile had meant dissolution. The Temple at Jerusalem, like many institutions on this earth, eventually disappeared ; but it has certainly left a blessing behind it, one reason being that in the Providence of God it was not allowed to survive its usefulness.

CHAPTER IV

THE LAW

The Law, not the Temple, united the Jews.—To an impartial observer it might have seemed that Judaism must disappear when the Temple at Jerusalem was destroyed. This, at least, was the opinion of many of the advisers of Titus during the siege. They argued that the Temple was the link which bound together the Jews of the Dispersion and the visible centre of their religion, and when it was gone there would be nothing to take its place. The cultus of the God of the Jews would then be numbered with other obsolete religions, and the people itself merged in the melting-pot of imperial Rome. But had our imaginary observer possessed exceptional foresight, he might have hazarded the prediction that Jewish monotheism—perhaps in the form of the new sect of the Christians—might survive as the religion of the future ; but only if it disregarded the bounds imposed by nationalism. Nevertheless, the great catastrophe of the capture of Jerusalem by the Romans and the ruin of the centre of the worship of the Jews increased, rather than diminished, the ties which united the people ; and it became evident that the real bond which kept them together was not the Temple but the Law. In fact, for many years before its destruction, the Temple had been losing its influence with the people, because it was increasingly felt that the God of Israel could not be confined to a sanctuary built by man, and was in truth enshrined in a law, which Josephus declared to be the infallible guide to all Jewish life, and the chief safeguard of the morals of the people. The fact, moreover, that the Law was known to every

Jew from his youth up, made transgression of its precepts inexcusable. The whole energy of Judaism was consequently devoted to making men and women conform to a rule of life which would render them acceptable to God.

The Law in the books of Moses.—To the question What is the Law ? the answer is not as simple as may at first sight appear. The obvious reply that ' The Law is to be found in the directions given by God to Israel through Moses, in the five books known to us as Genesis, Exodus, Leviticus, Numbers and Deuteronomy,' is unsatisfactory. The reason for this is, not that modern criticism denies the Mosaic authorship and the antiquity of his legislation, but because, taken as it stands, it does not fulfil the requirement of a complete guide to life and conduct. This can be shown by an analysis of the contents of the five books of Moses.

Genesis.—By both Jewish and Gentile theologians Genesis has been regarded as a perfect storehouse of morals and theology. In the first chapters they have recognised a supreme revelation of the nature of the Godhead and of its relation to humanity. But the legal element in the book is indeed scanty. The origin and sanctity of the seventh day is declared, but not the obligation to observe it. Certain precepts are given to Noah, which the later rabbis consider to be binding on Gentiles as well as on Israel. The one piece of actual legislation in this book deals with the obligation of circumcising all male children.[1]

Exodus.—Exodus, from i. to xix., continues the history of Israel, bringing the people to the foot of Mount Sinai where the legislative part of the book begins with the Twelve Commandments. The only laws found in the opening chapters relate to the observance of the Passover and the Lord's right to the first-born of men and cattle. The Sabbath rest is enjoined in the rules for gathering the manna.[2]

[1] The strictly legal parts of Genesis are (1) ix. 3–6 (against murder and eating the blood)—for a discussion of these commands see Lake, *Earlier Epistles of St. Paul* (1911), p. 55; (2) xvii. 10–14 (circumcision—in future to be on the eighth day). The rest is cosmology, history and poetry.

[2] The law of the Passover is in Exodus xii. 1–18, 43–49 and xiii. 3–10 ; the injunction that all males that are first born belong to

The Commandments in chapter xx. are followed by
the so-called ' Book of the Covenant,' a collection of very
ancient laws relating to worship and various social
relationships, interspersed with precepts regarding forbearance and kindness even to enemies. These are
comprised in about ninety verses from Exodus xx. 22 to
xxiii. 19.

The main part of the rest of Exodus xxiv.–xl., with
the exception of three chapters, is devoted to the directions
for making the Tabernacle, to the account of its erection,
and to the establishment of its priesthood.

Leviticus.—The Book of Leviticus is largely occupied
with the different offerings at the sanctuary, and to
questions of legal holiness or ceremonial purity. In
fact, except about half of chapter xxv., it is difficult to
use it as a guide for the conduct of ordinary life.[1]

Numbers.—Numbers is partly historical, with but
little hortatory matter. The legal portion treats of
offerings (chapter v.), Law of Nazarites (vi.), Levites
(viii.), vows, female inheritance, cities of refuge, etc.
Little is said in this book concerning the common duties
of life, the legislation being found in the midst of historical
narrative, lists of offerings made by the princes, and the
enumeration of the different halting places in the
wilderness.[2]

Deuteronomy.—Deuteronomy, as far as its laws are
concerned, is more of a prophetic exhortation than a
code. It appeals not only to the motive of fear in event
of its commands being disobeyed, but also to that of love
as a reason for observing them. Professedly consisting
of the last words of Moses to Israel before his death, it

the Lord (xiii. 11–16); the law of the Sabbath in conjunction with
the giving of the manna (xvi. 22–30). After the giving of the Ten
Commandments and the precepts which follow, on which Josephus
lays much stress, there is scarcely any strictly moral teaching in the
book.

[1] Of course, the book of Leviticus may be employed to teach
spiritual truths. What is here meant is that without interpretation
it suggests little or nothing except priestly duties, in which the majority
of the Chosen People could have no active part.

[2] The legal chapters of Numbers are iv., v., vi., viii., ix., xv., xviii.,
xix., xxvii.–xxx. Hardly any of these laws contain moral precepts
for the ordinary Israelite.

is more qualified to be a guide to personal holiness than the rest of the legislation under his name. Yet much of the book is a retrospect of the history of the wanderings, and prescribing laws as to how the nation of Canaan are to be treated, the duty of the king, the behaviour of the people in war, etc. The book is, however, of much value as expressive of the spirit of the Law, on which Josephus lays much stress.

Necessity for the Tradition to explain the Law.—Taking all this into consideration, the wonder is how a great body of law was extracted from such scanty material, for when we take out of the Pentateuch all that is not historical, hortatory, ceremonial or statistical, little indeed is found to remain. But by the first century the study of the Law had become the occupation of many a man's whole life, and the foundation was being laid for the great *corpus juris* known as the Talmud.

It must be borne in mind that the letter of the Pentateuchal Law, with the possible exception of parts of Deuteronomy, was incapable of producing a world-wide Judaism without being supplemented by traditional enlargements. The vitality of Judaism as a religion has been greatly assisted by its adaptability to changed circumstances, to which the elastic character of the Law has contributed not a little. The problem before the teachers of the nation has always been how to conserve the spirit of Judaism in a changing world, and they have tried to solve it by distinguishing between what is and is not essential. In theory there is no progress or development in the religion of the Law. It is inspired, perfect, and unchangeable.[1] In practice there has been a constant development owing to re-interpretation of its meaning. A Law designed for a nomadic people could not be carried out when they became a settled nation possessed of a considerable territory. When the people were later

[1] Judaism in the Law has a final, not a progressive legislation. See George Foot Moore, *Judaism*, Harvard University Press, 1927, vol. i. p. 269:
' The rabbinical doctrine could not be better expressed than in Matt. v. 18 : " until heaven and earth pass away (that is, never), not the smallest letter, not an apex of a letter, shall pass away from the Law till it all be done." '

scattered far and wide the Law had necessarily to be adapted to the change. A central sanctuary at one time appeared essential to the preservation of the great doctrine of the unity of God : it was destroyed, yet the doctrine remained unshaken. The powers of this world have repeatedly decreed that the Jewish nation should not exist as such, but be merged in the rest of humanity; the Law has made the decision of mankind impossible to enforce. This is greatly due to a code which, although rigid in principle, is, when expounded with wisdom, adaptable in practice.

Josephus and Tradition.—One reason why Josephus is of so much interest to us in this respect is because we have so little contemporary authority for the Judaism of the first century of the Christian era, the Jewish writers on the subject mostly belonging to a later age. It would be a valuable work to collect all Josephus says was enjoined and to see how far it is in accordance with the legislation embodied in Mishna and Talmud. Josephus was a Pharisee and therefore his interest lay mainly in the moral rather than in the ceremonial law, though as a priest he was proficient in the customs of the Temple. But when he dwells on the ritual, he is chiefly interested in its symbolism, regarding the priesthood to which he belonged as the proper conservators and expounders of the Law. From his intense desire to secure the Temple copies of the sacred writings, he evidently regarded them as of peculiar importance, although with the synagogue worship in full operation copies of the Scriptures must have been plentiful.[1] Speaking generally, however, the Priests' Code must have been of special interest to the Sadducees; whilst by the Pharisees, whose object it was to make the Law the rule of life for every Jew, the moral precepts applying to daily life were chiefly insisted upon. Josephus combines the views of both sects.

The Law as explained by Josephus in the ' Antiquities.' He promises repeatedly to write a treatise on the laws of the Jews ; but his intention was apparently not

[1] *Life*, c. 75 (418).

fulfilled.[1] It is therefore necessary to content ourselves
with what is found in his extant works. After giving the
story of Israel in the wilderness, Josephus recites the
law which he says ' appertains to our political condition.' [2]

There is but one holy city in the land of Canaan . . .
which God will choose for Himself ' by prophecy,' a temple
with one altar of unhewn stones which will have a fair
appearance when they are whitened. This altar is not
to be approached by steps but by an easy slope. In
no other city is there to be an altar or temple because
God is one, and the Hebrew race is one.[3]

All the inhabitants of Palestine are to meet thrice
a year at the Temple to celebrate the feasts and to
become known to one another.[4]

Tithe is to be paid in addition to the portions due to
the Priests and Levites. The tithed produce may be
sold, but the money must go to the maintenance of the
feasts in the Temple.[5]

Those gods which are acknowledged by other nations
are not to be blasphemed ; and gifts to any god are to
be respected.[6]

It is not necessary to go over these laws in detail,
as it will suffice to give a few specimens of the tradition
Josephus has preserved in interpreting them, remem-
bering, however, that he is writing not for Jews, but for
a Greek-speaking public ignorant of the Mosaic legislation.

The Jews are to inscribe on the doors the principal
blessings they have received—for thus he explains phylac-

[1] *Antiq.* Pref. sec. 4 (25); iii. 8 (223) ; iv. 8 (198), etc.
[2] This summary of the Law is in *Antiq.* iv. 8 *passim.*
[3] Exodus xx. 25. In saying that the stones were to be whitened
with mortar Josephus is possibly thinking of the altar to be made
when Israel should come to Mount Gerizim. Deut. xxvii. 4.
[4] Exodus xxiii. 15–17. The meeting for the purpose of becoming
acquainted is an addition of Josephus.
[5] For the law of tithe, see Deut. xiv. 22 and 28–29. See also *Antiq.*
iv. 8 (240).
[6] Exodus xxiii. 28. Josephus in the *Apion,* ii. 33 (237) quotes
this verse and says it is out of respect for the name ' God.' Philo says
much the same. See Thackeray's note in his translation. A Jew
was particularly liable to the charge of insulting the gods. *Cf.* the
remark of the ' town-clerk ' in Acts xix. 37. ' Ye have brought these
men, who are neither *robbers of temples, nor blasphemers* of your
goddess.' Almost the words of Josephus.

teries, or rather their contents—and on their foreheads
and arms, that God's favour for them may be seen by
all.[1] The testimony of women is not to be admitted
because of their levity and impudence, nor is that of
slaves.[2] An aristocracy is the best form of government ;
but if a king is desired he should do nothing without the
opinion of the High Priest and the Sanhedrin.[3]

A Jew may not marry a slave ; an erring damsel is
to be stoned, but if she is the daughter of a priest she is
to be burned alive.[4] It is a duty to show the roads to
those who do not know them, and not to regard it as a
sport to let them go astray.[5] Eunuchs, who have made
themselves such, are to be regarded with special detesta-
tion.[6] It is a crime to geld an animal.[7] No one is to
wear any garment of wool and linen, since these materials
are reserved for the priests.[8] The people are enjoined,
especially in battle, not to allow a man to wear a woman's
clothes, or the woman those of a man.[9] The above are
given as examples of the Jewish tradition as interpreted
by Josephus, whose *halakah* or rule of life should be
compared with that of rabbinic teachers or later date.

The Law as explained in the ' Apion.'—In the ' Apion '
Josephus repeats much he has already said in the
' Antiquities' ; but in dealing with ceremonial purifications following conjugal intercourse he betrays Essene
proclivities, which were later displayed in the Christian
idea that all Adam's descendants are conceived in sin.[10]
He reveals his Sadducean education in his mention of
the law that permitted the ungrateful son to be stoned.[11]
As a Pharisee he would have been shocked at the en-
forcement of so horrible an enactment. As a matter of

[1] Deut. vi. 9 ; Exodus xiii. 9.
[2] Not in the Law, but in accordance with rabbinic tradition. G. F.
Moore, *Judaism*, vol. ii. p. 185.
[3] Deut. xvii. 14. Nothing said of the king consulting the High Priest.
In the Talmud the king should consult the Sanhedrin before engaging
in war. Théodore Reinach's note on *Antiq*. iv. 17 (224).
[4] Later Judaism generally ignores the ferocious punishments prescribed by the ancient law.
[5] *Cf.* Juvenal, *Sat.* xiv. 103 : *Non monstrare vias eadem nisi sacra
colenti*. Deut. xxvii. 18.
[6] But see Matt. xix. 12.   [7] Where in the Law ?
[8] Lev. xix. 19.   [9] Deut. xxii. 5 ; *Antiq*. iv. 8 (301).
[10] *Apion*, ii. 24 (203).   [11] *Ibid*. ii. 27 (206).

fact, in rabbinic Judaism the penalty of stoning could only be inflicted for blasphemy of the NAME, for which crime the trial was to be most carefully conducted and the punishment to be made as painless as possible.[1] Many of the legal precepts declared to belong to Judaism have no warrant in Scripture and little in tradition of its great teachers.   An example of this may be selected from the ' Apion.' [2]

> ' We must furnish fire, water, food to all who ask for them (*not in the Law*), point out the road,[3] not leave a corpse unburied,[4] be considerate even to declared enemies.   For God does not allow us to burn up their country (*not in the Law*), nor to cut down fruit trees, nor even to despoil an enemy who has fallen in battle (*not in the Law*) ; He has taken thought for our prisoners of war, that they may not suffer outrage, especially the women.   So thoroughly did He train us to be gentle and humane that He will only allow us to use our dumb beasts in a legal way, and forbids misuse of them.   We are forbidden to kill creatures which take refuge in our houses, since thus they become our suppliants (*not in the Law*).   Moses has told us not to take the old birds with the young and ordered us not to kill domestic animals even in an enemy's country (*not in the Law*).   Thus in everything our legislator has an eye to mercy, enforcing the lesson by the aforesaid laws and has ordered penalties for those who transgress them without good cause.'

Josephus writes for Gentiles.—It must, however, never be forgotten that Josephus is not teaching Jews as a priest or rabbi would instruct the people, but is explaining the Law in such a way as to adapt himself to the capacity of his Gentile readers in order to persuade

---

[1] The treatise Sanhedrin in the Mishna gives elaborate directions. The criminal is cast into a deep pit and his sufferings are to be as brief as possible.   Sanhedrin, vi. 4 ; *Jewish Encyclopedia*, art. ' Capital Punishment.'

[2] *Apion*, ii. 29 (211–214).   [3] See Juvenal, *Sat.* xiv. 103 ff.

[4] Josephus may refer to Deut. xxi. 23, enjoining the burial of a criminal before sundown.   But the burial of the dead was reckoned as a pious action, Tobit i. 17 ff.   For rabbinic insistence on this duty see Moore, *Judaism*, vol. ii. p. 176.

them to receive his portraiture of Judaism with interest. In several of his expansions of the Law he is in accord with the later Jewish doctors ; but it would not be fair to estimate his qualifications for the rabbinate by what has survived of his writings, especially as he has not left us his oft-promised treatise on the Law. Nor is it perhaps unjust to say of him that his admiration for the Law was but little tinged with enthusiasm. He praises its antiquity, and the excellent qualities of Moses as the wisest of legislators, and says virtually that life under the Law properly observed would be one of ideal happiness. But Josephus could never have written the Hundred and Nineteenth Psalm, which expresses the fervid love of a truly pious Jew for the study of the Law. It is hard not to believe that at times he regards its observance as little more than a ceremonial obligation. In this spirit he declares that one of the worst crimes of Herod the Great was the expulsion of burglars from Palestine, because they were thereby prevented from fully discharging their religious duties.[1] Josephus is enthusiastic at the way his countrymen have died amid the most fearful tortures rather than consent to violate the Law ; [2] but he himself, as his career shows, regarded self-preservation as the chief law of life. Yet the fearful fate of his people, which he witnessed with his own eyes, made Josephus hate the extremists, whom he brands as ' robbers,' for the miseries they brought on the nation. As Professor G. F. Moore writes, ' It may, I think, be fairly inferred that Josephus, like most of the aristocratic priesthood to which he belonged, had little interest in religion for its own sake, and that his natural antipathy to all excess of zeal was deepened by the catastrophe which religious fanatics had brought upon his people.' [3]

Josephus advocates a pacific Judaism.—Josephus and many of his contemporaries regarded the Law as the essence of Judaism ; and the Law could only be rightly practised when the people were at peace. It is but justice to recollect that Johanan ben Zakkai, of whose

---

[1] *Antiq.* xvi. 1 (1).   [2] *Apion*, ii. 22 (232 ff.).
[3] *Judaism*, vol. i. p. 210.

devotion to Judaism there can be no doubt, also surrendered to Vespasian during the war, because he realised that the day of Judah as an independent nation was ended for his time, and that its future lay in the maintenance of the Law. Josephus, a less disinterested man, realised that Judaism could only now exist as a peaceful religion protected by the might of the Roman empire ; and that the day of heroic resistance was over. Circumstances, indeed, both in his own days and subsequently, justified Josephus' warnings against the party of violence. Terrible as was the issue of the war under Titus, that under Trajan and Hadrian was even more so. The national life of the Jews in the Roman Empire was then practically annihilated. What actually happened in Hadrian's war we do not know. The historical facts concerning this final struggle between Judaism and the Empire are few ; indeed, scarcely any contemporary records have come down to us ; and when we lament our ignorance, we are compelled to acknowledge our debt of gratitude to Josephus, but for whom we should have known as little about the fall of Jerusalem as we do of that of Bether in the days of Barcochba.

How the Law was preserved.—What, however, we want here to ascertain is, not historical details, but how it came to pass that the Law of God—the *torah* of Moses and the wise men of Israel, and one may add of Christian Scripture—survived the ruin of the Jews as a nation, and of the Roman Empire as a civilisation.

Contrast between Judaism and Christianity.—In a courteous dispute between a Jew and a Christian, both sides would admit that all that which was held to be common to the essence of both faiths was the true religion.[1] But the Christian would say : ' Your people have preserved it in an imperfect form,' and the Jew would retort : ' Among you Christians it has been continued in a perverted one.' The Jew may well claim that the Law was preserved by the Pharisees and the disciples of Hillel, and the Christian may say that this was done by

---

[1] I have developed this idea in my *Gentile Christianity* (New York, 1927).

Jesus of Nazareth and His followers in another manner. The two religions differed in one important respect, in that the chief object of the rabbis was to make the Law the bond of unity to conserve the people of Israel, and of the Christian teachers to make its precepts universal. The difference between the Jewish and Gentile *torah* is seen in the literature. The Jewish is preserved in what is known as the Talmud, a monument of the learning of many generations, abounding, no doubt, in sayings of great beauty and in profound observations as to the duty of man to God and to his neighbour, but requiring much learning to understand and patience to peruse, and consequently one of the least popular works ever produced. Christianity, on the other hand, has given to the world the Gospels, the first three of which at least are full of the spirit and ethics of Judaism and yet appeal to men of every race and in every age ; for the Christian may freely admit that the ethical system of Jesus is, as learned Jews maintain, to be found almost in its entirety embedded in the Talmud.[1]

Judaism saved by its students.—But here the question is not the respective merits of Judaism and Christianity as religions, but how the Judaism of the Law survived Jerusalem and the Temple. Judaism is the most remarkable example of a religion saved by its students. The wisest of the rabbinical teachers gave up the struggle with the powers of the world, threw cold water on fantastic hopes of a supernatural deliverance, and gave themselves up to the study of how the commands of the Law might be fulfilled. Not only so, but they gave up the culture of the West for a time, let their own Greek literature, including Philo, Josephus, and what Protestant Christians call the Apocrypha, fall into oblivion, and expounded the Law in Hebrew or Aramaic. Almost

---

[1] Klausner, *Jesus of Nazareth* (E.T., Macmillan Co., 1925), does justice to the ethical teaching of Jesus, but shows carefully how this can be found in the rabbinic literature—all the way after His time. This writer admits that Jesus has extracted the best ore from the vast mine of rabbinic literature. Jesus is criticised, not as an ethical teacher, but as one who paved the way to an inclusive morality, which did not rest on the exclusive principles inculcated by the patriotic Jews of His age.

simultaneously the Christians, with very rare exceptions, abandoned the study of Hebrew.

As a Jew, Josephus was the last for centuries to attempt to make the Old Testament accessible to Gentiles. The work begun by the translators of the Septuagint ended with him to be continued by the Christians. But although, as Josephus indicates, even after the fall of Jerusalem the work of proselytism continued, the movement was well-nigh spent ; and Josephus was not the man to revive it. When one reads his apology for the Law one is disappointed. It seems, despite some passages of real eloquence in the ' Apion,' to come from the head rather than the heart, and to resemble that of some modern apologists for both Judaism and Christianity, who loudly assert the excellence of their religion, without attempting to enter into its true spirit, and blame the zeal of those who err by excessive devotion.[1]

The new Judaism.—Having the Law without the Temple the Jews developed a religion for the individual of ordered prayer, study, and the practice of benevolence. It found a new centre in the synagogue, which from this time forward became the resort both of students and worshippers. Yet in all his voluminous writings Josephus does not mention the synagogue ; and we have to turn to the New Testament to see how vital a factor in Jewish life it had become long before the fall of the Temple.[2]

The Jew and the Christian parted company to all appearance finally after the middle of the second century. Down to the outbreak of the Jewish war Jews and such Christians at least as were of Hebrew origin agreed in their reverence for the Temple ; and both the believers

[1] I cannot resist quoting a verse written by a remarkably self-seeking English politician of the eighteenth century. It unconsciously reveals his own character and incidentally that of Josephus :
' Love thy country, wish it well,
Not with too intense a care.
'Tis enough that when it fell
Thou its ruin did not share.'
Quoted by the late Mr. Charles Whibley in his essay on Bubb Doddington.
[2] G. F. Moore, *Judaism*, vol. i. p. 210. The word ' synagogue' does not occur except in *War*, vii. 3 (44) ; a large Jewish place of assembly at Tiberias is called a *proseucha* (*Life*, c. 54 (280)).

in Jesus as the Messiah, and the peaceful section of the Pharisaic party under Johanan ben Zakkai, left Jerusalem either before or during the siege. It was the question of how the Law should be observed that made the break between the synagogue and the church irrevocable. As time went on the difference deepened, and mutual hostility became more and more marked. Yet it is a strange but indubitable fact that there was a striking similarity between the two rivals.

Jewish and Christian Scriptures.—In the first place they not only both retained the same Scriptures— for the Old Testament was for some generations the Christian Bible—but hereafter they both worshipped the God of Israel without animal sacrifices, and were the only great religions in the Roman world which completely broke with shedding the blood of victims in honour of the Deity. Their places of worship, whether synagogues or churches, became houses for prayer, study, and instruction. In other words, they were, as no other religions of the time were as yet, ' book religions.' They agreed in severing themselves from the society of the Hellenic and Roman world. It is true they made a different use of the same sacred books. The Jew with his intense nationalism tended to an increasingly rigid legalism ; the Christian under the influence of Greek thought inclined to an increasingly rigid dogmatic theology. These opposite tendencies made the divergence between the two faiths greater as time went on : perhaps both of them consequently suffered by a loss of spirituality.

But formalism cannot completely stifle Judaism, nor dogmatism Christianity, for there is no doubt that, despite appearances, any religion embodied in a literature is almost impossible to destroy. Judaism, had it relied on the priestly tradition of the Temple, on unwritten history and unrecorded sayings of the prophets, could not have survived, any more than the religion of Northern Israel actually did. It was to the written Law, Prophets, and Psalms that Judaism owed its vitality and also its power of adaptation. As times changed, and circumstances

altered conditions of life, men went to the old records
to see how the difficulties could be met; and found
a solution in constant reinterpretation. It is the
same with Christianity, the same with the religion of
Mohammed. The strength of each lies in the Torah,
in the New Testament, in the Quran. Critics may show
that these literatures are not absolutely free from defect,
and honest adherents may admit the fact; but to those
who know how to reject what is temporal and to recognise
eternal truths they are not only a sure foundation but also
a source of growth and progress.

CHAPTER V

The Hope of Israel in Josephus

Hope essential to every religion.—When St. Paul sent
for the elders of the Jewish community in Rome he
told them : ' For this cause did I intreat you to see
and to speak with me : for because of the hope of Israel
I am bound with this chain.' [1] In his allusion to the ' hope
of Israel ' the Apostle was using words as intelligible to
the men he was addressing as they were to himself.   The
question is whether such a hope would have appealed
to Flavius Josephus.   But among earnest men, whether
Jews or Christians, there must always be a belief that
the revelation of God which they have received, whether
as a nation or as a Church, has some great end in view.
To believe that Israel has no future, that the nation has
survived its purpose and will disappear, is as difficult
for a Jew, as it is for a Christian to say that the faith in
Christ may have been of use in its day, but that He will
be forgotten and has lived on earth for nothing.   No
cause can survive the abandonment of the conviction
that it has a work as yet unfulfilled to accomplish.   A
religion may survive its institutions, as Judaism did
the Temple sacrifices, and possibly an age-long rule of
life like the Law of Moses ; but it can never outlive its
hope.

Josephus not an idealist.—Josephus was assuredly
no idealist.   Brought up as a priest, he was anxious to
maintain the dignity of the national Temple ; educated
in the school of the Pharisees, he admired the Law.
But he was not a truly religious character ; rather he was
a far-sighted man who recognised that the best interests

[1] Acts xxviii. 20.

of the Jews in his day lay in submission to Rome, provided they might keep the Temple undefiled by the presence of Gentiles, and observe their law without molestation. In temperament this learned Jew somewhat resembled an English Whig of the eighteenth century. His patriotism was cold, and his religion under the strict control of reason and self-interest. Yet perhaps he served both his nation and his religion more efficiently than a better man could have done. Still we must naturally expect to search the voluminous writings of Josephus in vain to discover practical sympathy with ' the hope of Israel.' At most he believed that the excellence of its laws would be admitted by all the world, but felt none of that enthusiasm which for good or for evil had, at any rate since the days of the Maccabees, been burning in Judaism. This enthusiasm was, however, manifested in widely different ways. In its fiercest form it was seen in a fanaticism which made the insignificant Jewish nation produce armies formidable enough to force the kings of Syria to grant them independence, and imperial Rome to respect their religion and dread their displeasure. Surrounded by enemies anxious for his destruction, the Jew held his own and wellnigh became at least master of Palestine.

Literary and religious movements in Judaism.—That this outburst of energy ended in disaster, and that it was accompanied by much violence and injustice, can no more be denied than that it was also associated with a spirit of the loftiest patriotism, even though at times used without scruple by designing individuals. But the enthusiasm of Israel was manifested in a nobler form in greater spiritual movements culminating in the preaching of Jesus. These must for the present occupy our attention, since the vitality of a religion is displayed not so much in its unity as in its capacity to produce variety of expression. To this Judaism was no exception, and at this time there was a strange crop of divergent opinions—Sadducees, Pharisees, Essenes, Therapeutae, disciples of John, disciples of Jesus, only to name the best known. Education in religion was widespread, and disputation on points of law incessant. The diversity of the literature is manifested in apocalypses, books of wisdom, attempts to reconcile Judaism with the philosophy of Greece, liturgical utterances, letters genuine or spurious, and imitations of ancient literature. The Gospels, by themselves, testify to the mental and religious activity of this remarkable age.

The Sect of the Essenes in ' War,' Bk. II.—Josephus says nothing of the religious literature produced in his days, but he devotes some space especially in the ' War ' to explaining the tenets of the three great sects, although he never seems to perceive their real tendencies nor to appreciate their religious significance, except as regards those ascetic practices which he greatly admires.

The sect described most fully in a famous chapter in the ' War ' is that of the Essenes, who practised what Josephus evidently regarded as the most ideal and perfect form of Judaism, one which his Gentile readers would readily confess to be in every way admirable. It is consequently important to have before us what Josephus says of this curious sect, and to bear in mind that we have no evidence of its existence outside Palestine, and that the name Essene only occurs in the three ancient sources from which we derive our information— namely, Pliny the Elder, Philo, and Josephus.[1] In his account of Essenism Josephus is evidently concerned to describe it in such a way as to be intelligible to his Gentile readers and sympathetic to their religious ideals. Essenism has been presented in modern times as a precursor of Gnosticism, as an ideal of life not dissimilar to that of the primitive Christians, or as an extreme form of Pharisaic Judaism. But from the standpoint of his age Josephus seems to be appealing to the non-Jewish world to see that Judaism included a mystery religion, an association for philosophic life, and a means of obtaining supernatural powers by the pursuit of ascetic purity. Here, however, we must let Josephus speak for himself, or at any rate give a summary of his remarks on the Essenes without comments or additions.

---

[1] See *Beginnings of Christianity*, vol. i. p. 91 ; Pliny, *Nat. Hist.* v. 7.

Essene life and piety described in the ' War.'—The Essenes are Jews; and the object of their discipline is seemliness (σεμνότητα ἀσκεῖν). They are more loving to one another than are the members of other sects. They practise temperance and eschew marriage. They adopt children in order to train them in their principles. Their distinguishing feature is that they have all things in common (τὸ κοινωνικόν). No one is richer than another, since all who enter the sect surrender their property to a common fund, which elected officers (χειροτονητοὶ δ' οἱ τῶν κοινῶν ἐπιμεληταί) are appointed to administer. The use of oil as an unguent is strictly forbidden.

The Essenes are to be found in different cities, and whenever one of them comes to a strange town he is received with brotherly hospitality. They carry no provisions for their journey, but take weapons because of the brigands. (Were these peaceful Jews liable to be attacked by their more patriotic countrymen?) Their dress and demeanour is like that of children led terrified to school (παιδαγωγουμένοις παισίν). They neither buy nor sell ; but have all things in common.

They have a piety towards the Divine peculiar to themselves. Before the sun rises they utter no word on mundane matters, but offer to him certain prayers which have been handed down from their forefathers, as though entreating him to rise.[1]

Having performed these devotions they go to work at their several occupations, after which they bathe in cold water ; and after this purification assemble in their own apartment, where no outsider is allowed. The food is served in silence, and no one begins to partake of it till the priest has uttered his prayer over it. At the beginning and end of the meal they do homage to God.

---

[1] *War*, ii. 8 (128). Does this difficult sentence mean that the Essenes worshipped the sun ? It is as hard to explain the passage otherwise as it is to believe that Josephus would reveal the fact that the sect was acting contrary to a fundamental law of Judaism. Can he mean no more than that the Essenes just before sunrise turned eastward and said the regular Jewish prayers (πατρίους δέ τινας εἰς αὐτὸν εὐχάς) like men who implore that the sun may rise ? In his description of the Essenes St. Hippolytus, in his *Philosophumena*, bk. ix., who follows Josephus almost verbatim, omits this allusion to sun worship.

After this they work till evening, when there is another meal at which guests, not Essenes, are allowed to be present. At this meal their behaviour and their moderation excite the admiration of all. ' No clamour or disturbance ever pollutes their dwelling ; they speak in turn, each making way for his neighbour.' Their silence and gravity suggest an awful mystery (ὡς μυστήριόν τι φρικτόν).

The Essenes practise unbounded charity to the needy, but they may not help their relatives without the permission of the stewards of their property. They prohibit swearing to observe a contract, because every word they speak is of more force than an oath. They study ancient writings to discover what will assist the soul and the body, and enable them to find out how to heal disease by means of medicinal herbs, and the properties of stones.

Grades in Essenism.—Before joining the Essenes, a candidate has to undergo a probationary period for a year, and is given a small axe, a linen girdle and a white garment. When the time comes he enters upon the second stage for two years, and is allowed to share in the lustrations, but not to partake of the sacred meal. When the proper period has elapsed he has to swear awful oaths (ὅρκους φρικώδεις) to be just in his dealings, to obey those in authority, to be moderate if called upon to rule, to keep his hand from theft and his soul from base gain, to have no secrets from his brethren and not to reveal those of the order even at the risk of his life, to communicate the rules exactly as he has received them, never to become a robber, to preserve the books of the order and the names of the angels.

If a man is expelled, he generally ends his life in misery. By his oath he may not eat ordinary food, and as none of the order may give him any sustenance he is forced to eat grass. But as death approaches he is generally compassionated and pardoned. Blasphemy against Moses and God is punished with death. A court of a hundred members is needed to pronounce sentence, which must be unanimous. The sabbath is kept with

exaggerated scrupulosity. It is particularly noticed that
a sanitary law prescribed in Deuteronomy is observed
by the Essenes, as though it may have been otherwise
disregarded in the days of Josephus.[1]

Like many sects with an esoteric philosophy, the
Essenes kept a strong line of demarcation between the
higher and lower grades. If anyone of the rank of a full
initiate is touched by an inferior, he has to take a purifi-
catory bath. The members of the community are very
long-lived ; many reach their hundredth year. They
are extraordinarily constant as martyrs ; in the war with
Rome they suffered anything rather than deny the
lawgiver. In the midst of their tortures they are seen
to smile, so certain are they that they will receive their
lives again.

Essene philosophy.—Finally, Josephus deals with
what he calls the Essene philosophy. They consider
that the soul is imprisoned in its perishable body. When
it is released from its prison it flies joyfully upward.
The good go to the abode of the blessed beyond the
ocean, the bad to a dungeon where punishment never
ceases. In a word, their view of the future life is that
of the Greeks. The object is to make men moral
by the hope of reward and the fear of punishment.
Men who study the holy books so earnestly and practise
so many ritual purifications are often gifted with the
power of prophecy, and the predictions of the Essenes
are rarely in error. There are other Essenes who
marry, but only for the purpose of maintaining the race
of man.

Essenism in the ' Antiquities.'—In the eighteenth
book of the ' Antiquities '[2] Josephus refers to what he has
already said about the Essenes in the ' War ' ; but by a
few important particulars he supplements his remarks
in this briefer notice of the sect. The Essenes are
determinists, they submit themselves to the dispensation
of God. They consider the soul immortal, and strive for
the reward of the righteous man. They separate themselves from the people when they send their offerings to

---

[1] Deut. xxiii. 12–14.   [2] *Antiq*. xviii. 1 (18 ff.).

the Temple, considering their own rites to be superior.[1]
No other people, Greek or barbarian, have excelled them
in virtue. There are about 4,000 Essenes. They have
neither wives nor slaves. They appoint good men and
priests to receive the fruits of their lands and to prepare
their food.[2] They live in complete harmony (οὐδὲν
παρηλλαγμένως), resembling mostly the Dacae, called
Polistae (dwellers in cities).[3]

Josephus' admiration of Essenism.—Josephus has
evidently a high admiration for Essenism. In the ' Life '
he says he made trial of the three great sects, Pharisees,
Sadducees, and Essenes, at the cost of no small self-denial,
and spent three years with Bannus, the strictest of ascetic
solitaries.[4] That a young man with a mind naturally
so enquiring should have studied the leading currents
of Jewish life is quite probable ; and from his long
intercourse with Bannus it is evident that his manner
of life had its attractions. We can therefore appreciate
the interest he takes in the Essenes, whom he constantly
credits with exceptional gifts, notably that of prophecy.

Eminent Essenes in Josephus.—His first mention of
an Essene is in his account of the death of Aristobulus
(104 B.C.), which, as has been subsequently noticed,
an Essene, named Judas, foretold would take place at
Strato's Tower.[5] But a more famous prediction was made
by the Essene Manaem, who saluted Herod the Great
when he was a schoolboy and promised that he should
become King of the Jews. When this prophecy had
been fulfilled Herod sent for Manaem, and enquired as
to the length of his reign.[6] It is to be noted that Herod
had an almost extravagant admiration for the sect ;

[1] This is a very difficult passage. Philo, in *Quod omnis probus
liber*, 12, says expressly that the Essenes did not sacrifice animals. But
the negative is omitted in the best MSS. of Josephus. See *Beginnings
of Christianity*, vol. i. p. 92. It was not a breach with Judaism to
abstain from animal sacrifices.

[2] Who are these priests ? Were they necessarily Aaronic ? In
War, ii. 8 (131), one says a grace before meals.

[3] Strabo speaks of the Clistae and Daci in *Geog.* bk. vii., and says
that the Mysi in Getica practise a continence similar to that of the
Essenes.

[4] *Life*, c. i. (11). See above, p. 6.

[5] *Antiq.* xiii. 11 (312–313). See below, p. 117.

[6] *Ibid.* xv. 10 (373 ff.).

when the Jews were forced to take an oath of allegiance
to him he specially exempted the scholars of Sameas and
Pollio and the Essenes from the obligation to do so.[1]
An Essene named Simon foretold to Herod's son
Archelaus the termination of his rule by interpreting a
dream.[2]

The favour shown by the Herods for these men in
part explains the character of Essenism as a world
renouncing sect, indifferent to the question of the political
independence of the Jews, provided they were allowed
to practise their rites and to live their own lives. In
this respect they were in sympathy with those Pharisees
who, like Josephus, accepted without protest the domination of Herod and his family.

Josephus commends an ascetic Judaism.—It has been
thought desirable to give Josephus' account of this
sect by itself because this is the best way of showing
our author's ideal of Judaism at its best. To him the
religion of Moses was truly perfect when practised by
ascetics zealous for the Law and for nothing else, men
more ready to die for their cause than to fight for it, a
remnant of righteous persons, living in the Jewish world
but not of it, intent only on attaining personal holiness.
The description we have here is intended to set before the
Gentile world the truest observance of the principles
of Mosaism. Whether Josephus has given an accurate
portraiture of the sect or drawn largely upon his
imagination is another question. His account is similar
to, but not identical with, that of Philo, who wrote before
him, or the brief statements of the heathen contemporary
of Josephus, Pliny the Elder.

Disappearance of Essenism.—It is remarkable that so
interesting a religious confraternity should be entirely
ignored, not only by the writers of the New Testament,
but in Jewish rabbinical literature : a conclusion one
seems forced to adopt, despite the ingenuity and real
learning expended in the attempt to see Essene ideas
and influences in the teaching of Jesus, and in dis-
covering allusions to Essenism in the Talmud under

[1] *Antiq.* xv. 10 (370 ff.)   [2] *Ibid.* xvii. 13 (345 ff.)

different names. What is of importance to the modern
reader is that in Josephus and Philo there is such abundant
evidence that Judaism had long been developing an ascetic
movement, similar to that displayed in the Christianity
of the fourth century. Its existence is in itself a proof
that the Judaism of the period from the days of the
Maccabees to the fall of Jerusalem was not only an active
religion but one prolific in different ideals of life and
conduct.

Proselytism.—Josephus recognises that Judaism
has a future as a religion that will spread throughout
the world ; in the ' Apion ' he triumphantly points to
those Gentiles who had at least partially accepted its
tenets.[1] But there are fewer mentions of proselytes
than one might expect, nor can I find the actual word
proselyte in his vocabulary.[2] But there is one example
of royal personages embracing Judaism ; and the story
of Izates of Adiabene and his mother Helena is too
interesting and instructive not to be given at some length.

Izates, King of Adiabene.—The little kingdom of
Adiabene [3] lay east of the Tigris and a little to the south
of the ancient Nineveh. It was bounded by two rivers,
the great and the little Zab, which flow into the Tigris.
Within its territory was Arbela, where Alexander defeated
Darius and overthrew the Persian Empire. Monobazus,
King of Adiabene, had a favourite son named Izates,
who was sent to the country of Carrae, where the
remains of Noah's ark were still shown, to protect him
from his jealous brothers. From thence, on his father's
death, Izates was summoned by his mother Helena to
the throne. In his absence from Adiabene he had met
with a Jew, Ananias, who persuaded him of the excellence
of the Mosaic dispensation ; and, later, Helena was converted. So convinced was Izates of the truth of Judaism,
that he demanded the rite of circumcision. His mother,

---

[1] *Apion*, ii. 38 (282 ff.).   There is not a Greek nor barbarian city
in which the sabbath is not observed.
[2] My friend, Mr. G. A. Taylor, a student in the Union Theological
Seminary, N.Y., has pointed out that in *Antiq*. xviii. 3 (82), the verb
is used of Fulvia, a Roman lady, becoming a Jewess.
[3] *Antiq*. xx. 2 (17 ff.).

however, endeavoured to dissuade the king from taking a step which might alienate his subjects. In this she was supported by Ananias, who declared that observance of the Jewish Law was more essential than circumcision. But a Jew of a less accommodating disposition, named Eleazar, now appeared, maintaining that the Law could not be observed properly by any uncircumcised person, whereupon Izates submitted and became in every respect a Jew. After a prosperous, if uneventful, reign of twenty-four years, Izates died, leaving his kingdom to his brother Monobazus, who sent his body with that of Helena to be buried under a pyramid outside the walls of Jerusalem.

Missionary activity.—No one can fail to see in this remarkable conversion to Judaism that there was great zeal displayed before A.D. 70, and probably long after, to spread the principles of the religion of Israel, which implies a belief, confirmed by the ancient prophets, that it would one day become the faith of mankind. The Christian legend of Abgar of Edessa has a resemblance to the story of Izates of Adiabene. Abgar, when he first hears of the miracles of Jesus, like Izates has Jews at his court. Thaddeus, or rather Addai,[1] one of the Seventy whom Jesus sent, stays with Tobias, the son of Tobias ; and the messenger of Abgar to Jerusalem is named Ananias. In both the Western and the Eastern world in the first century of Christianity there seems to have been a form of proselytising Judaism. Hence the violence of the opposition to Paul, not so much in Jerusalem as throughout the Empire, which may have been in part due to the rivalry of other missionaries of Jewish monotheism.

Different sorts of proselytism.—It is also noticeable that there were two forms of proselytising Judaism which are analogous to those we find in the early dissemination of the religion of Jesus. Izates' masters, Eleazar and Ananias, may be said to represent in Judaism the schools of James and of Paul in Christianity. To

---

[1] [Addai is the constant Syriac tradition of the name ; it is only Eusebius who identifies ' Addai ' with Thaddaeus. I believe Addai was the native name of ' Tatian ' (Tatianos).—F. C. Burkitt.]

Eleazar circumcision was essential to true conversion to Mosaism. Ananias, on the other hand, almost re-echoes Paul's words: ' Circumcision is nothing and uncircumcision is nothing ; but the important thing is the keeping of the commandments of God.' There were consequently different aspects of Jewish as well as primitive Christian proselytism ; for though the distinction between ' proselytes of the Gate,' *i.e.* those who accepted Jewish monotheism and morality, and proselytes of righteousness or those who conformed to Judaism in every respect, is of much later date,[1] there were in the days of Josephus a large class of Gentiles who sympathised with Judaism, and a more select body who boldly declared themselves uncompromisingly to be Jews. Still, many devout Jews hoped that their religion would become that of all humanity and that this end would be compassed by peaceful persuasion and penetration.

Josephus not interested in religious movements.— But, with the exception of Essenism, Josephus apparently took little interest in any religious movement of his day. The work of the Baptist had been evidently a powerful religious awakening force in Palestine, although the only reason the historian has for mentioning the preaching of John and his baptism is in connection with Herod Antipas and his dispute with Aretas. It may be the same with his silence as to the work of Jesus, which may have had little or no immediate political results,[2] and therefore could easily be ignored.

Messianism as Josephus may have viewed it.—The famous passage, together with Josephus' brief alleged notice of Jesus as the Christ, must be a subject for a separate discussion ; but it seems worth consideration whether the preaching of the Gospel of the kingdom

[1] If, indeed, it ever existed ; see G. F. Moore, *Judaism*, vol. i. p. 341, who finds no occurrence of the phrase ' proselyte of the Gate ' before the 13th century.

[2] I confess to a certain doubt concerning the persecutions of the Christians under Nero and Domitian, and I am inclined to hazard the opinion that organised attacks on the Church began in the days of Trajan ; see my *Peter, Prince of Apostles* (R. Smith, N.Y., and Hodder & Stoughton, London).

of heaven by John the Baptist and Jesus would have
appeared to Josephus in any sense a Messianic movement.
The word Messiah, as is well known, is the equivalent
of anointed, and was later rendered by the Greek word
χριστός. According to ancient Hebrew usage, anointing
meant setting apart for a special purpose persons or
even things. We may best describe it as consecration.
Priests, kings, and prophets were Messiahs, because
they had been literally or even metaphorically anointed
to their offices. Even a heathen is called a Messiah
in the person of Cyrus, whom God had chosen to permit
the Jewish exiles to return from captivity (Isaiah xlv. 1).
A Messiah came to mean someone appointed to deliver
Israel as the great saviours of the nation had done in
the days of the Judges. Ultimately, when the hope of
Israel lay in a final triumph when its deliverer would
come at the end of the world and judge or vindicate
the nation by victory over all the kingdoms and peoples
of the earth, this universal conqueror was looked for not
merely as a Messiah but as pre-eminently *the* Messiah.[1]
Christians have naturally seen prophecies of this promised
deliverer in the Law and the ancient Scriptures of Israel,
notably in the book of Isaiah, who is often spoken of as
' the evangelical prophet.' Yet if the ancient seers
spoke of the coming deliverance, the utterances concerning

---

[1] The subject has been discussed by Foakes Jackson and Lake,
Beginnings of Christianity, vol. i. pp. 345 ff., chapter on ' Christology.'
The editors owe much to the assistance in preparing the chapter freely
given by Professor G. F. Moore of Harvard, whose views now appear
in his monumental work on *Judaism*, vol. ii. pp. 323 ff. As the present
writer has been criticised for making a distinction between *a* Messiah
and *the* Messiah, he feels bound to give a fuller explanation of this
remark. (1) The word Messiah or Anointed (Greek χριστός), generally
' the Anointed of the Lord,' is applied to kings, especially Saul, to a
prophet, Elisha (1 Kings xix. 16), and to the later priests. (2) The
times of the Assyrian invasions and the ruin of Jerusalem led to
prophetic predictions of a restored monarchy under a strong deliverer
of the House of David. This was renewed after the Captivity, and
hopes were perhaps centred in Zerubbabel, the scion of David. But
these deliverers were all human, the man to whom the title Messiah
or Anointed is specially applied is the Gentile king Cyrus (Is. xlv. 1).
As he restored Judah to Jerusalem so might another monarch whether
Davidic or otherwise ; therefore one may speak of *a* Messiah. (3) After
Daniel the apocalyptic Messiah appears in connection with the restoration of the dead to life, a series of divine catastrophes, etc. Such a
conception of *the* Messiah we owe mainly to Jewish non-Hebrew
literature of which Josephus takes no notice.

the person of the Deliverer are uncertain and we must look for the Messianic hope of the salvation of Israel in the Jewish Apocalypses before and after Josephus, from which, as from the Christian Gospels, we can gather that there was a widespread expectation that some Saviour would appear and establish a kingdom of God either on earth, or in a recreated world ; but such a hope was probably confined to enthusiasts and mainly to the uneducated. The leaders of the nation, however, the commonsense Sadducees, and the practical Pharisees cherished no such illusions. The priestly rulers had the Temple, the scribes, the Law ; if God was properly worshipped, and His will interpreted and understood, what more was required ? Of all the men in Judah, Josephus was least inclined to look for or even to desire a Messianic deliverance. Therefore, it need cause no surprise to find that he studiously avoids any mention of a Messianic deliverer except with disapproval. Once, or at most twice, does the word Christ occur in his later history : in the famous disputed passage about Jesus, and in his account of the death of James, ' the brother of Jesus who was called Christ.' [1]

Would Josephus have regarded Jesus as a Messiah ?— Whether we deny or accept the genuineness of the passage about Jesus, it is doubtful if Josephus would have classed Him among those who pretended to be the Christ, though in the Gospels of Mark and Matthew we have warnings that false Christs and false prophets were to be expected, and that the disciples of Jesus would hear of men proclaiming that the Christ had come and was actually on earth. That these rumours were to be disregarded almost goes without saying. We hear more of false prophets than of false Christs, as is but natural. If we may trust a single passage in Acts, pretended prophets were to be found throughout the Jewish world. But a false prophet may be no more than a man of words ; a false Christ must be a man of action. In a country seething with rebellion almost any enthusiast who raised the standard of revolt might claim Divine

[1] *Antiq.* xx. 9 (200).

authority and either proclaim himself to be a Messiah,
a man anointed by God to deliver Israel, or be welcomed
as such by his enthusiastic disciples. The greatest
example of a Messianic movement was in the second
century of our era in the terrible outbreak in Palestine
in the reign of Hadrian (117–135).

Barcochba, or Simon Barcoziba, is only known as a
man of obscure origin who became the leader of the
insurgent Jews of Palestine. Tradition represents him
as a mighty warrior of gigantic physique. He was
evidently a consummate master of irregular warfare
and held the Roman generals long at bay. The saintly
Rabbi Akiba was so excited by his successes that he
hailed him the Messiah foretold by Balaam as the Star
which should rise out of Jacob—hence his name Barcochba—son of the Star.[1]

Here we have an idea of the Messiah hoped for by
enthusiasts of Palestine ; and, although we have the
most meagre of sources, Jewish, Christian, and Gentile,
for reconstructing the story of the revolt, we may be
allowed to imagine the course of these obscure events,
and the underlying motives. The Gospels are sufficient
evidence for the belief that terrible cataclysms were
to precede the Messianic deliverance ; and the ruin of
Jerusalem, and the disasters of the wars against the Jews
of Egypt and of Cyprus in the days of Trajan (98–117),
clearly indicated to the nation that the time of redemption
must be at hand. A great and successful warrior had
arisen in Judah itself, and at any time the Parthians
might come and roll back the boundaries of the Roman
Empire in the East. No wonder that the venerable
Akiba saw in Barcochba a Messiah—perhaps the Messiah
of victorious Israel—and that after the disastrous end of
the war Messianic hopes were dissipated, only occasionally
to revive.

---

[1] Barcochba, called in Jewish literature Barcoziba, either because
of his birthplace, or on account of his having deceived the people.
Akiba is said to have addressed him as ‘ King Messiah.’ The passage
in Numbers xxiv. 17, if messianic, predicts a Messiah resembling a
victorious Asmonaean prince : ‘ There shall come a star out of Jacob
and a sceptre (cf. Ps. 11. 9), and shall smite through the princes of
Moab (A.V. margin) and destroy all the children of Seth,’ etc.

Possible Messiahs in Josephus' day.—This leads us to enquire what sort of leaders of the revolts before the Jewish war were virtually Messiahs or Christs in the eyes of Josephus. At the death of Herod there was a general outbreak of lawlessness and fanaticism, in which Josephus relates that three conspicuous leaders arose in the persons of Judas, the son of Hezekiah, a robber chieftain, whom Herod had executed in his early days; Simon, a slave of the king entrusted with important duties, who was acknowledged as king by his adherents; and the shepherd Athronges and his four brethren.[1]

The very fact that Simon and Athronges ' put on the diadem ' may indicate that they each claimed to be a sort of Messiah. The vigour of Varus as procurator of Syria made such rebellions temporarily abortive; but, under Pilate, there was a small outbreak among the Samaritans due to a man promising to reveal the treasures hidden by Moses on Mount Gerizim.[2] The procurator evidently thought this might herald a serious revolt, and took stronger measures to suppress it than the occasion warranted. Theudas, who appeared later in the days of Fadus, one of the last of the proconsuls, claimed to be a prophet with power to bring people dryshod over the Jordan, and may well be recognised as a false Christ also, as may the Egyptian who persuaded his followers that he could cause the walls of Jerusalem to fall down.[3]

Such men as these were regarded by Josephus with the utmost abhorrence as the most dangerous of impostors and traitors to the best interests of Judaism. It is remarkable that in his account of John the Baptist as a preacher of righteousness, whose execution by Antipas was popularly regarded as a crime, there is no hint that he proclaimed the coming of a Messiah. When James is mentioned as the brother of Jesus who is called Christ it is highly probable that Josephus may have considered the appellation as derisive rather than

---

[1] *Antiq.* xvii. 10 (278).   [2] *Ibid.* xviii. 4 (85 ff.).
[3] *Ibid.* xx. 5 (97 ff.); xx. 8 (167 ff.).   See p. 262.

otherwise.   For Josephus, and it may be added the most
important Jewish teachers of his day, indulged in no
messianic hopes.

The disputed passage about Jesus.—The famous
passage in the eighteenth book of the ' Antiquities ' in
which Josephus alludes to Jesus is the subject of a controversy on which no agreement is likely to be reached.
The arguments on either side turn on the undoubted fact
that Origen, writing in the first half of the third century,
says that Josephus does not mention Jesus, and yet
remarks that the Jews were punished by the destruction
of Jerusalem among other reasons for putting to death
James ' the brother of Jesus who was called Christ.'
About a century later Eusebius, in his ' Church History,'
quotes the words of Josephus ; and consequently one
may infer that as Origen, a man of great learning, is silent
as to this testimony about Jesus, the passage was inserted
into the ' Antiquities ' by some one between A.D. 250 and
300.   For our present purpose, however, it is sufficient
to quote the section and see whether it appears to be
possible that such an author as Josephus could have
written it.

In the third chapter of the eighteenth book of the
' Antiquities,' Josephus gives two paragraphs relating
how Pilate offended the Jews by bringing the Roman
ensigns bearing the effigy of Caesar into the city, and by
using the Temple treasure to improve the water supply.
These are followed by the disputed section, after which
Josephus abruptly tells an unpleasant story about a lady
being seduced in the temple of Isis in Rome.   Why he
goes out of his way to interrupt the account of Pilate's
government is not clear, for he resumes it in the succeeding chapter.   Anyhow, all known MSS. have the
following statement preceding Josephus' account of what
happened in Rome :

' About this time lived Jesus, a wise man—if
indeed one may call him a man.   For he, as a teacher
of those men who receive the truth joyfully, did
marvellous things.   And he attracted many Jews
and men of Hellenic birth.   He was the Christ.

And when Pilate had condemned him to be crucified on the evidence of our leaders, those who had loved him from the first did not desert him. For he appeared to them on the third day alive, the prophets having foretold this and ten thousand other wonders concerning him. And to this day the tribe of the Christians, who are so called after him, has not failed.' [1]

Controversy as to the passage.—Since the Revival of Learning in the sixteenth century, scholars have taken three courses : (1) they have denied that Josephus could possibly have written these words ; (2) declared that, if he did, they have been interpolated by later hands in a Christian direction ; (3) maintained that Josephus wrote them as they stand. As those who take the third view are liable to incur the reproach either of ignorance or prejudice, one is naturally provoked to attempt to defend the genuineness of the section, bearing in mind that the case for the historicity of Jesus is not prejudiced or advanced by what Josephus has said or not said. The question is really one of the comparative value of the universal testimony of all MSS. and versions and ' the almost universal testimony of the best critics.' All turns on whether Josephus could possibly have written the words ' This man was the Christ.'

Militant Messianism impossible for Christians.— Whether Jesus believed Himself to be the Messiah or not, He certainly desired that, at any rate during the greater part of His ministry, the people should not acknowledge Him as such, being fully as much opposed to militant Judaism as Josephus. Without doubt the more ardent disciples of Jesus acknowledged Him whilst yet with them to be the Messiah, and His enemies accused Him of claiming to fulfil the hope of Israel in that capacity. Nor did Jesus deny the charge when tried before the priests, knowing full well that ·He must die. His death and resurrection made any hope of a militant Messiah impossible among His followers ; for once they confessed Jesus

---

[1] Euseb. *Hist. Eccl.* i. 11. *Demonstr. Ev.* iii. 5 (124 b). In both the text is virtually the same as *Antiq.* viii. 3. See Appendix B.

to be the Christ, they could not acknowledge any man who might arise to claim to deliver Israel. Their Saviour was in heaven, whence He would return in God's good time.

Jews practically abandon Messianism.—With the overthrow of Barcochba, the Jews also generally ceased to look for the appearance of a Messiah ; and, even before that, a large portion of the nation had remained contented with the Law as their guide in life. It became a proverb that ' If the Law were kept for a single day by all Israel, Messiah would come.' In other words, the world would become God's kingdom, if His people would but acknowledge His claim to be obeyed.

Messiahs dreaded by Josephus.—To a man of the temperament of Josephus the hope either for a Messiah as a Jewish world conqueror, or a Christian Saviour at the end of the world, was practically impossible ; and anyone who claimed to be a Messiah, let alone *the* Messiah, was eminently undesirable. The word Christ must have been to Josephus a term of contempt, and even of reproach. If he wrote the disputed passage he meant it probably to be inferred that in the days of Pilate a very wonderful man, named Jesus, had appeared, and that if all that was related of him were true he was more than mortal, and this was the Christ. The rulers of the Jews persuaded Pilate to have him crucified, but he appeared the third day to his followers and there is still a sect bearing his name. Elsewhere, in speaking of the death of James, Josephus adds that this man was the brother of ' the so-called Christ,' a name according to the Gospels applied to Jesus by his enemies and judges.[1]

The hope of Israel, according to Josephus, seems to have been that neither of a worldly nor of an eschatological kingdom. If he had looked for a Messiah in any sense of the word, he would have been satisfied with someone of the type of Vespasian, an emperor who would restore peace to a distracted world. A Jewish patriot, whom he would call a ' brigand,' was the worst evil ; as for the world to come, as a Pharisee Josephus might

[1] See above, p. 87, and Matt. xxvii. 22.

acknowledge its possibility, but to him as a man of the world it probably meant little, especially if understood in a Messianic sense.

SUPPLEMENTARY NOTE

Among the pretenders to the Messianic office mentioned by Josephus, the members of two distinct families appear conspicuously ; and I believe that there were two centres of rebellion, one in Galilee and the other in Judaea.

Hezekiah the robber chief in Galilee was defeated and put to death by Herod the Great, who showed himself throughout his life a relentless enemy of the brigandage so prevalent in Galilee. This was in 48 B.C., and so far as one can judge from Josephus there is no trace of this Hezekiah having been a patriot. That Herod was haled before the Sanhedrin for the summary execution of his prisoner, appears to have been a party move by the opponents of Antipater. Judas, the son of this Hezekiah, who seized the arsenal at Sepphoris, is mentioned by Josephus among other brigand chiefs who caused disturbances in the anarchy in Palestine after the death of Herod.

The other family which proved a centre of rebellion was that of the ' sophist,' Judas of Galilee the Gaulonite. Apparently he incited the people of Judaea in revolt, but did not succeed in causing them actually to rise in rebellion (A.D. 6). Two of his sons, Jacob and Simon, were crucified in A.D. 44 (?) by Tiberius Alexander ; the third, Menahem, seized the palace of Herod at Masada (A.D. 66), marched to Jerusalem ' as a king ' and was ultimately put to death.[1]

[1] For Hezekiah, cf. *Antiq.* xiv. 9 and *War*, i. 10 ; for his son Judas *Antiq.* xvii. 10 and *War*, ii. 4 ; for Judas of Galilee, *Antiq.* xviii. 1 ; for his sons Jacob and Simon, *Antiq.* xx. 5 ; for Menahem, *War*, ii. 17, *Life*, 5 (21).

PART III
INDEPENDENCE OF THE JEWS

CHAPTER VI

THE HIGH PRIESTS AS WARRIOR PRINCES

Obscurity of the Jews in Palestine.—Herodotus lived from 484 B.C. to about 409, and was consequently a contemporary of Ezra and Nehemiah.[1] But Herodotus, the most persistent and inquisitive of globe-trotters, who went about seeking information from every source, tells us nothing about the Jews. This, as we have seen, perplexed Josephus, who in vain tried to show that Herodotus had information concerning this people whose customs were so different from those of the rest of mankind.[2] The silence of Herodotus is still a problem to some, but its solution is perfectly simple. Judaea was so small a district and its inhabitants were so insignificant that the most intelligent traveller in the fifth century before Christ might even visit what was then called *Syria Palestine*, or Syria of the Philistines, and never hear of the Jews.[3] In the time of Nehemiah Jerusalem must have been a very insignificant city, in which the inhabitants of the neighbouring villages were only with difficulty persuaded to dwell ; and no place mentioned in his book as Jewish was much more than ten miles away. As the prophet says, it was ' the day of small things.'[4] What is more remarkable than the insignificance of the Jews in Palestine in the days of Nehemiah (445–432 B.C.) is that their territory remained restricted, nor do they seem to have multiplied in the country for nearly three centuries. The Temple at

[1] Josephus first mentions Herodotus in *Antiq*. viii. 10 (260).
[2] *Apion*, i. 22 (168).
[3] Palestine is found in the Authorised Version in Exodus xv. 14, the Song of Moses, and in Isaiah xiv. 29 and 31. Herodotus mentions Syrian Palestine in iii. 5, vii. 89 (the catalogue of the fleet of Xerxes) : ' this part of Syria . . . is known by the name of Palestine.'
[4] Zech. iv. 10.

Jerusalem increased in splendour, and, probably, the city in population, but the Jews did not become a power in the land till nearly the middle of the second century B.C. They were no doubt numerous in Babylonia and Egypt ; but in Palestine they were wellnigh negligible.

The sons of Tobias.—The first symptom of political vigour among the Jews was seen in the remarkable adventures of the Tobiades, an aristocratic priestly family in Jerusalem. Whether the story as Josephus tells us may be regarded as serious history or not, it is very significant, despite a flavour of Oriental extravagance which makes it read as if it were a tale out of the ' Arabian Nights.'

In the days of Ptolemy Euergetes (247–222 B.C.) [1] the High Priest Onias, a covetous man, refused to pay tribute due to his overlord. The king threatened to quarter his soldiers on Judaea as colonists, but Onias still refused to find the money. Whereupon his nephew Joseph, the son of a man named Tobias, who had married the High Priest's sister, offered to go to Egypt and see Ptolemy. Joseph first won over the king's ambassador, whom he feasted sumptuously for many days ; and then went to his friends in Samaria ; [2] and having borrowed all the money he could, started for Alexandria. There his friend Athenion, who had been sent to Jerusalem to demand the tribute, gave Joseph an excellent character to Ptolemy, who invited him to remain as his guest, till the day arrived when the farmers of the taxes of Coele-Syria, Phoenicia, Judaea, and Samaria, bid for the privilege of

[1] This might appear to be a suitable date but for the fact that Josephus represents the King as having a wife named Cleopatra. But it was not till 193 B.C. that a Cleopatra shared the Egyptian throne as the wife of Ptolemy V, Epiphanes. This was after Palestine had been annexed by Antiochus III in 198 B.C. Consequently, the whole story cannot be historically accurate as the Ptolemies could not collect the revenues of their lost province. At the same time the fact that the family of Tobias made their fortune and incidentally enriched the Temple as farmers of the revenue is not impossible.

[2] Note that the friendliness of the priestly nobles and the Samaritans existed as it had done in the days of Nehemiah. It may perhaps be suggested that the Tobiades have some connection with Tobiah the Ammonite, the friend of Sanballat mentioned in Neh. iv. 7 ; vi. ; xiii. 4–8. It is impossible to forget that Josephus has placed Sanballat a century later than Nehemiah.

collecting the revenue. As no one offered more than eight thousand talents,[1] Joseph boldly told Ptolemy that the bidders had conspired to bid an inadequate sum, and said he was prepared to pay double for the monopoly. When asked for security, he named the king and queen as his sureties. His impudence so delighted Ptolemy that he gave Joseph the concession, who thereupon set to work to collect the tribute. In the words of Josephus :

> ' Joseph took with him two thousand foot soldiers from the king, for he desired he might have some assistance, in order to force such as were refractory in the cities to pay. And borrowing of the king's friends at Alexandria five hundred talents, he made haste back to Syria. And when he was at Askelon, and demanded the taxes of the people of Askelon, they refused to pay anything, and affronted him also ; upon which he seized upon about twenty of the principal men, and slew them, and gathered what they had together, and sent it all to the king ; and informed him what he had done. Ptolemy admired the prudent conduct of the man, and commended him for what he had done ; and gave him leave to do as he pleased. When the Syrians heard of this, they were astonished ; and having before them a sad example in the men of Askelon that were slain, they opened their gates, and willingly admitted Joseph, and paid their taxes.' [2]

As Joseph met with rude treatment at Scythopolis, he dealt with its chief men as he had done with those of Askelon. By these vigorous measures he amassed an immense fortune, taking good care to remit large sums to Ptolemy and his wife Cleopatra. For twenty-two years Joseph enjoyed his great prosperity ; and Josephus says of him : ' He was a good man, and of great magnanimity ; and brought the Jews out of a state of poverty and meanness to one that was more splendid. He retained

---

[1] Jerusalem must have been indeed insignificant, if Onias had been asked for only twenty talents. But one of the provocations which led to the outbreak of the war with Rome was the action of Gessius Florus in taking from the treasury seventeen talents at a time when the Temple wealth was immense, *War*, ii. 14 (293).

[2] *Antiq.* xii. 4 (180–182) (Whiston's translation).

the farm of the taxes of Syria and Phoenicia and Samaria twenty-two years.' [1]

Hyrcanus, the son of Joseph.—Hyrcanus, the son of Joseph, went to Egypt as a mere boy, and won the favour of Ptolemy by his wit and profusion. On the birthday of the king's son, when the nobles offered presents, none of which exceeded in value twenty talents, Hyrcanus introduced a hundred boys and a hundred girls each with a talent, and presented the boys to the king and the girls to the queen. The youth went back to Palestine to find his father and his brothers wild with jealousy. He fought and killed several of his brethren, and finally established himself in a splendid palace beyond the Jordan, which he named Tyre (the rock). For seven years he was practically an independent potentate ; but when Seleucus the son of Antiochus the Great was dead, and Antiochus Epiphanes his brother had succeeded him, Hyrcanus, fearing that he would be called to account for his tyranny over the Arabs of Moab, killed himself.[2]

The Jews as tax farmers for Egypt.—Whether what Josephus relates is historically accurate or not, it is extremely significant. It would appear that the Jews up to the middle of the third century remained poor and obscure, till the sons of Tobias agreed to become the tax farmers of the Ptolemies. As long as the Egyptian kings were dominating Palestine the aristocracy of Jerusalem conducted the farming of the taxes of Syria with systematic thoroughness. In so doing they naturally incurred the violent antipathy of their victims, the Syrians and Greeks in Palestine ; but their energy showed the possibility, in the event of the Greek kingdoms degenerating, of the Jewish priesthood becoming the

---

[1] *Antiq.* xii. 4 (224). From this I think it legitimate to infer that the real prosperity of Jerusalem and the Temple dates from the rise of the Tobiades, and that the description of the splendour of the Temple in the so-called ' Letter of Aristeas ' belongs to the second or first and not to the third century B.C. See Büchler, *Tobiaden und Oniaden*, pp. 91 ff.

[2] *Antiq.* xii. 4 (236). According to 2 Macc. iii. 11. Hyrcanus had deposited his money in the treasury of the Temple. See the note to Théodore Reinach's translation of Josephus, *ad loc.* p. 93.

rulers of the country. There is no hint in this section of Josephus of any religious consideration influencing their conduct.

Palestine annexed by the Seleucids of Syria.—In the days of the Tobiades the Ptolemaic empire was deprived of its Asiatic dominions by the victory, won in 198 B.C., by Antiochus the Great's general Scopas at Panion (the ancient Dan). The Jews, and probably the house of Tobias, went over to the Seleucid kings. When Antiochus IV (Epiphanes) came to the throne (175 B.C.), and it was probable that disorder in Palestine might be suppressed with a heavy hand, we are told that Hyrcanus committed suicide ; but it would appear that his brethren in Jerusalem were ready to support Epiphanes in his policy of pacifying and also Hellenising his dominions in Palestine. Incidentally this accounts for the religious indifference of the higher priesthood, whose object it was at any cost to retain the wealth of the sanctuary at Jerusalem, even though the price for doing so was a temporary apostasy from its God.

Antiochus Epiphanes.—Antiochus Epiphanes is one of the comparatively few men in the ancient world who can be said to live, move, and have his being in our imagination. His character is full of interest from its contradictions. His very genius and versatility made his contemporaries call him ' the madman.' He had lived in Rome as a hostage and was acceptable to the best society in the city. During his short reign (175–168 B.C.) he proved an able general, an Oriental tyrant, and a patron of arts and letters. His manners were democratic, his disposition was arbitrary, and he has gone down to posterity as the typical persecutor of the true religion. To Josephus he is little more than a name : to the Greek Polybius and to the writer of the book of Daniel a surprising character, with a fascination terrible to contemplate.[1] Yet when one remembers what sort of men

[1] I have deliberately omitted to describe the well-known persecution of the Jews by Antiochus Epiphanes, the object of this chapter being to show how the High Priesthood passed from the priestly aristocracy of Jerusalem to the priests of Modin. I suggest that the Jerusalem hierarchy did not object greatly to the dedication

the leading priests at Jerusalem were in that day, and
that some of them had virtually invited the king
to make Jerusalem a Greek city, it is not easy to blame
Antiochus for supposing the Jewish religion could be
easily suppressed.

Revolt of the Maccabees.—To the historian, however, there are times when what is recorded in the
documents is of less importance than the inferences which
can be drawn from events. If we judge Jerusalem by
what Josephus has set down from the days of Nehemiah
to the appearance of Antiochus IV, there was very little
enthusiasm for religion among the people. But directly
the king interfered with the habits of the common folk
he aroused a fury of fanaticism, which can only be
accounted for by the fact that they had for generations
been trained to the service of the God of Israel and had
devoted their energies to obeying His commands as
embodied in the Law of Moses. Thus the Maccabean
revolt against Antiochus Epiphanes was essentially a
peasant uprising. Jerusalem was apparently Hellenised
without serious difficulty, the Temple was heathenised
for a while, and the young priests took part in the sports
of the gymnasium.[1] But when Antiochus began to force
Hellenism on the neighbouring cities he met with a
stubborn resistance ; and the common people showed a
heroism which none of the ruling hierarchy had dared
to display.[2] During the persecution Judas the Maccabee
seems to have gone round the villages inciting the people
to revolt.[3] At last at Modin, a small town north-west of

of their Temple to Zeus of Olympus, any more than the Samaritans
(*Antiq.* xii. 5 (258–264)) did to that of Gerizim to Zeus Hellenios. This
religious syncretism, identifying Zeus with Jehovah, is found in the words
of Aristeas as reported in *Antiq.* xii. 2 (22). For the character of
Antiochus see Polybius, bk. xxvi. (fragments quoted by Athenaeus,
Loeb Library, vol. vi. p. 480) ; and Dan. vii. 8 ; viii. 9–23 ; xi. 21 ff.
(J. A. Montgomery, *International Critical Commentary*.)

[1] 2 Macc. iv. 14.
[2] 2 Macc. vi. *passim*, but note v. 8.
[3] 2 Macc. viii. 1. Nothing is said of the sudden outbreak of
Mattathias and his sons at Modin. The village is not mentioned
earlier, but the Talmud says that a place called Modiim or Modith is
15 miles from Jerusalem. St. Jerome (A.D. 400) was shown the ruins
of the tombs of the Maccabees. See Neubauer, *Geog. du Talmud*,
p. 90.

Jerusalem, an aged priest named Mattathias declared war by killing an apostate Jew who was offering sacrifice at the local altar, together with the king's commissioner who was compelling him to do so. Mattathias then cried with a loud voice : ' Whosoever is zealous for the law, and maintaineth the covenant, let him come forth after me.' [1]

The rising of the peasantry even of a small tract of mountainous country like Judaea is bound to be formidable, especially when the people are maddened by oppression and intoxicated by religious fanaticism. A disciplined force is almost certain to meet at first with disasters when, in a rugged country, it encounters a foe to whom every pass is known and every cavern can become a fortress. At first, however, under Mattathias, who survived the outbreak of the rebellion for no more than a year, the insurgents went round the country destroying the idolatrous altars, and forcing all the children to be circumcised. Owing to some Jews having been massacred rather than fight on the Sabbath, it was decreed that in extreme necessity the holy day might be broken by resistance to the enemy.[2] The next incident in the war is not mentioned by Josephus and is only found in 1 Maccabees. There was evidently a sect, who were called Assidaeans, devoted to the strict observance of the law. They had formed themselves into a company of warriors, ready to fight to the uttermost for a religious object, but for none other, and their accession to Mattathias and his son at this time was of great importance.[3]

Dying speech of Mattathias—Religious aspect of the revolt.—At the beginning the war was characterised by all the fervour of fanatical piety. The dying Mattathias exhorts his sons to fight bravely, reminding them of Abraham, Joseph, Phinehas our father, Joshua, Caleb, David, Elijah, Ananias, Azarias, and Misael, who were

---

[1] 1 Macc. ii. 23–27.   [2] 1 Macc. ii. 28–41, 45.
[3] The Assidaeans are perhaps the predecessors of the Pharisees. Anyhow, their attitude of zeal for the Law, and coldness towards the ambition of Asmonaean ambition, was the same ; 1 Macc. ii. 42 ff. ; vii. 13 ff.

delivered from the fiery furnace as Daniel was from the mouth of the lions. Judas Maccabeus is to lead them in war and his brother Simon in counsel. He ends thus : ' Avenge the wrong of your people. Render a recompense to the Gentiles, and take heed to the commandments of the law.' [1] The same tone of exalted piety is found in the story of the first part of the war related in 2 Maccabees up to the restoration of the Temple and its worship, after which the history, both here and in Josephus, becomes almost entirely secular. This is what might be expected, for the career of Judas falls into two periods. The first may be called a war of liberation, the second was one of conquest.

Early victories of Judas.—The first two battles were fought north-west of Jerusalem in the neighbourhood of Modin, the home of the family of the Asmonaeans. Apollonius, the general of the Samaritan forces, attacked Judas and was defeated and killed, Judas taking his sword as David had Goliath's. This battle does not seem to have been important, as the place is not mentioned. But when Seron, the *strategus* of Coele-Syria, came, Judas exhorted his people to remember that God could save even by a small company, and suddenly attacking the Syrians, drove their discomfited army down the pass of Bethhoron where Joshua had destroyed the army of the five kings, and where the Jews later defeated Cestius Gallus the *legatus* of Syria.[2] Antiochus Epiphanes was in Persia, having left Lysias as regent in Syria. It was now resolved seriously to undertake the suppression of the rebellion in Judaea ; and an army of forty thousand infantry and seven thousand cavalry was collected. But, though the army of Judas was ill armed and numbered only three thousand men, the suddenness of their attack defeated one of the generals, named Gorgias, whose army

---

[1] I. Macc. ii. 52–68. Josephus puts a very different sort of speech in the mouth of Mattathias. [He has obviously the speech in the Maccabees before him.] He is going on a predestined journey (τὴν εἰμαρμένην πορείαν). The Divinity (τὸ θεῖον) will not forsake them, their bodies are mortal, but their fame will live. See *Antiq.* xii. 6 (279 ff.). The discourse throws light on the method of Josephus. He himself makes very similar speeches.

[2] I Macc. iii. 1–26 ; *cf.* Josh. x. 10–11.

was pursued into the Philistine plain. Judas had now
become a power in the land, and his victories having been
attended by the capture of his enemies' camps, he was able
to collect and equip an army of ten thousand men. At
Bethzur in the south of Judaea, on the road between
Jerusalem and Hebron, Judas defeated Lysias so
thoroughly that the Syrian general was compelled to
return to Antioch. Thus the land was cleared of its
heathen invaders.[1]

Dedication of the Temple.—Then came the re-dedi-
cation of the Temple, and the fortification of ' Mount
Zion ' with the destruction of the profaned altar, the
stones of which were preserved ' till there should come
a prophet to show them what should be done with them.'
Thus was instituted the feast of Lights. ' I suppose,'
writes Josephus, ' because this liberty beyond our hopes
appeared to us.' Blameless priests were appointed, the
necessary vessels for worship restored, and the sacrifices
resumed.[2] Two facts, however, must be borne in mind,
namely, that if Judas had restored and fortified the
Temple hill, he was not in full possession of the city,
since the Syrians, or apostate Jews allied to them, held
the *Acra* or citadel which overlooked it.[3] Nor could
Judas remain in Jerusalem, but had had to fortify
Bethzur in the south.

With the dedication of the altar a new era in Judaism
had commenced. Henceforward the nation was distinguished by an intense vigour and devotion. Its former
leaders, men like Jason and Menelaus, had been replaced
by such leaders as Mattathias and Judas ; and all compromise with heathenism was out of the question. The
new priests were enthusiasts, and the family of Asmon

[1] I Macc. iii. 27–iv. 35. Notice the close and perhaps intentional
parallel in the account of these wars with that in I Samuel. Josephus
follows I Maccabees pretty closely in *Antiq.* xii. 6–7.
[2] *Antiq.* xii. 7 (325). In Macc. iv. 59 the feast is called ' the days
of the dedication of the altar ' ; see John x. 22.
[3] It seems to be the general opinion that the *Acra* or citadel of
the Syrian fort was on the south side of the Temple. It is mentioned
in I Macc. i. 33–36 ; iv. 37–41 ; vi. 18 ff., etc. It may have been at
one time higher than the Temple Hill. Simon the Maccabee is said
to have had the hill of the *Acra* lowered (*War* i. 2 (20)). See G. A.
Smith, *Jerusalem*, vol. i. pp. 157–8.

were virtually, if not in name, in possession of the chief priesthood.[1]

Judas in Eastern and Northern Palestine.—Henceforward we enter upon what may be termed the less distinctly religious part of the career of Judas. Having dedicated the altar, he embarked upon wider schemes of conquest ; and 1 Maccabees v. is very significant of what was to prove the future development of the power of his family. The Jewish people were scattered throughout what we now speak of as Transjordania, and a few were in Northern Palestine. To relieve these from the oppression of the heathen Judas made an expedition beyond the territory of Judaea ; for, as in the days of Nehemiah, the neighbouring nations viewed the restoration of the Temple and its fortification with indignation ; and Judas being temporarily relieved of danger from the Syrian Greeks could turn his attention to the Edomites, the near kinsmen and deadly foes of Israel in the days of yore. He conquered and despoiled them, after which he attacked a tribe, otherwise unknown, called the sons of Baean, burning their towers and massacring their men. His next objective was Ammon, on the east side of the Jordan and the Dead Sea, where he defeated the native leader, named Timotheus, and sacked the city of Jazer.[2] The record of the campaigns outside Judaea reads like an extract from the book of Joshua. The Jews took Bosora and ' slew all the males with the edge of the sword.' They defeated Timotheus and killed eight thousand men. Judas next took Maspha and slew all the males and burned it. Carnaim was captured, and its temple burned ; at Ephron, which refused the Jews a passage, all the males were slain. Hebron was taken, and its towers were burned. Finally, Judas attacked the Philistines and destroyed

---

[1] 1 Macc. v. 6–52. The exploits of Judas were performed in Gilead, those of his brother Simon in Galilee.

[2] It is interesting to compare the language of Josephus, *Antiq.* xii. 8 (329), and 1 Macc. vi. 8, which has τὰς θυγατέρας αὐτῆς, which the most rudimentary knowledge of Hebrew would show that the writer meant, as the Authorised Version has it, ' Jazar and the towns belonging thereto,' *i.e.* her daughters. But in Josephus we have ' and their women and children he took captive.' This looks as if the historian had given a copy of 1 Maccabees for some scholar to turn into elegant Greek.

the heathen altars and their images. In the meantime, Simon had delivered the Jews settled in Gilead and Galilee from the heathen. Thus Judas and his brothers had declared war on every non-Jewish nation in Palestine, though they had not attacked any of the Greek cities. The Jews who had been rescued were settled in Judaean territory. This policy of concentration evidently made the Maccabeans a formidable power in Palestine.

Not all Jews attached to Judas.—Judas, on his return to Judaea, was at the height of his power and influence. He had repeatedly defeated the Syrian armies in the district, and had conducted more than one successful raid in Edom and Ammon. He had crossed the Jordan, entered Galilee, and returned in triumph with those Jews he had delivered from among the heathen. Because of his heroic achievements we are disposed to regard Judas and his brethren as patriots, backed by the whole Jewish population around Jerusalem. But even in this tiny province there was a religious party strongly opposed to the Maccabees, viewing their progress with a suspicion which, as events proved, was not wholly unjustifiable. All desired the continuation of the Temple-worship and permission to observe their ancestral customs; but many felt no desire to exchange the yoke of the kings of Syria for that of successful native adventurers, who might not be able to secure them peace and tranquillity, surrounded as they were by hostile Samaritans, Edomites, Arabs, Syrians, and the Greek settlers in Palestine. Jerusalem was occupied by two hostile camps : the city and the *Acra* by the Syrian faction, and the strong fortress of the Temple by the patriots.

Antiochus V, Eupator.—Antiochus Epiphanes died in Persia, leaving a son, a boy named Antiochus Eupator, of whom Lysias assumed the guardianship. It was not possible to sanction the state of affairs in Judaea with a chieftain as able as Judas organising an independent principality, which might at any time bid for the support of the Ptolemies of Egypt. Accordingly Lysias, taking with him the young king and an army of 120,000 men, invaded Judaea, utterly defeated Judas at Bathzacharias,

and took the city, but not the Temple, of Jerusalem.
Then occurred one of those frequent incidents which were
to contribute so effectually towards the establishment of
the independence of Judah.

The Syrian kings recognise the Jewish religion.—A
rival general opposed to Lysias, named Philip, was
returning from Persia, and, owing to its being the sab-
batical year, there was great scarcity in the country.
The army of Lysias made terms with the Jews and retired
from besieging the Temple, after destroying its forti-
fications.   In this way freedom of worship was secured,
and the whole policy of Antiochus Epiphanes abandoned, Judaism being henceforward recognised, and the
Hellenisation of Israel no longer insisted upon.

From this time began a series of civil wars which ended
in the ruin of the Seleucidae and the incorporation of
their once vast dominions into the Parthian and Roman
empires.   Demetrius Soter, who had been a hostage at
Rome, escaped and made his way to Antioch, where he
was crowned king.   Lysias and the young Antiochus
were executed ; and the new monarch resolved on making
a skilful compromise with the Jews.   They were to have
their city and Temple, and the high priesthood was to be
restored to them.   In this way it was hoped that the
Asmonaean rule would be ended.

In recording the events which followed the accession
of Demetrius Soter, Josephus follows the guidance of
1 Maccabees, on which his statements are mainly based.
It must be remembered, however, that for the life of
Judas we have also the weighty testimony of 2 Maccabees,
which is an independent work, later than 1 Maccabees,
and not known to Josephus.[1]   The reason for keeping
these narratives apart is that, when they are skilfully
combined, they give an impression of a greater agreement
than is warrantable, though 2 Maccabees in places
supplements what we learn from the first book.

[1] See 2 Macc. xi.–xiv. This book concludes with the victory of
Judas over Nicanor, leaving the patriot triumphant over the enemies
of Israel, and says nothing of his defeat and death. In this respect
2 Maccabees may be compared with the conclusion of the Acts of the
Apostles.

Demetrius wisely resolved to give the Jews religious liberty whilst endeavouring to prevent the possibility of the establishment of the freedom which the Maccabean patriots desired. He appointed Bacchides, one of his ablest generals, to suppress any symptom of revolt, and gave the Temple an Aaronite High Priest in the person of Alcimus,[1] who like Jason and Menelaus had changed his Jewish name into a Greek one. Alcimus was thoroughly pro-Syrian, ready to carry out any policy his masters at Antioch might desire. But there can have been no doubt as to his being of the genuine stock of Aaron ; for the people received him, and the Assideans, believing that nothing was to be gained by war now that the High Priesthood was restored, offered to welcome Alcimus, who forthwith murdered seventy of them and cast their bodies into a pit.[2]

Defeat of Nicanor and death of Judas.—Bacchides left Alcimus to administer affairs in Judaea, but finding Judas too strong for him, the High Priest petitioned the king for help, and Nicanor was sent. Judas fought two battles with Nicanor, one at Carpharsalama, where apparently the Jews were badly defeated,[3] the other at Adasa, where Nicanor was killed and his head brought away in triumph and set up outside Jerusalem. This victory, the greatest gained by Judas, was kept yearly as the Day of Nicanor on the 13th of the month Adar.

But Bacchides was too strong for Judas. A battle was fought at Eleasa, where Judas was killed, but his brethren rescued the body and buried it in the ancestral sepulchre at Modin 160 B.C.[4]

Jonathan.—Jonathan, another son of Mattathias, took the place of Judas ; with him we enter upon a new

---

[1] In his catalogue of the High Priests (*Antiq.* xx. 10 (235)) Josephus says that Jacimus (*i.e.* Jehoiakin or Alcimus) was a member of the House of Aaron, but not of the same family as the high priests before him.

[2] 1 Macc. vii. 8–20.

[3] Dr. Oesterley in Charles' *Apocrypha and Pseud-epigrapha* on 1 Macc. vii. 31 says : ' According to Josephus, Nicanor " beat Judas, and forced him to fly to that citadel which was in Jerusalem," an obvious error, since the citadel (" Acra ") was in the hands of the enemy.' Where Capharsalama was is a matter of pure conjecture.

[4] 1 Macc. ix. 19.

BATTLES OF JUDAS THE MACCABEE

1 Macc. iii–ix

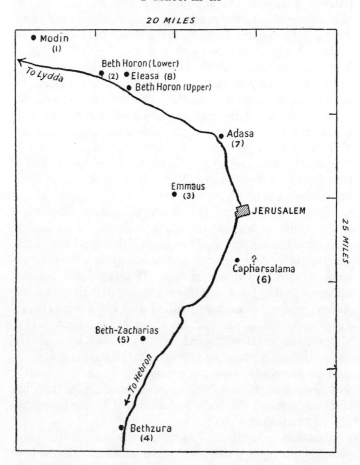

(1) Defeat of Apollonius at place unknown, possibly near Modin (1 Macc. iii. 10–12).

(2) Defeat of Seron at Bethhoron (1 Macc. iii. 16–24).

(3) Defeat of Gorgias at Emmaus (1 Macc. iii. 38–iv. 25).

(4) Besieged by Lysias at Bethsura (1 Macc. vi. 31 ff.).

(5) Judas defeated by Lysias at Bethzacharias. His brother Eleazar and the elephant (1 Macc. vi. 33 ff.).

(6) Capharsalama (?) (1 Macc. vii. 31, 32).

(7) Nicanor defeated and killed at Adasa (1 Macc. vii. 39–47; 2 Macc. xv. 20–30).

(8) Bacchides defeats Judas at Eleasa (1 Macc. ix. 5 ff.).

period, in which diplomacy effected more than arms for the advancement of the house of Asmon. The Maccabees had become heads of a formidable robber principality— for as such their territory would undoubtedly be regarded at Antioch ; but, when empires or kingdoms are in a state of dissolution, a robber chieftain has only to prove himself sufficiently formidable to be recognised as a legitimate prince. Thus it was inevitable that the Seleucid kings would in time acknowledge the brothers of Judas as the rulers of Judaea, especially as they had an army capable of materially aiding the various pretenders to the Syrian throne. But before his death Judas had sought and secured alliance with the power which was real master of the East.

Embassy to Rome.—The Jews, even those cooped up in the narrow territory of Judaea, must have heard of the Romans, who, as yet with few eastern possessions, were already really masters of the western empire of Alexander the Great. It is probable that Jewish traders had already found their way as far westward as Rome, if they had not already drifted into Spain. At any rate, Judas and his friends were fully aware that the Seleucid monarchs were in awe of the great Republic, which had annihilated the army of Antiochus the Great at Magnesia, turned back Antiochus Epiphanes on his victorious march into Egypt, and held the sons of the kings of Syria as hostages in Rome.

After the defeat of Nicanor, Judas resolved to bid for Roman support in his contest with King Demetrius ; and the story of the embassy is delightfully told in I Maccabees, and is certainly not improved by Josephus in his brief account of the transaction.[1]

The embassy to Rome was a wise and politic step on

---

[1] I Macc. viii. ; Josephus, *Antiq.* xii. 10 (413 ff.). According to Josephus, in the treaty Judas is called ' High Priest of the Jews,' and Simon their ' general.' These words are not in I Maccabees. The two versions of the story deserve careful comparison, as here we have an example of Josephus' method in dealing with an original document. The very naïve description of the Roman republic, the Senate, and the consul (I Maccabees thinks there was only one, viii. 14–16) reflects the impression the Roman government might have made on a remote nation, to which it was known only by hearsay.

the part of Judas, nor do its results appear to have been entirely futile. The small territory of Judaea had at least a powerful people on its side, and its rulers had shown foresight in recognising that the future lay with the great Republic. For it is worth noticing that, for all this artless description of Rome, the Jews had grasped the fact that a government existed far superior to anything else in the world. The kingdoms of the successors of Alexander the Great had either ceased to be, or were distracted like those of Antioch and Alexandria by intestine divisions. Rome as yet had no provinces in Asia. It was not till 133 B.C., or twenty-eight years after the treaty with the Jews, that the dominions of Attalus of Pergamus were bequeathed to the Roman people, thereby giving them a footing in the East ; yet the fact had been recognised that the Asiatic potentates were already only puppets in the hands of the Roman senate, since ' all that heard of their fame were afraid of them : moreover whomsoever they will to succour, and to make kings, these do they make kings ; and whomsoever they will, do they depose.' [1] Nearly a century elapsed before the Romans interfered in the affairs of Palestine ; and in the interval the family of the Maccabees, at any rate, were perfectly able to look after their own interests.

Desperate condition of the patriots after Judas' death.— The careers of Jonathan and Simon, the brothers who succeeded Judas, can only be related if we keep in our mind the history of the Seleucid and other kings at Antioch. The course of events is by no means clear, nor are the exploits of the two brothers of particular interest compared with those of Judas. But it is evident that both Jonathan and Simon were as resourceful and able as their famous brother, though circumstances make their adventures less heroic. After the defeat and death of Judas the state of the patriotic party was wellnigh desperate, and Jonathan and Simon showed their greatness in restoring all that had been lost.

The friends of Judas chose Jonathan as their leader and retreated east of Jerusalem to the wilderness of

---

[1] I Macc. viii. 12, 13.

Tekoa by the pool Asphar. They were later attacked by
Bacchides among the marshes of Jordan just north of
the Dead Sea, and forced to escape across the river.
Bacchides then fortified the cities of Judah and Alcimus
prepared to pull down the wall of the sanctuary. In
this the High Priest was prevented by death ; but in the
end Bacchides made a treaty with Jonathan, who was
now able to establish himself at Michmash just north of
Jerusalem.[1] ' And the sword ceased from Israel.'

Disintegration of the Syrian monarchy.—The Syrian
monarchy now became a prey to civil war. After the
death of Antiochus Epiphanes in 164 B.C., kings come
and go with amazing rapidity. Antiochus V reigned but
two years before he was killed by Demetrius I (Soter), who
occupied the throne twelve years (162–150 B.C.). But
in 153 a rival appeared who professed to be the son
of Antiochus Epiphanes. He is known as Alexander
Balas ; and from this time forward the Maccabees became among the most important people in Palestine. A
man who could put a trained army into the field, disciplined by a long course of patriotic and, one may perhaps
add, predatory warfare, was not to be despised when
there were two claimants to the crown ; and both sides
vied with one another in bidding for the support of
Jonathan. Alexander Balas acknowledged him as High
Priest of the Jews ; and, in the words of the Book of
Maccabees, ' Jonathan put on the holy garments in the
seventh month of the hundred and sixtieth year at the
Feast of Tabernacles ' *i.e.* in the autumn of 153 B.C.
' And '—a strange contrast to our minds—' he gathered
together forces, and provided arms in abundance.'[2]
Privileges were heaped upon Jonathan, and he was given
the right of wearing the insignia of a prince. As High

[1] 1 Macc. ix. 32–73. The events in these verses cover the period
160-153 B.C., 160 being the 160th year of the Seleucidae. The whole
account is obscure. According to Josephus, Alcimus died before the
defeat of Judas, and the people conferred the high priesthood upon Judas,
who retained it for three years (*Antiq.* xii. 10 (413, 434)). Jonathan
seems to have been driven across the Jordan and become a sort of
bandit chief. In spite of the opposition of the unpatriotic Jews and
Bacchides he managed to get back to the south of Judah, and at last
made an agreement which placed him near Jerusalem.
[2] 1 Macc. x. 21.

Priest he was recognised as the head of the Jewish people, and with his formidable little army he was able to work havoc in the Philistine towns, breaking their idols, destroying their temples, and showing himself to be the champion of Israel's God against the heathen.[1]

It would be tedious to relate how Jonathan, and after him Simon, added to the power and prestige of their family by supporting the different rivals for the Syrian throne.   All that appears as necessary is to trace how the High Priests attained first independence, and finally princely, and even royal, power.

The *Acra* taken by Simon.—The great object of the brothers was to get possession of the *Acra* in Jerusalem, which was still in the hands of the disaffected Jews of the Syrian faction.   Twice did Jonathan make an effort to take the fortress ; on the second occasion he tried to cut it off from the city by a wall which collapsed whilst it was being built.   It was not till after his capture and death that the *Acra* ceased to be a menace to the Temple.   Simon demolished it and levelled the ground on which it stood.[2]

Prosperity under Simon.—' In the hundred and seventieth year (143 B.C.) was the yoke of the heathen taken away from Israel.   And the people began to write in their instruments and contracts, In the first year of Simon the great high priest and captain and leader of the Jews.' [3]

Simon reaped the fruits of the exertions of his heroic brothers, all of whom had fallen in the cause of Israel. Eleazar, at Bethzacharias, crushed by the elephant which he had slain ; Judas, surrounded and fighting to the last at Eleasa ; John, captured and killed by the Arabs ; Jonathan, slain as a captive by the treachery of Tryphon.[4] In honour of them and of his father and mother, Simon

---

[1] 1 Macc. x. 84–86 ; xi. 4–6.

[2] The *Acra* was built by Antiochus Epiphanes (1 Macc. i. 33), and was held by the enemies of the Maccabees continuously for about 27 years.   For its fall see 1 Macc. xi. 41 ff. ; xii. 35 ff. ; xiii. 49 ff., and the parallel passages in the *Antiquities*, xiii. 4 (133) ; 5 (181 ff.) ; 6 (217). See above, p. 103.

[3] 1 Macc. xiii. 41.   *Antiq.* xiii. 6 (213 ff.).

[4] 1 Macc. xvi. 10–16 ; ix. 38 ; xi. 13–19 ; vi. 43–46.

erected a splendid tomb at Modin with a pyramid for
each, the seventh being reserved presumably for himself.
On the pillars of the tomb ' panoplies ' and ships were
sculptured ; and the whole edifice formed a conspicuous
object for the sailors on the Mediterranean.[1]

Embassies to Sparta and Rome.—In the days of
Jonathan and Simon further embassies were sent to the
Spartans, with whom the Jews claimed kinship, and also
to Rome. It seems reasonable to infer that these Roman
missions were advantageous to the Jews, as the influence
of the Senate may have caused the Syrian kings to have
made several concessions ; and even to have given way
when Jerusalem was virtually in their power. A hint
from Rome would be a command to any occupant of the
precarious throne of Syria in the days of the Maccabees ;
nor would the Senate be less inclined to help the Jews
who promised to become a formidable power led by a
succession of such experienced *condottieri* generals as
their High Priests really were.[2]

Simon extended his conquests into the Philistine
territory and became master of Gadara (or Gezer),
Jamnia and Joppa, so that Jerusalem now had access
to the sea. The grateful people now declared the High
Priesthood to be hereditary in the family of their deliverers ' until there should arise a faithful prophet.'
Simon was definitely accepted as ' General and Ethnarch
of the Jews and of the priests, and to be protector of all.'[3]
This decree was set up in the Temple. Thus the secular
as well as the priestly authority in Judaea was formally
placed in the hands of a single man. From Antiochus VII
(Sidetes) Simon received the right to coin money, a valuable concession, as it recognised him as an independent
prince.[4]

[1] 1 Macc. xiii. 29. ' It is there unto this day.' The sepulchre of
the Maccabees was shown in the early fourth century in the days of
Eusebius and Jerome. See Josephus, *Antiq.* xiii. 6 (211).

[2] The embassies to Rome are related in 1 Macc. viii. ; *Antiq.* xii.
10 (415 ff.), (Judas) ; 1 Macc. xii. 1–23 ; *Antiq.* xiii. 5 (163 ff.) (Jonathan);
1 Macc. xiv. 24 (Simon). Simon and Jonathan also sent to Sparta.
Hyrcanus I. sent to Rome, *Antiq.* xiii. 9 (259 ff.).

[3] 1 Macc. xiv. 25–47. Protector in the same sense as Oliver Cromwell
was ' Lord Protector.'

[4] 1 Macc. xv. 6. See Madden's *Jewish Coinage* (London, 1864).

The First Book of the Maccabees is loud in the praise of the felicity of the land under Simon. In a lyrical strain the historian declares that Simon ' took Joppa for a haven, and made it an entrance for the isles of the sea ' : the people ' tilled their land in peace, and the land gave her increase, and the trees of the plains gave their fruits.' ' The ancient men sat in the streets . . . and the young men put on glorious and warlike apparel. . . . ' ' Israel rejoiced with great joy : and they sat each man under his vine and his fig tree, and there was none to make them afraid.' [1]

Simon's death was less glorious than his life and exploits would have seemed to warrant. He was murdered by Ptolemy, his son-in-law, together with his sons Mattathias and Judas at a banquet at a little stronghold called Dok, near Jericho.

It is not without regret that one finds a guide no longer in the First Book of the Maccabees, which closes with the murder of the last of the five heroic sons of Mattathias. Its Hebraic style lends itself to enhance the interest in the story of how Judah became free ; and, despite the reserve with which the author suppresses even the word God in recording the course of events, there is an undercurrent of piety which contrasts with the coldness with which Josephus deals with this crucial period of the history of his people. With him as our sole authority we trace the careers of the two last great high priestly warriors of the house of Asmon, John Hyrcanus and Alexander Jannaeus.

Antiochus VII and John Hyrcanus.—Since the death of Demetrius I in 150 B.C. the Syrian kingdom had been the prey of dissension between rival kings and sometimes fell into the hands of usurpers. Now it was to be for a brief time ruled by a legitimate sovereign, worthy of the best traditions of the Seleucid race. Antiochus, the son of Demetrius I, called ' of Side,' from the city in which he had spent his youth, came to Seleucia in 138 B.C., married his sister-in-law Cleopatra, widow of Demetrius II, and daughter of Ptolemy Philometer,

[1] I Macc. xiv. 4 ff.

King of Egypt, and was acclaimed as Antiochus VII
(Euergetes). The usurper Tryphon fled ; and by grace
of the new king was allowed to become his own executioner. Of Antiochus VII it has been well said : ' One
more man capable of rule and of great action, one more
luminous figure, the house which had borne the empire of
Asia had to show the world before it went out into
darkness.' [1]

John Hyrcanus, a worthy son and successor of
Simon, had to prove his metal at once. Antiochus was
not the sort of king to permit Judaean encroachments.
In the days of Simon he had sent to demand the cession
of Joppa and Gazara, or a payment of a thousand talents
for all the damage he had done to the nations outside the
Jewish territory. Simon had offered to pay one hundred
talents for the two cities. The king's friend, Athenobius,
seeing the immense wealth of Simon, reported the facts
to Antiochus, who had sent his general Cendebeus to
bring Simon to reason. Cendebeus had been defeated
by Judas and John, the sons of Simon, just before
their father's murder. Thereupon Antiochus in person
besieged Jerusalem.

Thus John had plenty of difficulty to contend with.
The Jews acclaimed him as their High Priest, but
Jerusalem was closely invested by Antiochus. Suddenly
the king of Syria changed his policy. The Feast of
Tabernacles, the joyous autumn festival, was being
celebrated in the starving city, when the king generously
contributed to the Temple, made peace with the High
Priest, and contented himself with demolishing the
walls the Maccabeans had erected. John accompanied
Antiochus on his expedition to Parthia ; but fortunately
returned before its disastrous issue in 128 B.C. Henceforward there was nothing to hinder the High Priest in
his career of conquest and ambition. To satisfy the
demands of Antiochus VII, we are told that Hyrcanus
had opened the tomb of David which contained much
treasure. We also learn that he was the first Jewish
prince to employ mercenary troops, though in this he

[1] E. R. Bevan, *The House of Seleucus*, chapter xxx.

must have imitated David's practice of employing Cherethites and Pelethites.[1]

Further successes of Hyrcanus.—The Asmonaean family was, now that the Syrian kingdom was rapidly declining, at the height of its power. John Hyrcanus attacked the Edomites, the ancient foes of Israel, reduced them to subjection, and made them accept Judaism as the price of retaining their territory.[2] He then turned on the Samaritans, demolished their temple on Mount Gerizim, and laid waste the city of Samaria. Hyrcanus ruled Judah for thirty years, from 135–105 B.C., and was regarded as the recipient of three proofs of divine favour, the rule over the nation, the office of High Priest, and the gift of the Spirit of prophecy, which enabled him to foresee future events. Of his spiritual influence Josephus tells us nothing.

It must be evident to the reader that the rise of the Asmonaeans had been regarded with anything but favour by many Jews. The lax semi-heathen party to which some of the priestly leaders belonged regarded them as enemies and disturbers of the peace, preferring the rule of Antioch to the tyranny of Jerusalem. But all the enemies of the Maccabees were not the ' lawless ' and ' impious ' men we read of in the record of 1 Maccabees. We have already seen that earnest pietists, like the Chasidim, looked on the progress of a worldly Jewish state with apprehension, desiring only the right to exercise their religion in peace. To these a High Priest whose main qualification was warlike ability was an anomaly hardly to be endured.

Pharisees and Sadducees.—In the days of Hyrcanus the two famous Jewish sects came into prominence. The Pharisees, if not the same as the Assidaeans or Chasidim, carried out their principles. Deeply religious and fanatical observers of the Law, they cared little for the sort of patriotism displayed by the Asmonaeans.

---

[1] *Antiq.* xiii. 8 (247–249). Hyrcanus rebuilt the walls; *cf.* 1 Macc. xvi. 23. It seems probable that the Romans had something to do with the easy terms Hyrcanus received from Antiochus VII.

[2] *Antiq.* xiii. 9 (257). His son Aristobulus did the same. *Antiq.* xiii. 11 (318).

Hyrcanus, however, admired and honoured them, till they revealed the real tendency of their tenets in an incident dramatically related by Josephus. At a banquet given to the leaders of the Pharisees, Hyrcanus asked their candid opinion of his government. All united in his praise except one, named Eleazar, who said that he ought to resign the High Priesthood and be content with the secular authority. The reason Eleazar gave was that Hyrcanus was the son of a woman whom Antiochus Epiphanes had made a captive. Josephus says that this was untrue ; and a certain Sadducee, named Jonathan, suggested that Hyrcanus should ask what punishment Eleazar deserved. The Pharisees, always averse to the death penalty, declared for his imprisonment. This deeply offended the High Priest, who thenceforward transferred his patronage to the Sadducees.

Aristobulus I, Philhellene.—Without entering here upon the subject of their respective views and practices, it is enough to say that the Pharisees represented the popular party which often regarded the priestly rule as unjustifiable and oppressive, whilst the Sadducees supported the ideas of the house of Asmon. The fatal effects of the mutual hostility of the two parties in Judaism appeared when the strong hand of Hyrcanus was removed. Hyrcanus left five sons. The two elder, Aristobulus and Antigonus, were on good terms ; but Aristobulus became jealous, and permitted his brother to be killed under the following circumstances. Antigonus returned to Jerusalem after a successful foray ; and on the Feast of Tabernacles officiated in place of the High Priest, who was ill. Aristobulus was assured that his brother was aiming at the chief power ; and the courtiers persuaded the High Priest and king, for Aristobulus was the first of his house to assume the royal title, to allow Antigonus to be killed if he came armed into his presence. Aristobulus warned his brother not to come armed, but the queen and her confederates altered the message ; and Antigonus was killed by the guards in a dark passage of the fortress called Strato's Tower. Aristobulus never recovered from the remorse occasioned by his brother's

death, and only reigned one year. He had his mother
starved to death in prison, and thus his short reign is
marked by crimes characteristic of the court of an
Oriental despot. King Aristobulus was known as *Philhellene*, Lover of the Greeks ; but his Greek name and
title did not make him less zealous for the Law, for he
conquered the Itureans and insisted on the vanquished
accepting circumcision.

Alexander Jannaeus.—Alexander Jannaeus, who succeeded Aristobulus, reigned for twenty-seven years.
Dean Milman describes him as ' Always unfortunate in
battle,' [1] but if he could lose battles he could certainly win
campaigns, for his gains in cities and territory were
enormous. Josephus enumerates twenty-eight towns or
fortresses in Syria, Idumaea and Phoenicia, many with
Greek names. True to the traditions of his house he
destroyed Pella because its inhabitants would not embrace
Judaism. A rough sketch map will show that at his death
in 79 B.C. Alexander was virtually master of the whole of
Palestine.

In character he seems to have been a ferocious despot.
The Jews were terrified into submission, but at times
showed pride in his exploits. On one occasion when he
was acting as High Priest at the Feast of Tabernacles the
people pelted him with citrons, and a riot ensued in which
six thousand were massacred. Later he captured eight
hundred rebels of the sect of the Pharisees, and crucified
them in Jerusalem, whilst he looked on, feasting with his
concubines. Before he died he advised his wife Salome-
Alexandra to make terms with the Pharisees, and the fact
that this able woman could, with their support, hold her
own till her death in 69 B.C. is a testimony to the sagacity
of her ferocious husband.

The record of the Jewish High Priests as the heads of
the people is indeed painful to read. From Eliashib in
the days of Nehemiah to Menelaus in those of Antiochus
Epiphanes there is much darkness, and when it is lifted
for a while, despite here and there a bright spot, we are
not sorry that the curtain should fall once more. Capital

[1] *History of the Jews*, ii. 38.

has been made out of such incidents as the story of the
Tobiades to discredit the Jewish nation;[1] and indeed,

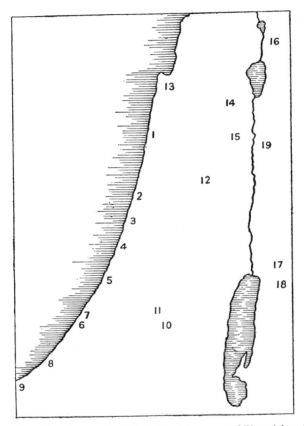

Antiq. xiii. 15 (395–397). Of Syrian, Idumean and Phoenician cities
the Jews possessed :

(1) Strato's Tower.	(11) Marissa (Mareshah).
(2) Apollonia.	(12) Samaria.
(3) Joppa.	(13) Mount Carmel.
(4) Jamnia.	(14) Mount Tabor.
(5) Azotus.	(15) Mount Scythopolis.
(6) Gaza.	(16) Seleucia.
(7) Anthedon.	(17) Heshbon.
(8) Rhinocoura.	(18) Medaba.
(9) Raphia.	(19) The Valley (αὐλῶνα) of
(10) Adora.	Pella

except for the early exploits of Judas, the story of the
Maccabees is not inspiriting. Yet their worldly prudence

[1] Klausner, *Jesus of Nazareth*, Book II. chap. i.

and skilful use of the dissensions of their enemies made the inhabitants of a somewhat barren tract around Jerusalem masters of Palestine.

But such reflections are entirely unjust unless one takes into account that the people at large were inspired by the Book of Daniel, the later Psalms, the study not only of the Law, but of the Prophets whether as historians or preachers of righteousness, not to mention the sober wisdom of Jesus the Son of Sirach (Ecclesiasticus). The record of the exploits of the High Priestly warriors is on the surface, below it is the obscure but indubitable fact that the period is marked by a great spiritual revival of the People of God.[1]

[1] For the Greek kings of Egypt and Syria see Appendix C.

CHAPTER VII

THE FALL OF THE ASMONAEANS AND THE RISE OF THE HERODS

Rivalry of the sons of Alexander Jannaeus.—The Asmonaean priesthood, like the older line, suffered from dissension between brothers. After the death of Hyrcanus I, Aristobulus and Antigonus were rivals; and Alexander Jannaeus, when he succeeded, instantly put one of his brothers to death. When Queen Alexandra died, a fraternal strife between her sons began, which lasted for three generations, and resulted in the ruin of the house which had delivered Israel from the yoke of the heathen.

Alexander's two sons were very different in character; the elder, Hyrcanus, was of a mild and peaceful disposition, and Aristobulus the younger a man of energy and ambition. The Pharisees gave their allegiance to Hyrcanus, whilst the party of the Sadducees favoured the more enterprising Aristobulus. But Hyrcanus was made a match for his warlike brother by the support of an Idumaean sheik, who with the rest of his countrymen had embraced Judaism, namely Antipater, who was later excelled both as a warrior and as a statesman by his sons, especially Herod, known as ' The Great.'

Power of Rome in the East.—For more than a century, since the battle of Magnesia in 190 B.C., Rome had been the dominant factor in the politics of the Near East; and she was rapidly exchanging her role of a powerful influence for that of the recognised mistress of the different countries which made up Asia Minor, Syria, and the territory west of the Euphrates. Palestine was in fact rapidly drifting into the vortex, to be lost in the *imperium Romanum*. The history of the Jews after 65 B.C. involves some of the greatest names in history. Pompey, Crassus, Cassius, Caesar, Antony, and Augustus, successively become the pivots on which all events connected with the fortunes of Israel turn.

Pompey.—The career of Pompey in Asia had been unusually brilliant. He had cleared the Eastern Mediterranean of the Cilician pirates and had given permanence to his victory by the wise moderation shown to the vanquished. Mithradates, King of Pontus, the most formidable enemy Rome had known since Hannibal, was at last subdued. Pompey increased the Roman dominions in Asia fourfold ; and when Mithradates in despair ordered an attendant soldier to kill him (63 B.C.), the Romans became masters of the East for many centuries to come. From the appearance of Pompey in Palestine we may date the destruction of the Jewish state.

The rivals appeal to Pompey.—The sons of Alexander Jannaeus and Alexandra Salome were soon at variance. Hyrcanus was made king ; but Aristobulus, despising the peaceful character of his brother, resolved to seize the throne. A peace was arranged and Hyrcanus retired to his private house in favour of Aristobulus. Shortly after this, under the influence of Antipater, who had become his adviser, Hyrcanus withdrew to the protection of the Arab king Aretas at Petra. Aristobulus took refuge in the Temple fortress ; and Jerusalem was besieged by the Arabs and the party of Hyrcanus. But Scaurus, Pompey's legate, arrived, and ordered the siege to be raised. Then both sides, after offering bribes to the rapacious Scaurus, appealed to Pompey, who had already reached Damascus.

There were three suppliants for the support of the all-powerful Roman, the partisans of Hyrcanus, those of Aristobulus, and the representatives of a Jewish section, who petitioned for the abolition of the kingship at Jerusalem, and permission to live at peace under their own

priests.[1]   In fact, since the first victories of Judas, many
Jews were content to surrender civil liberty.   If only
they could be free to obey the Law, they were ready to
submit to any master who would respect their religious
customs.   Jewish patriotism, so called, attracted energetic
enthusiasts, but was never universal.   The Messianic hope
that God would bring about the deliverance without
human aid kept many a pious Jew from avenging his
country's wrongs upon the heathen.   But it is wellnigh
impossible to conjecture what Judaism might have become
in the world had it renounced all secular ambition and
remained content with Roman domination.

Aristobulus and his sons were patriots ; had they had
the chance they would have retained and perhaps extended
the Jewish hegemony over Palestine ; but they had very
different people to deal with from those encountered by
John Hyrcanus or Alexander Jannaeus.   The dominant
power was, not the Macedonian kingdom of Antioch in its
dotage, but the Roman Republic and its armies commanded by some of the greatest generals in history.   The
Jews made a brave resistance to Rome, but in doing so
they courted inevitable ruin.

The family of Antipater consistently pro-Roman.—
Antipater and his sons, in whose hands Hyrcanus was
a puppet, saw things clearly.   These knew the Romans
must win ;   and they saw that the only hope of the
Jewish nation was in submitting and courting their
favour.   They became the loyal partisans of the Republic,
and supported its officers through bad as well as good
fortune.   True to no Roman, they were never faithless
to Rome, with the result that they emerged from the
wars of the triumvirate, wealthier, stronger, and masters
of a larger realm than any Asmonaean prince could have
dreamed of.   How they accomplished this unscrupulously,
if sagaciously, the sequel will show.

---

[1] *Antiq.* xiv. 3 (41).   Much the same thing happened when the
sons of Herod appealed to Augustus about their father's inheritance.
The Jews sent a request to be embodied in the empire and allowed
to manage their affairs under their own magistrates (see *infra*, p. 143).
Earlier the Chasidim had deserted Judas the Maccabee, when Alcimus,
a lawful priest, was sent to Jerusalem.

Pompey besieges Jerusalem.—Aristobulus made trouble from the first : he submitted, then he revolted against Pompey, who, after imprisoning him at Jericho, himself marched on Jerusalem. The party of Hyrcanus in the city welcomed the Romans, but the Temple held out. Like Titus and others who besieged Jerusalem Pompey attacked the Temple from the north side ; and it would have been impossible to occupy it had not the Jews scrupulously abstained from attacking Pompey's engineers as they erected mounds against the wall on the Sabbath. The heroic priests, who performed its services regardless of danger, were slain at the altar. When the Romans poured into the sanctuary Pompey and his officers insisted on entering the Holy of Holies ; but scrupulously refrained from plundering the Temple of its treasures.[1]

In this Pompey showed his wisdom, and indeed his whole eastern policy proves that he is not called Pompey the Great for nothing. The victories gained by Sulla, Lucullus, and himself over Mithradates had really been the triumphs of the civilisation of the West over the disorder of the East ; for the King of Pontus was an Oriental with a veneer of Greek culture. Pompey had fought as a Roman to secure the triumph of Greek ideas. Palestine was full of Greek cities, and the Jews had tried to Hebraise the country by forcing the districts which were conquered by their kingly priests to adopt their religion, and had not scrupled to put to the sword those who refused to do so. In their way John Hyrcanus and Alexander Jannaeus were at least as great persecutors of other religions as Antiochus Epiphanes had been of Judaism. Pompey's policy was thoroughly Roman : he sought to force no special religion upon a conquered people, nor did he desire to change any customs, provided they did not disturb the peace, diminish the revenue, or otherwise cause the Roman people any inconvenience. For this reason few provinces were formed in the East ;

---

[1] *Antiq.* xiv. 4 (58 ff.).   Jerusalem was taken, after a siege of three months, in the 179th Olympiad in the consulate of C. Antonius and Marcus Tullius Cicero, *i.e.* 63.

and local potentates whether kings, priests, or ethnarchs were left undisturbed, on condition that they gave no trouble.

Pompey's Jewish policy.—The Jewish question was complicated by two factors. In the first place, the Jews were allies of the Romans and the treaties made in the days of the early Maccabees still remained valid. Their peculiar customs were always recognised, and as far as possible respected by the Roman authorities, and their independence was partly acknowledged. But, on the other hand, the Romans, whilst they recognised the rights of their Jewish allies, could not disregard those of the rest of the inhabitants of Palestine, and they saw in Aristobulus and his sons the type of patriot who would continue the encroachments of his father Alexander. Accordingly, Pompey decided in favour of Hyrcanus and his prudent adviser Antipater, and at the same time restored the liberty of the Greek and Syrian cities, subdued by the forward policy of the priest-kings. After the siege of Jerusalem Pompey restored to their inhabitants such cities as Hippos, Scythopolis, Pella, Dion, Samaria, etc. To quote the words of Josephus :

> ' We lost our liberty and became subject to the Romans. We were obliged to give back to the Syrians all the territory which our arms had acquired ; and further the Romans exacted from us in a short time more than 10,000 talents, and in addition the royal authority, which had formerly belonged to those of the race of the high priests, was henceforward entrusted to men of the people.' [1]

Pompey confirmed Hyrcanus in his high priesthood, and taking with him Aristobulus and his sons Antigonus and Alexander sailed for Rome to celebrate one of the best deserved triumphs of the Republic.

Gabinius.—The settlement as arranged by Pompey was completed by his friend, the proconsul Gabinius, who came to Syria 57 B.C. Alexander, the elder of the two sons of Aristobulus, had managed to escape, and

[1] *Antiq.* xiv. 4 (77 ff.).

was now in Palestine. Apparently he had driven
Hyrcanus out of Jerusalem ; and in the end he shut
himself in the fortress of Alexandrium, where he was
besieged by the Romans, Mark Antony, then a young
officer, being particularly distinguished for his bravery.
Gabinius defeated Alexander and went throughout
Palestine restoring the cities ruined by the Maccabees.

> ' Every time he met a ruined town on his journey,
> he ordered it to be restored.   Thus Samaria, Azotus,
> Scythopolis, Anthedon, Raphia, Adora, Gaza,
> Marissa, and many other towns were rebuilt.   And
> as their populations obeyed Gabinius' orders, towns
> which had been long deserted were able to be re-
> peopled in perfect security. . . .'

Gabinius then received from Alexander the fortresses
of Alexandrium, Machaerus, and Hyrcania, restored
Hyrcanus to Jerusalem, and gave him the custody of
the Temple.   He constituted the government of the Jews
in Palestine, abolishing the central authority of Jerusalem
and establishing five separate councils at Jerusalem,
Gazara, Amathus, Jericho, and Sepphoris.   ' Thus the
Jews delivered from monarchical rule were organised
under an aristocracy.' [1]
Aristobulus escaped from Rome, but was again
captured by Gabinius.   His son Alexander then seized
the government, ' marched over the country with great
force, and slew all the Romans he could light upon.'   In
vain Gabinius sent Antipater to negotiate for peace, and
in the end Alexander was utterly defeated on Mount
Tabor.   Some time later Aristobulus was poisoned and
Alexander beheaded at Antioch, Antigonus the younger
son being the only one left to claim the Judaean throne.

The Idumaean influence in Jewish affairs.—For several
years Josephus relates nothing of importance except

---

[1] *Antiq.* iv. 5 (87–91).   I have pointedly refrained from trans-
lating so common a word as συνέδριον by Sanhedrin.   I see Whiston
does the same ; but even such an excellent historian as Milman calls
Gabinius' councils ' Sanhedrin.'   For councils in the Roman world
see the late Professor Duckworth in Foakes Jackson and Lake's
Beginnings of Christianity, in the chapter on the ' Roman Provincial
System.'

the pillaging of the Temple by Crassus the triumvir in 54 B.C., his subsequent defeat by the Parthians and the restoration of the Roman authority in the East by Cassius, later one of Caesar's murderers.   This brings us to the arrival of Julius Caesar in the East after the defeat of Pompey in 47 B.C. at Pharsalia.   Henceforward for many years to come interest centres in the Idumaean Antipater and his sons, a family, Jews by religion rather than by birth, which long remained powerful in Palestine.   It is often asserted that the Jews were miserable under these Edomites, and had been happy under their Asmonaean predecessors.   But, judging by what Josephus records, there seems to have been very little difference between the government of priest-kings and that of their successors. From the death of John Hyrcanus to that of Herod the Great 105–5 B.C. the record of Josephus is one of almost continuous bloodshed.   As for the spiritual condition of the Jewish people, it is entirely ignored by the historian, despite the fact that the century is of the utmost interest in the development of Jewish ideas.

Antipater.—The historian Nicolaus of Damascus, a friend of Herod the Great, tried to convince the world that the family of Antipater was descended from a noble race, which had returned from Babylon.   But whether they were by birth Jews or Edomites, Antipater and his clan seem to have been just as devoted to the religion of Israel as the High Priest, Alexander Jannaeus, who feasted as he watched eight hundred Pharisees in agonies on their crosses, or Alexander, who marched throughout Palestine massacring the Romans.   The only difference between Asmonaeans and Herodians is that the one pursued a policy of patriotism which could only end in disaster, and the other hoped by submission to Rome to secure some benefits for the Jewish people.

Antipater at once declared for Julius Caesar, and gave him valuable assistance in the Egyptian campaign, not only securing the allegiance of the Syrian princes and cities when Mithradates, King of Pergamum, was bringing up reinforcements to aid Caesar, but displaying the virtues of a tried soldier.   The partiality Caesar showed to the Jews, and the privileges granted to them, were probably due to the influence of Antipater, and the honours heaped upon Hyrcanus prove his loyalty to the son of his old master, Alexander Jannaeus. Antipater for these services was made a Roman citizen. After the murder of Caesar in March, 44 B.C., Palestine came under the leaders of the aristocratic republicans represented by Cassius. Antipater, always a supporter of the Roman cause, whoever represented it, threw the whole weight of his influence on the side of Cassius. But before Cassius left Syria, Antipater was poisoned by a Jewish rival, named Malichus. ' So died Antipater,' says Josephus, ' a man truly eminent for his piety, justice, and patriotism.'

Herod the Great.—The career of Antipater's son Herod is told by Josephus at great length,[1] a fact which is more remarkable when we find that after Herod's death, as we approach Josephus's own time, several years are often dismissed almost in a few lines. The historian had good authorities to work with here, notably the account of Herod by Nicolaus of Damascus, and besides he enjoyed the patronage of Herod Agrippa II, a descendant of the king. Much of Herod's career is of thrilling interest and could be made a theme for several tragedies ; and most writers on this period devote much space to the subject.

Nevertheless, it may be permitted to hasten over the rise and reign of this monarch ; for it is well to remember that the reason Josephus has survived, is not because he gives the record of the secular fortunes of the Jews up to his day, but on account of the religious interests which underlie them. The Jewish teachers recognised this fact when they passed over the reign of the king, who made their Temple one of the wonders of the world, in almost complete silence. Here, therefore, without further apology will be presented a mere sketch of the significance of Herod on the stage of the world.

[1] In my copy of Whiston's translation of the *Antiquities* there are 1014 columns ; of these 170, or one-sixth of the entire work, are devoted, with a little other material, to Herod's life. As the *Antiquities* relate the history of the creation and end in A.D. 66 the reader may judge how disproportionate it is to devote so large a part of the narrative to the events of some forty years. Seventy-six columns of the first book of the *War* are devoted to Herod.

Brigandage.—The curse of Palestine was the pre-valence of brigandage. Even the heroes who under Judas routed the armies of Gorgias and Lysias were raised from the villagers, and probably welcomed the prospect of irregular warfare. The raids of Judas in eastern Palestine increased the appetite for predatory expeditions. By the time of John Hyrcanus the priest-kings had hired mercenary soldiers, and when these were disbanded or scattered by a defeat, they were liable to recombine as robber bands. A misguided belief that the confederates were fighting the battles of Israel increased the evil, which till the Jewish war seemed to be ineradicable, and revived in a more terrible form in the days of Hadrian. Herod when appointed by his father governor of Galilee, though a young man, realised the need of vigorous measures, and attacked and put to death a notorious brigand named Hezekiah. Haled before the Sanhedrin at Jerusalem, he convinced the assembly, presided over by Hyrcanus as High Priest, that he was not a man to be trifled with, and with the support of the Romans he soon became one of the most important men in the country.

Herod and his brother Phasael appear to have loyally supported one another, and though Hyrcanus was ready to be their friend he was too weak in character to give reliable assistance. The Jews accused the brothers to Mark Antony at Antioch, but to no purpose, and they were appointed tetrarchs of Judaea (42 B.C.). At this time Herod married Mariamne, the daughter of the Alexander who had been put to death by the Pompeians at Antioch, and on her mother's side the granddaughter of the High Priest Hyrcanus.

The Parthian invasion.—And now in 40 B.C. came the Parthian invasion of Syria. Barzapharnes the satrap and Pacorus the king's son overspread the country. Antigonus, according to the ' War ' through Lysanias, son of Ptolemy,[1] or according to the ' Antiquities ' directly, had offered the Parthians a thousand talents and five hundred women if they would invade Syria and put him

[1] *War*, i. 13 (248 ff.) ; *Antiq.* xiv. 13 (331).

on the throne. Jerusalem was invested, and Phasael was induced to bring Hyrcanus to Barzapharnes to negotiate for a peace; but the treacherous Parthian held both in captivity. Phasael might have escaped; but, with a magnanimity which was displayed on other occasions by his family, he refused to desert Hyrcanus. In the end, Phasael in despair dashed out his brains on the wall of his prison house; and the brutal Antigonus, according to the ' War,' bit off the ears of the uncle of Hyrcanus, though in the ' Antiquities ' Josephus softens the act by saying he caused the old man's ears to be mutilated to disqualify him for the High Priesthood.[1]

Herod proclaimed king.—Herod had to escape from Jerusalem as best he could. With Mariamne, her mother, the daughter of Hyrcanus, and a numerous company he made his way to the fortress of Masada, where he left the ladies, and betook himself to Malchus, King of Arabia, who was supposed to be his friend. But finding no succour from Malchus, Herod went first to Egypt, and thence after a stormy passage to Rome. There he was received by Octavian and Antony. Josephus says in the ' Antiquities,' but not in the ' War,' that Herod asked that the crown should be given to his future brother-in-law Aristobulus, son of Alexander; and this is not incredible, for Herod from prudence as well as generosity may have preferred to rule in the name of the youngest member of the high-priestly house. But Octavian and Antony agreed that the best solution of the troubles of Palestine was to place the supreme power in the strong and experienced hands of Herod. In the words of Josephus :

' And when the session (of the senate) was over, Antony and Caesar went forth with Herod between them, with the consuls and other magistrates leading the way, to offer sacrifices and to deposit the decree

[1] This practice of injuring the ear was a recognised means of disqualifying a man for the priesthood. In the Tosephta to the treatise *Parah* (Heifer) in the Mishna, Rabbi Johanan ben Zakkai nipped the ear of a High Priest, to whose ritual in the matter of the Red Heifer he objected, to make it impossible for him to officiate in the Temple. I found this in an article in the *Harvard Theological Review*, July 1929, by Louis Finkelstein.

in the Capitol. And on the first day of Herod's reign Antony made a great feast. Thus did he obtain his kingdom in the 184th Olympiad, in the second consulship of Gaius Domitius Calvinus, and Gaius Asinius Pollio.' [1]

Herod, now officially King of the Jews, returned to Palestine to fight for his kingdom. One of the great difficulties of warfare in the country was the impossibility of forcing an engagement with irregular troops who could disappear into caves unknown to any but themselves and there deposit their booty and emerge for future raids. Herod had not failed to profit by his early experiences against Eleazar in Galilee. He lowered great chests, full of soldiers with hooks to harpoon the defenders of the caves. When they asked for mercy Herod accepted their surrender ; but one old man, though Herod had promised him a free pardon, killed his seven sons and his wife sooner than yield.

Herod marries Mariamne.—Herod now found time formally to celebrate his marriage with Mariamne at Samaria. Jerusalem was invested by Herod and the Roman general Sossius, and taken after a desperate resistance. Sossius was resolved to punish the city with true Roman ferocity, but Herod strongly remonstrated against such vengeance, declaring that he was resolved not to reign over a desert. Antigonus threw himself at the feet of Sossius, who contemptuously addressed him by the female name of Antigone, and sent him to Antony. At Herod's request Antigonus, the last to claim the Asmonaean kingdom, was executed. This, says Josephus, was a fitting end to an inglorious career. Hyrcanus, the aged High Priest, was also a victim to the cautious cruelty of Herod a little later. In this way the race of the Asmonaeans perished but for two survivors—Herod's bride Mariamne, and her younger brother Aristobulus.

Herod and Augustus.—Herod maintained good re-lations with Mark Antony, despite the fact that he warned the triumvir against his infatuation for Cleopatra,

---

[1] *Antiq.* xiv. 14 (388–389). This was in the 184th Olympiad, or 40 B.C. The account is virtually the same in the *War*, i. 14 (285).

incurring thereby the queen's hostility. The battle of
Actium (Sept., 31 B.C.) was the crisis in his career. As a
partisan of Antony he had little to hope for, but he
resolved to face the danger of confronting Octavian.
He came to meet him at Rhodes, appearing as a private
person without his crown—as Josephus says, ' dressed
as a private person with the demeanour of a king.'   He
confessed he had been a loyal friend and counsellor of
Antony, and was prepared to be as true to Caesar as
he had been to his rival.   Thereupon Octavian instantly
placed a diadem on Herod's head, and gave him in
addition Gadara, Anthedon, Joppa and Strato's Tower.
In 23 B.C., ' after the first period of the Actian era,'
Octavian, now Augustus, added to Herod's the district
of Zenodorus Trachonitis, Batanaea and Aurantis out of
which the new ruler knew well how to clear the brigands
who were the curse of the country.   When Zenodorus
died, the rest of his territory was assigned to Herod ;
he was further made ' procurator of all Syria.'   It was
said that Augustus regarded Herod as only second to
Agrippa as a friend, and Agrippa placed Herod next to
Augustus.[1]

Splendour of Herod's reign.—Herod was now to
show the world what a Jewish king protected by Rome
was capable of accomplishing.   It must be remembered
that since the days of the Tobiades the priestly rulers in
Jerusalem had accumulated stores of unpopularity among
the inhabitants of Palestine, and after the Maccabean
revolt the Asmonaeans had made themselves more
detested by their intolerant attitude towards those who
would not accept the Jewish religion.   Herod's dominions
included many Greek and Syrian cities, and to retain
them he had to show himself as not only an impartial
ruler, but an impartial benefactor, to all his subjects.
In place of his career, like that of his predecessors, being
marked by ruined cities, it was signalised by new or
restored towns, fortresses and temples.   The great
colonnades of his new temple at Jerusalem, overlooked
by the palace and fortress, called Antonia after his patron

[1] *Antiq.* xv. 10 (361–362).

Antonius; his own palace, with its Caesareum and Agrippeum, testified to his desire to adorn Jerusalem. Samaria, which had been destroyed by John Hyrcanus, was restored and surrounded by a great wall, and renamed Sebaste (the city of Augustus). A temple was built at the source of Jordan at the ancient Panium in honour of Caesar. But almost as wonderful as the Temple of Jerusalem itself was the harbour of what we have spoken of as Strato's Tower, now known as Caesarea, the chief port and civil capital of Palestine for many centuries. Herod's bounty was shown far beyond the frontiers of his own dominions. Athens and Sparta, Rhodes and Pergamum benefited by his liberality, and he paved the great street in Antioch and adorned it with a colonnade, rendering it a chief resort in the capital of the East, whereas it had been previously impassable for the mud. Thus Herod reigned in unexampled splendour, enhanced by his own noble presence and his reputation as a warrior and as a mighty hunter. His glory, however, had the darkest of backgrounds in the sorrows and crimes which attended his home life.

It is, of course, a commonplace with most writers on this period to represent Herod as a fiend in human form and to contrast his recorded crimes with the supposed virtues of the family of the priest-kings whom he had betrayed and ruined. But as one reads the record in Josephus—and, be it remembered, we have no other authority—one is convinced of the injustice of such a verdict. Judged by any standards, Herod cannot be called a virtuous man. He could be ruthlessly cruel; his religion was that of an opportunist; he often showed himself to be utterly unscrupulous. But when we compare him with other rulers of his age, with the later Ptolemies and Seleucids, with the Romans of the last stages of the Republic, and even with the priest-kings whom Herod supplanted, he does not appear in an unfavourable light; and if he did more harm, he certainly did more good than any of his predecessors. His life is such a tragedy because he naturally possessed many fine qualities, and, surprising as it may appear, he was

a man of strong natural affection. To his brothers and
sisters Herod seems to have been sincerely attached.
He practised polygamy and married ten women, but
none of them had, so far as we know, any influence over
him except Mariamne. Nor did any of the children of
the other wives cause him trouble, with the sinister
exception of his eldest son Antipater, the child of Doris
of Jerusalem. Herod's domestic difficulties were centred
in Mariamne, and her two sons Alexander and Aristobulus.
The two evil influences at work were Herod's sister
Salome and his eldest son Antipater. The family history
was not exceptional in any Oriental kingdom. Harem
intrigue, the mutual jealousy of brothers of one another,
and the desire of an heir regardless of filial piety to succeed
his father at once were evils common to every Eastern
monarchy.

Herod's domestic troubles.—Mariamne was evidently
a very beautiful woman with all the pride and spirit
of an Asmonaean. Her mother Alexandra, daughter
of the High Priest Hyrcanus, encouraged her in her
growing hatred and fear of Herod, who nevertheless
was devotedly attached to his wife. On behalf of
her son, Aristobulus, Alexandra tried to set Antony
against Herod and with the aid of Cleopatra to procure
his deposition. It was generally believed that Herod
out of policy had compassed the death of Alexandra's
father, the venerable Hyrcanus. Mariamne and her
mother also incurred the deadly enmity of Salome, Herod's
sister, and the other female members of the family. To
allay the rising enmity of Alexandra and her children,
Herod appointed the young Aristobulus High Priest.
The youth officiated at the Feast of Tabernacles, but the
delight of the people crowned the suspicions of Herod.
A feast was held at Jericho, and while the guests diverted
themselves by bathing in the water around the palace,
Aristobulus was drowned. His death was naturally
attributed to the machinations of Herod.[1] This happened

---

[1] The narratives in a shorter form in the *War*, and as expanded
in the *Antiquities*, are so full of confusion that it is not easy to say
whether Aristobulus was murdered or died owing to an accident. The
death of the aged Hyrcanus is equally mysterious.

35–34 B.C., and for six more years Herod and Mariamne lived a life of unrequited affection on his part, and constant provocation on hers. Their estrangement was fomented by Salome till Herod, persuaded of his wife's infidelity, ordered her to execution. Mariamne's mother taunted her unfortunate daughter as she was led to her death ; but Mariamne proved worthy of her high birth and suffered with the dignity of a queen. Herod, when the deed was done, went wellnigh mad with remorse, but at last recovered and found Alexandra plotting against him in favour of her grandsons Alexander and Aristobulus, the sons of Mariamne. It is satisfactory to record that Herod put her to death.

Herod and the sons of Mariamne.—Twenty-two years after Mariamne's death Herod had her sons tried before Saturninus the *legatus* of Syria on the ground of a conspiracy, and they were led to execution 7 B.C. Their story, as told at length by Josephus, is a sad one. The villain in the plot of the tragedy of the closing years of Herod is his eldest son Antipater, whose guilt was made manifest to the dying king. Thus, during a career of otherwise constant success, Herod put to death the wife whom he loved tenderly and her two sons, as well as his first-born whom he had designated as heir to his vast dominions.

The descendants of Herod must be considered later. At the king's death the Jewish kingdom reached its greatest extent. Never had the people enjoyed such peace and prosperity since the days of Solomon. If the iron hand of the tyrant had not annihilated the disorderly element in the country, it had at least been driven underground. The population was evidently increasing, and with it the worldly prosperity of the land. Galilee seems to have become almost entirely Jewish, and to have been full of teeming villages. Jerusalem prospered as it had never done before. It may be said that this was at the expense of liberty ; but what liberty had the Jews enjoyed since the Captivity, save a brief and precarious one whilst the Syrian Empire was in the throes of dissolution ? If it is urged that the price was the loss of religion, it may be justly asked, What does Josephus tell us of the piety, beliefs and hopes of Israel from the day of the rededication of the Temple, 165 B.C., to when Herod the Great expired in 4 B.C. ? Yet we know that there was a strong and warm undercurrent of piety, revealed here and there in the literature of the period, and later in the Christian Gospels. Still, we have no evidence that the priest-kings with their mercenaries, or Herod supported by the legions of Rome, contributed to advance the piety of the nation, though the land had enjoyed at least rest for a while at the time of the birth of Jesus Christ ' in the days of Herod the king.'

PART IV
THE ROMAN YOKE

CHAPTER VIII

The Descendants of Herod

(*Archelaus—Antipas—and Agrippa I*)

The Herodian family.—Thanks to Josephus, we have a more complete record of the family of Herod than of almost any other in antiquity. The pedigree is prefaced by these words :

> ' I desire therefore to speak at some length about Herod and what happened to his family both because an account of them is suitable in the history, and also because it affords an example of God's providence. In this we have proof that in human affairs there is no stability except in piety. For within a century although Herod had many descendants all but a few had entirely disappeared.' [1]

Importance of the descendants of Mariamne.—As we know, Herod rested his claim to rule over the Jews on his marriage with Mariamne, the last survivor of the old priest-kings ; and, although she and her two sons had been the victims of the jealousy of the tyrant, her descendants were regarded both by the Jews and the Romans as belonging to a class distinctly different from the rest of his numerous family. Nearly every petty king and prince around Palestine sought to marry some one sprung from Mariamne.[2] So great, moreover, was the partiality of the Romans for what may be called the legitimate stock of Herod that the failure of their Jewish policy is in part due to their determination to secure the peace of Palestine by furthering the interests of this house.

---

[1] *Antiq.* xviii. 5 (127–128).   [2] See map and table annexed.

JOSEPHUS, *Antiq.* xviii. 5 (130 ff.).

Matrimonial alliances (some only temporary) of the descendants of Herod the Great and Mariamne, the last of the Asmonaeans, with map showing how these were connected with the royal and princely rulers of the East.

d. = daughter.   s. = son.   gs. = grandson, etc.

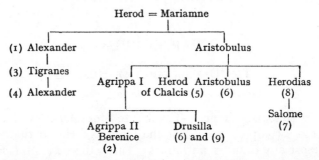

Herod = Mariamne

(1) Alexander   Aristobulus

(3) Tigranes

(4) Alexander   Agrippa I   Herod   Aristobulus   Herodias
                      of Chalcis (5)   (6)   (8)

                                              Salome

    Agrippa II   Drusilla   (7)
    Berenice   (6) and (9)
      (2)

(1), (2), (3). These numbers indicate the countries into which the Asmonaean Herods were connected by marriage. The three successors of Herod the Great, Archelaus, Antipas, and Philip, all sought an alliance with their Asmonaean relatives.

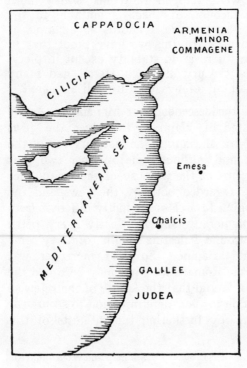

(1) *Cappadocia*— Alexander s. married Glaphrya d. king.

(2) *Cilicia*—Berenice ggd. m. Polemon.

(3) *Armenia Minor*— Tigranes V gs.

(4) *Commagene*— Alexander ggs. m. Jopata d. of king.

(5) *Chalcis*—gs. king.

(6) *Emesa*—Aristobulus s. m. Jopata d. of king. Drusilla ggd. m. king of.

(7) *Ituraea*—Philip tetrarch m. gd. Salome.

(8) *Galilee*—Antipas tetrarch m. gd. Herodias.

(9) *Judaea*—Archelaus m. Glaphyra d.-in-law Felix the Procurator m. Drusilla ggd.

Herod's fortune.—Herod the Great at his death left an immense fortune and a multitude of greedy relatives to contend for it. His dominions in Palestine were estimated as yielding a revenue of more than nine hundred talents, Judaea and its dependencies being assessed at 600, Galilee and Peraea at 200 and the northern districts of Batanaea and Trachonitis at 100. In addition, there were several rich cities. Herod made a personal bequest to Augustus of 1500 talents, which the emperor gave back to the family, reserving only a few art treasures as souvenirs of his friend.[1]

Josephus devotes a large section to the litigation about Herod's will. The family hastened to Rome to lay their claims before Augustus, who appointed his youthful grandson Gaius as his assessor and heard the case with due deliberation.

Jewish riots against Archelaus. Herod's family plead the cause of Antipas before Augustus.—Herod had made two wills : the earlier leaving his Kingdom to his son Antipas, and one executed just before his death making an elder son, Archelaus, his heir. On the decease of Herod, Archelaus had acted as his representative, given him a splendid funeral, and practically assumed his position. But the people of Jerusalem regarded him as nothing better than a tyrant and a usurper ; and scenes of bloodshed and disturbances occurred throughout the city.[2] After the celebration of the Passover, which ended in

---

[1] There are several discrepancies in the *War* and the *Antiquities* in Josephus' estimate of the value of Herod's property. In the *Antiquities* the wealth of the king appears far greater than in the earlier book of the *War*. It is not possible to estimate the value of money in ancient times. Indeed, in our own day we realise that £1,000 is not the equivalent of the same sum before the War. We must be satisfied with the fact that Herod was a very rich man, and also that Josephus' figures are more rhetorical than reliable. See *War*, ii. 6 (93–100); *Antiq.* xvii. 8 (190) and xvii. 11 (317–320). Whiston on *Antiq.* xvii. 2 thinks Herod must have been much richer than Josephus represents him to have been.

[2] We gather from Josephus that Herod the Great was almost insane at the time of his death owing to the mental agony caused by the domestic tragedies of his latter days, and the intense physical pain of his malady. Otherwise it is impossible to account for the fact that, after having done all in his power to conciliate his Jewish subjects, he should needlessly have provoked them by setting up the image of an eagle in the Temple, etc. (*War*, i. 31 (647–665) ; *Antiq.* xvii. 6–8 (146–195).

tumult and confusion, Archelaus started for Rome to
be confirmed in his inheritance.   His brother Antipas
demanded that the earlier will should be followed,
his claims being supported by the entire family, and
especially by his aunt Salome.   Josephus says that he
relied most on the eloquence of an advocate called
Irenaeus, who, however, is not mentioned in the account
of the trial.[1]

Josephus reports three speeches : (1) an attack on
Archelaus by Antipater, the son of Salome ; (2) the
defence of Archelaus by Nicolaus of Damascus ; and
(3) the plea of the Jews.   These are of importance,
because they illustrate the state of affairs in Palestine,
and the relation of the Herods to the Emperor.

(1) **Speech of Antipater, son of Salome.**—Antipater [2]
was the spokesman for the family, who seem to have
been unanimous in their dislike of Archelaus.   The
argument was best calculated· to prejudice Augustus.
The chief offence of Archelaus was declared to be that
on the death of his father he had presumed to assume the
position of the successor to the kingdom without com-
municating with his Roman overlord.   His conduct
towards the inhabitants of Jerusalem had further proved
his unfitness to control them.   He had provoked riots,
which he suppressed by massacres, and had disgusted
everyone by his hypocrisy in feigning grief for his father
in public, and in private exulting over his death.   Finally,
Antipater contended that Herod the Great was not himself
when he made his second will and that the first in favour
of Antipas was valid.

(2) **Nicolaus defends Archelaus.**—Nicolaus,[3] who had
been the counsel for the prosecution when Herod's
son Antipater was condemned, argued that Archelaus
had been driven to suppress the tumult with violence ;
and, in proof that he had no intention of usurping
authority without Caesar's consent, he had hastened to
Rome to plead for his kingdom.   Herod himself could

---

[1] *War*, ii. 2 (14 ff.) ; *Antiq*. xvii. 9 (206 ff.).
[2] *War*, ii. 2 (26–32) ; *Antiq*. xvii. 9 (230–239).
[3] *War*, ii. 2 (34–36) ; *Antiq*. xvii. 9 (240–247).

not have been incapable of making the second will,
because in it he had made Augustus, his friend as well
as his master, his executor, and had thereby submitted
the decision of the ultimate disposal of his estate to
Augustus.[1]

(3) **Petition of the Jews.**—Augustus deferred judgment : and soon afterward a Jewish deputation arrived
which recalls the parable in the New Testament of
the nobleman who went abroad to receive a kingdom :
' But his citizens hated him, and sent an ambassage
after him, saying, We will not that this man reign over
us.' [2] The main argument advanced by the Jews was
the atrocious character of Herod the Great, who had
found their country prosperous, and had grievously
impoverished it by lavishing money on decorating heathen
cities to the ruin of his Jewish subjects. Their petition
was that the dominions of Herod should be incorporated
in the province of Syria and the Jews allowed to show
their loyalty by managing their own affairs.[3]

Partition of Herod's dominion among his sons.—
Augustus then gave his decision.[4] He handed the
country, which had been subdued and pacified by Varus,
to the Herod family, giving the rich provinces of Judaea
and Samaria with several cities on the coast to Archelaus,
chargeable, however, with an annuity of sixty talents
for Herod's sister Salome. To Antipas, the brother of
Archelaus, was assigned Galilee and Peraea, whilst Philip,
another son of Herod, was given the northern parts of
his father's dominions. Archelaus was to be called an
' ethnarch ' and was promised the rank of king if he gave
satisfaction ; his brothers were to be styled ' tetrarchs.'

Whether Augustus would have been wise to accede to
the seemingly moderate proposals of the Jews is open to
question. At first sight nothing could be more reasonable

---

[1] *War*, ii. 6 (80–92) ; *Antiq.* xvii. 11 (299 ff.).
[2] Luke xix. 12 ff.
[3] ' The Jews,' so ended their petition, would then show that,
calumniated though they were as factious and always at war, they knew
how to obey equitable rules' (Thackeray's translation). The Jewish
deputation arrived later than the members of the family of Herod ; and
after Varus (*vide infra*, p. 156) had pacified the country.
[4] *War*, ii. 6 (93–100) ; *Antiq.* xvii. 2 (317–323).

than the request to be incorporated in the Syrian province. It was virtually a return to Pompey's policy of freeing the Greek cities of Palestine from Jewish control, and leaving the nation to govern itself.

But Augustus did not trust the Jews, after the anarchy and bloodshed which had followed the death of Herod the Great. He suspected, as many Western rulers of Eastern lands have had good reason to do since, that ' self-government ' meant a return to disorder ; and he knew the Herods to be, if Orientals, at least accustomed to Roman ideas ; and in a measure he considered them likely to provide the best available solution of the Jewish difficulty.

Archelaus in Judaea.—As regards Archelaus,[1] his choice was disastrous ; but virtually nothing is related by Josephus about the period during which he administered the affairs of Judaea. All the historian tells us is that an Essene, named Simon, predicted that he would reign only ten years, and that his wife Glaphyra had a remarkable dream. Archelaus had married her, though she was the widow of his brother Alexander, the son of Mariamne. Alexander appeared to her and told her that for this impiety she must die, as she did, within a few days.[2] If the Lucan parable of the ' Pounds ' refers to Archelaus, it would appear that on his return to Judaea after being confirmed in his authority by Augustus he had executed those who had opposed his appointment. Anyhow, in A.D. 6 Augustus deprived him of his government and all his property, and sent him into exile to Vienna in Gaul.[3]

Antipas as tetrarch of Galilee.—The bare fact that Antipas held his government from about 4 B.C. till A.D. 39, shows that he was possessed of qualities which made him at least acceptable both to Augustus and to

---

[1] *War*, ii. 7 (111–116) ; *Antiq.* xvii. 13 (339 ff.).

[2] In the Slavonic Josephus John the Baptist was brought before Archelaus ! Later he rebukes Antipas for his incestuous marriage with Herodias. It is possible that this discrepancy is due to the confusion with the stories of Archelaus and Glaphyra and Herod Antipas and Herodias.

[3] Like all his family, Archelaus was anxious to improve his dominions. He rebuilt the palace at Jericho and was careful to provide water to irrigate the palm trees he had planted there, *Antiq.* xvii. 13 (340).

Tiberius ; and, as no serious outbreak is related of having occurred in Galilee, he must have displayed capacity as a ruler. Both Antipas in Galilee and his half-brother Philip inherited their father's taste for building ; and to Antipas Galilee and the shores of its lake probably owed their population and prosperity. From the Gospels we gather that the country was largely inhabited by Jews ; and Josephus enlarges on the size of its villages and the density of their inhabitants. The two greatest cities of Galilee, Sepphoris and Tiberias, the last-named his own foundation, owed their subsequent eminence to Antipas. Philip, who built Bethsaida-Julias and Caesarea Philippi, is described by Josephus as a model governor of his province. He died in A.D. 34.

Our two authorities for the life of Antipas are the Gospels and Josephus, and from them a fairly consistent picture can be drawn. Both Antipas and Archelaus were sons of a Samaritan woman named Malthace, and were, if on that account alone, probably distasteful to their Jewish subjects ; but whilst Jerusalem and Judaea were almost entirely Jewish, Galilee contained several Greek cities, and Peraea was scarcely Jewish at all.[1]

Antipas marries Herodias.—Antipas,[2] so Josephus and the Gospel tell us, married his niece Herodias, who had deserted her husband, another Herod, called Philip by Mark. This marriage, which Josephus as well as the Gospel pronounce to have been illegal, allied Antipas with the Asmonaean branch of his family, and Philip, tetrarch of Iturea, late in life married Herodias' daughter Salome. As both Antipas and Philip were grown up at the time of their father's death in 4 B.C., they must have been comparatively elderly men in the days of the Gospel ; and Herodias cannot have been very young when she deserted her first husband for Antipas. It is consequently an open question whether the real motives of these alliances were not due to ambition rather than to affection, the whole

---

[1] Josephus has nothing but praise for Philip in Iturea. The sons of Herod had been brought up in Rome and found it comparatively simple to rule a partially Hellenised population. Dr. Klausner recognises this in his *Jesus of Nazareth*, pp. 165 ff. (E.T.).

[2] *Antiq.* xviii. 5 (109 ff.) ; Mark vi. 17 ff.

territory and kingship of Herod the Great being the object for which his descendants were constantly striving.

Antipas in the Gospels and in Josephus.—The four Evangelists state, directly or indirectly, that Herod Antipas put the Baptist to death, and this is confirmed by Josephus, though he gives an account entirely independent of Matthew's and Mark's narrative.[1] Luke, in both the Third Gospel and the Acts, shows some acquaintance with the Herod family, which is partly confirmed by Josephus. The most notable example of this is a detail peculiar to Luke's account of the trial of Jesus. In his Gospel it is said that Pilate, hearing that Jesus as a Galilean was of Herod's jurisdiction, sent Him to Herod.[2] Of course this incident may have been inserted to emphasise the fulfilment of the words of the Second Psalm, ' The kings of the earth set themselves in array and the rulers were gathered together, against the Lord, and against his Anointed,' which is explained in Acts as alluding to Herod and Pontius Pilate.[3] But the Gospel adds that Pilate and Herod from henceforward became friends, ' for before they were at enmity between themselves.'[4] That, however, there was hostility between Antipas and the Roman officials is confirmed by Josephus, who says that Vitellius, the governor of Syria, was greatly annoyed at Antipas forestalling him by sending the news of the treaty with Parthia to the emperor before the official report could be dispatched. From this we may infer that Tiberius was accustomed to encourage the native princes to watch his officials and report their conduct to him.[5]

Antipas and Jesus.—Elsewhere in the Gospel Antipas is represented as very curious about Jesus, and desirous to see Him. The reason is obvious from the fact that Chuza, his steward (ἐπίτροπος), an important official, has a wife named Joanna, who was one of the women who ministered to Jesus,[6] and Manaen the foster-brother of the tetrarch was one of the Christian prophets associated

---

[1] *Antiq.* xviii. 5 (117 ff.).
[2] Luke xxiii. 7.
[3] Acts iv. 27.
[4] Luke xxiii. 12.
[5] See below, chapter x.
[6] Luke viii. 3 ; xxiv. 10.

with Barnabas at Antioch.[1] An Essene of the same
name had saluted Herod the Great as a boy as King of the
Jews [2] and it is quite conceivable that the connection
with Manaen's family may have been continued by the
appointment of one of them as foster-father of one of the
king's sons.

According to Luke the Pharisees warned Jesus that
Antipas sought to kill Him.[3] This is by no means
impossible, for if we may trust Josephus, the tetrarch
dreaded popular religious teachers, and had offended the
Pharisaic party, among other things by building Tiberias
on the site of a graveyard. Jesus on receiving this warning called Antipas ' a fox '—no bad description of so crafty
a man, though in other respects we have little real information as to his character. Mark's interesting story of
the death of the Baptist implies that Antipas was by
nature superstitious and easily influenced.

War with Aretas.—As long as Tiberius was alive
Antipas was secure both against the hostility of the
Roman officials and that of his own family ; but the
emperor was an old man, and Antipas was only safe so
long as he lived. His marriage with Herodias had been
the cause of a war with Aretas, an Arab king whose
daughter had been divorced, and having betaken herself
to Machaerus on the frontier of the tetrarchy of Antipas,
she was passed on from one sheik ($\sigma\tau\rho\alpha\tau\eta\gamma\acute{o}s$) to another
till she reached her father. Antipas and Aretas had also
a dispute about their frontiers and did not openly wage
war but employed their subordinate chieftains to fight.
It may be legitimately inferred that neither dared offend
the Romans by declaring open war, but each stirred up
the sheiks in their dominions to make raids on his rival's
territory. The defeat of an army of Herod made Tiberius
resolve to put an end to further disturbances by ordering
Vitellius, the *legatus* of Syria, to capture or kill Aretas.

Deposition of Antipas.—The death of Tiberius altered
everything. Vitellius owed Antipas a grudge for his
behaviour about the Parthian treaty, and perhaps deemed
it imprudent to continue the war without orders from

[1] Acts xiii. 1. [2] *Antiq.* xv. 10 (373). [3] Luke xiii. 31.

the new government, which would probably be less friendly to this Herod. Accordingly he withdrew his troops and proclaimed Caligula emperor at Jerusalem. He had judged rightly, for the fall of Antipas was now imminent.[1]

For this his wife Herodias was responsible. She had helped her brother Agrippa in the days of his poverty ; but could not bear to think of him as a king when her husband, to whom she was evidently genuinely attached, was only a tetrarch. Accordingly she urged Antipas to go to Rome and beg the new emperor to give him the title of royalty. But Agrippa, now in a position of influence, hearing of his uncle's ambition, sent his freedman, Fortunatus, to prevent his design. On learning of the preparations for war which Antipas had made, Caligula deprived him of his tetrarchy and banished him to Lugudunum (Lyons) in Gaul, telling Herodias that as sister of Agrippa she could keep her property and need not suffer for her husband's faults. But Herodias magnanimously replied that, having shared in her husband's prosperity, she was not going to desert him in his adversity, and accompanied him in his exile. Whilst the Herods could be both cruel and licentious, they were also capable of generous actions.

Fortunes of Herod Agrippa.—Another important member of the Herodian family appears in Agrippa, the grandson of Mariamne, who seems to have been the ablest and most unscrupulous of the descendants of Herod the Great, and as dexterous a politician as his famous grandfather.

Agrippa, whose son was the patron of Josephus, is the historian's hero, and the Jewish nation regarded him with veneration and even affection. Despite the fact that the only things recorded of him in the New Testament are the execution of James the brother of John and the imprisonment of Peter, his popularity with the Jews has made even Christian writers consider him a patriotic king. Yet an impartial survey of his career reveals that one of the indirect consequences of his promotion to the kingdom

[1] *War*, ii. 9 (181 ff.) ; *Antiq.* xviii. 7 (240 f.).

of Herod the Great was the Jewish war and all its terrible consequences.

Early life of Herod Agrippa.[1]—The story of the life of Herod Agrippa is one of the best examples of Josephus' power as a narrator, and is full of interesting material, not to be found elsewhere.[2] Agrippa was born in 11 B.C.; his mother Berenice was an intimate friend of Antonia the daughter of Mark Antony, widow of Tiberius' brother Drusus, mother of the Emperor Gaius (Caligula), and grandmother of Nero. Agrippa was consequently in close touch with the imperial family and the great Roman aristocracy, and was educated with Drusus, the son of Tiberius. Drusus died in A.D. 23; and, according to report, the Emperor was by no means satisfied with the conduct of his son and his profligate companions, of whom Agrippa was one. After the death of Drusus (A.D. 23), Tiberius, so says Josephus, forbade any of the young man's friends to come into his presence; and Agrippa, whose extravagance had loaded him with debt, was forced to leave Rome for his native land. So desperate were his affairs that at one time he thought of suicide and was only prevented by his wife Cypros, who induced his sister Herodias to give him a pension and a small office at Tiberias. But he soon quarrelled with her husband, the tetrarch Antipas, and betook himself to Flaccus, then *legatus* of Syria, who befriended him and also his brother Aristobulus.

Herod Agrippa returns to Rome.[3]—Aristobulus soon discovered that Agrippa, with whom he had quarrelled, had been taking bribes to use his influence with Flaccus, and informed the *legatus* of his duplicity. Driven away from Antioch, Agrippa decided to return to Italy and for some time his career was the not uncommon one of a man borrowing money from one creditor to pay another.

[1] *Antiq.* xviii. 6.
[2] There is nothing concerning Agrippa I's early life in the *War*. Probably Josephus derived much of his information from Agrippa II when they were together at Rome. The story of this Herod is admirably told by Thomas Lewin, *Life and Epistles of St. Paul* (1874), ch. vii.
[3] *Antiq.* xviii. 6.

Antonia helped him to pay his debt to the Roman treasury; and, for a time, he enjoyed the favour of Tiberius.

It was to his intimacy with the family of Antonia that Agrippa owed his later success; and he had the foresight to attach himself to his patroness's grandson Gaius, popularly known as Caligula, instead of the Emperor's grandson, Tiberius; and when Gaius proved impossible as emperor, he transferred his allegiance to Claudius the son of Antonia.

Agrippa in disgrace with Tiberius.—But at the end of the reign of Tiberius, Agrippa was under a cloud, and at one time actually in peril of his life. Eutychus, a freedman of Agrippa's who drove his carriage, was accused of stealing his master's clothes. When haled before the magistrate he declared he had a warning message for Caesar, whereupon he was sent to Capreae, where Tiberius had made his home in his declining years.[1]

Tiberius as described by Josephus.—Josephus here gives an interesting digression in a sketch of the character of the Emperor Tiberius. The awful descriptions which are found in Tacitus and Suetonius of his perfidy and cruelty in public life, depicting him as a monster of iniquity in his old age, must not blind our eyes to the fact that, before he became emperor, he had proved himself a great Roman general, and that he was an excellent administrator of his provinces. He was often criticised for his dilatory methods of business, which made him keep prisoners too long in custody when they were awaiting trial, for refusing to give audience to ambassadors, and especially for his delay in appointing new governors to provinces. Josephus attributes his hesitation to give prisoners a hearing to his innate cruelty; but he also tells the well-known story of how Tiberius excused himself for keeping men so long in office in the provinces. A benevolent stranger found a man tormented by a swarm of flies, and began to drive them away. But the sufferer begged him to desist as these flies had satisfied their appetites and would only make way for more hungry bloodsuckers. This certainly shows Tiberius to have

[1] *War*, ii. 9 (178 ff.), and more fully *Antiq*. xviii. 6 (168 ff.).

possessed a grim sense of humour, and not to have
been entirely destitute of humanity.[1]

Arrest of Herod Agrippa.—In the affair of Agrippa
the tyrant appears in a singularly amiable light. Agrippa
had the folly to press Antonia to ask the emperor to bring
Eutychus to a speedy trial. The old man, who had a real
affection for his sister-in-law, begged her not to press
him ; and warned her that if he examined Eutychus her
protegé Agrippa must take the consequences. When the
emperor heard that Eutychus had reported a conversa-
tion in which Agrippa, while out driving with Gaius,
had expressed a hope that Tiberius might soon die,[2]
he ordered Agrippa to be arrested and kept in prison.
A false report that Tiberius was dead caused the jailor to
invite Agrippa to a banquet, but on finding that the
rumour was false he thrust his prisoner into closer confine-
ment than ever.

Herod Agrippa given a royal title.—When, however, it was certain that the old emperor was no more and
Caligula was his successor, Agrippa was liberated, given
a chain of gold of the same weight as that which he had
borne in prison, and made a king of the districts formerly
administered by his uncle Philip, which were then known
as the tetrarchy of Lysanias. Agrippa then went to
Palestine to take possession of his kingdom, and having
done so returned to Rome.

Riots in Alexandria.—Whilst Caligula was heaping
honours on his friend Agrippa, a violent outbreak against
the Jews occurred at Alexandria.[3] The Greek inhabitants
attacked the Jews, with the connivance of Flaccus Avilius,
the governor of Egypt ; and when Agrippa arrived at the
city on his way to Palestine he was treated with gross
insult by the populace. This led to Philo's *Embassy to
Gaius* and apparently to the emperor's order to place his
statue in the Temple. Josephus makes Agrippa the hero
in the transaction and attributes the recall of the order
to his boldly claiming it as a favour of Caligula. Thus

---

[1] *Antiq.* xviii. 6 (174 f.).
[2] In the *War*, Agrippa at a dinner is said to have expressed a
desire that Tiberius might die.
[3] *Antiq.* xviii. 8 (257 ff.).

he won the highest reputation for piety among the Jews, which facilitated his rapid advance under Claudius.

Claudius enriches Herod Agrippa.—The murder of his friend Caligula enhanced the fame of Agrippa ; for, whilst the Senate was debating whether it should restore the Republic or elect someone outside the Julian family, Agrippa, true to the family of his faithful patroness, Antonia, declared for her son ; and it was largely through his instrumentality that Claudius became emperor.[1] In gratitude for his assistance Agrippa was given all the country over which Herod the Great had reigned and Claudius confirmed the grant of Abila of Lysanias which Caligula had made, with the addition of other imperial territories. Thus Agrippa became one of the powerful subject kings in the eastern part of the empire. His brother at his request was made King of Chalcis.

Jewish enthusiasm for Herod Agrippa.—The Jews naturally regard the brief reign of Agrippa I (41-44) as one of the brightest periods of their history. In him they had a king of undoubted Asmonaean descent and approved piety, who had risked all to save the Temple from profanation. The Talmud relates that when at a feast he showed diffidence as one sprung from an Edomite family, the people with one voice shouted ' Thou art our brother.' It is hard not to endorse the modern Jewish verdict that the untimely death of so good a monarch was one of the worst calamities that could have befallen the nation. Yet reading between the lines of Josephus it is not difficult to see that Agrippa, though a national hero, was as unfit for his sudden promotion as Tiberius had long foreseen. He was one of those dissipated and extravagant men, whose loose lives and constant impecuniosity make people underrate both their abilities and their power for evil.[1]

Character of Herod Agrippa.—The Acts of the Apostles relates that he ' killed James the brother of John with the sword. . . .' This has prejudiced all Christians against him, but to the historian the significance of the remark lies, not so much in the fact that he executed

[1] *War*, ii. 11 (206 ff.) ; *Antiq.* xix. 4, 5 (236-277).

a leading disciple of the Christ, as that on coming to Jerusalem he sought popularity by executing those whom the people of the city, and especially the priesthood, disliked. The Roman government had only to relax its vigilance, for vengeance to be wreaked on any person unpopular with the Jewish rulers. Agrippa's attempt to fortify Jerusalem, frustrated by the imperial *legatus* Marsus, is an indication that he meant if possible to make an attempt to restore the empire of his ancestors; and Marsus was probably right in seeing signs of a conspiracy against Rome in a gorgeous entertainment given by Agrippa to the neighbouring princes. A Jewish war backed by Parthia might have proved the ruin of the *Imperium Romanum* in the East.[1] The indecent joy of the Greek inhabitants of Caesarea when they heard of Agrippa's death shows how unpopular the Jews were, and what serious apprehensions the sight of a Hebrew king had aroused in the non-Jewish population of Palestine. How far Agrippa was from being an ardent adherent of the Law is evident from his giving at Berytus a popular entertainment to which the most accomplished musicians contributed, and no fewer than fourteen hundred malefactors were exhibited in the act of killing one another. In order, remarks Josephus, ' that both the malefactors might receive their punishment, and that this operation of war might be a recreation in peace.' [2]

The High Priesthood.—After the death of Agrippa at Caesarea in A.D. 44 the Roman government reverted to the policy of placing Judaea once more under a procurator, leaving the rest of Palestine to the members of the Herodian family, to whom also was committed the charge of the priestly vestments, and the appointment of the High Priests, who were changed as frequently as they had formerly been by the procurators.

[1] See below, chapter x.
[2] *Antiq.* xix. 7 (335–337). For the death of Herod Agrippa *vide infra*, chapter xvi.

CHAPTER IX

THE ROMAN GOVERNMENT OF PALESTINE

(The Legati of Syria and the Procurators of Judaea)

Romans fail in Palestine.—The Roman rule in Palestine is one of the tragedies of history, the more so because the Romans had no natural antipathy to the Jews and upon the whole showed a disposition to treat them fairly. In the end the complete antagonism between the Western conception of order and Oriental fanaticism manifested itself in one of the most ruthless wars in human history and in consequences which are operative to the present day.

Rapid decline of the Asmonaeans.—During the revolt against Antiochus Epiphanes and his successors, the Asmonaean family, by their determined resistance on behalf of the laws and customs of Israel, consolidated the nation and founded a veritable empire in miniature. But the princes of the dynasty rapidly degenerated from the lofty patriotism of Judas the Maccabee to the rapacity of a brutal adventurer of the type of Alexander Jannaeus. The Jewish conquests were characterised by forced conversions of Greek and Syrian cities and the destruction and massacre of those whose inhabitants refused to accept circumcision. In this way the Asmonaean rule had become odious to the great majority of the people of Palestine. After the deaths of Alexander Jannaeus and his prudent wife Alexandra, the ruling family became hopelessly divided; and, on the appearance of Pompey the Great in 63 B.C., the Roman power had to endeavour to appease the dissensions of a distracted country.

Pompey's Eastern policy.—Pompey's idea was not so much to annex the East, as to compose and civilise its rival nationalities. The Romans regarded, not their own, but Hellenic culture as the best remedy against barbarism, and had long declared themselves in favour of it. Consequently their object was to deliver the Greek and Macedonian cities from Jewish domination, and to confine the Jews to their own sphere. To the religion of Israel Pompey showed no hostility. On the contrary, though he insisted on penetrating to the Inner Sanctuary, the Holy of Holies, he refrained from plundering the Temple. His successor Gabinius (57–54 B.C.) placed the Jewish inhabitants of Palestine under five synods each with its separate Sanhedrin, and left them to manage their own affairs.[1] Caesar, grateful for the support he had received from Antipater, the real ruler of Jewish Palestine in the name of their feeble High Priest Hyrcanus, granted the nation extraordinary privileges, but after his murder, the Parthians who supported Hyrcanus's rival and nephew, Antigonus, burst into Syria and took Jerusalem. The Romans, despite the mutual hostility of the factions during the civil war, pursued a singularly consistent policy in Eastern affairs, recognising that the peace of Palestine depended on a strong native ruler acceptable to the Jews by religion, and at the same time liberal enough to acknowledge the claims of the Greek cities. They considered they had found a suitable person in Herod the son of Antipater, who had married into the Asmonaean family, professed Judaism, and yet was loyal to the Roman rule, and a liberal patron of Greek culture. Herod, a barbarian with a veneer of civilisation, despite the frightful dissensions of his own household, managed by severe methods to preserve a show of order ; but at his death, Augustus, considering that none of his sons could be entrusted with their father's extensive dominion and powers, divided his kingdom between three of them, giving Judaea and Samaria to Archelaus. He, however, proved so distasteful to his Jewish subjects, that it was necessary to remove him in A.D. 6 and to

---

[1] Thus, as Josephus says, the Jews were given an aristocratic government. The synods were at Jerusalem, Gadara, Amathus, Jericho, and Sepphoris. *War*, i. 8 (170) ; *Antiq.* xiv. 5 (11).

place his tetrarchy in the hands of a Roman administrator. From henceforth Judaea and Samaria, except for a few years (A.D. 41–44), were incorporated in the Roman Empire as part of the great province of Syria, governed by a Roman official of the highest rank, appointed by the Emperor as his *legatus*, or deputy.

The *legati* of Syria.—As the dominions of which Archelaus was deprived were under a subordinate representative of Caesar it is necessary to mention only those rulers of Syria whose names occur in the pages of Josephus. Their intervention in Jewish affairs will help to determine somewhat the character of Roman provincial government in the eastern frontier of the empire, and will also give some idea of the problems which confronted it. A map indicating the boundaries of the province of Syria gives no notion of the complexity of the problems of its government, which, speaking generally, exercised jurisdiction over the vast territory between the eastern coastline of the Mediterranean and the river Euphrates. Of this province it may be said that in it the authority was Roman, the common language Greek, and the religion Syrian. Of the Jews, whose religious community was a marvel of organisation, it may justly be said that they regarded the worship of Syria, the customs of Greece, and the discipline of Rome as equally incompatible with their national aspirations. But the position of Jerusalem, their religious centre, was not unique in Syria at this period —the sanctuary at Emesa, for example, was likewise under the control of a priest who had an authority similar to that of the High Priest at Jerusalem. The Syrian province included a number of petty princes, recognised as kings or tetrarchs by Rome, and enjoying an independence similar to that of the rulers of native states in British India. Herod the Great had been one of these, as were his three sons among whom his territory was divided.

Varus B.C. 4.—When Herod died Syria had been entrusted to Quintilius Varus, who later lost his army and his life in Germany. Archelaus had gone to Rome to plead his cause in the dispute about his father's will, and

Augustus had sent Sabinus, his steward for Syrian affairs, to Jerusalem to protect the property of the Herods. At the Passover there was a fearful riot against the Romans in the Temple, and Sabinus was regularly besieged in the city, and only delivered by the approach of the army of Varus. The whole of Palestine was in disorder; and Varus had no little difficulty in dealing with such irregular leaders as the son of Hezekiah, killed by Herod the Great,[1] Simon, a slave of Herod the Great, and Athronges the shepherd king. The two last of these rebels gave trouble till they were suppressed by Valerius Gratus, procurator of Judaea in the days of Tiberius. Finally, having partially pacified the country, Varus left for Antioch.[2]

Quirinus, A.D. 6.—After the deposition of Archelaus, who was banished to Vienna in Gaul A.D. 6, Quirinus (Cyrenius) was appointed, and Judas the Gaulonite of Gamala and Sadduc, a Pharisee, made an attempt to cause a revolt, but succeeded only in founding a new sect which in after days was to have a fatal influence.[3]

Flaccus, A.D. 32.—Josephus mentions Flaccus, to whom Agrippa I and his brother Aristobulus paid court, shortly after Agrippa's banishment from Rome following the death of Drusus the son of Tiberius in A.D. 23.[4]

Vitellius, A.D. 35.—Flaccus' successor, Vitellius, was ordered to assist Antipas against Aretas and reached Jerusalem, where he showed great deference to Jewish prejudices; and, on hearing that Gaius was Emperor, made the people take an oath of fidelity.[5] He had been to Jerusalem previously when Pilate was deprived of his office, and it was then he surrendered the High Priest's garments to the Jews. On both occasions he deprived the High Priest: first Caiaphas, then his successor Jonathan.[6] By order of Tiberius he made a peace with

---

[1] *Antiq.* xiv. 9 (159); see chapter xvi. Judas the son of Hezekiah cannot be identified with the Judas of Galilee of Acts v. 37.
[2] *Antiq.* xvii. 10 (*passim*); *War*, ii. 3, 4, and 5 (*passim*).
[3] *Antiq.* xviii. 1 (3 ff.); *War*, ii. 8 (118 ff.). On Quirinus see chapter xvi.
[4] *Antiq.* xviii. 6 (150 ff.). L. Pomponius Flaccus, d. A.D. 34, is just mentioned by Tacitus, *Ann.* ii. 32; vi. 27. Velleius Paterculus says he was a man of strict probity. Suetonius says that Tiberius found him a most congenial companion (*Tiberius*, xiii.).
[5] *Antiq.* xviii. 5 (120 ff.).   [6] *Antiq.* xviii. 4 (90 ff.).

the Parthians.[1] He was deeply offended by the conduct
of Antipas.

From the foregoing it would appear that Vitellius was
anxious to conciliate the Jews; and also that, in the
absence of a procurator from Judaea and whenever he
came to Jerusalem, his authority superseded all others.
Subject to no superior but Caesar himself, he exercised
the regal power of the Seleucids. Under Tiberius, however, who watched the provinces with keen attention, it
is evident that the governor of Syria was constantly
receiving orders from Rome.

Petronius, A.D. 39.—P. Petronius, the successor to
Vitellius, played a very creditable part in his dealing with
the Jews in an affair the circumstances of which are
extremely difficult to disentangle. The Emperor Gaius
(Caligula), despite his friendship for Herod Agrippa, a
strict Jew, showed his insanity by ordering his statue to
be placed in the Temple of Jerusalem, and threatened the
nation with war unless it was admitted within the precincts
of a sanctuary which, in itself, was a standing protest
against any form of image worship. The evidence for
the story is scanty. Josephus relates it in both his
histories,[2] Philo[3] alludes to the intention of the emperor
to erect the statue in the Temple, and Tacitus mentions
the attempt in a single sentence,[4] remarking that it caused
a rebellion, of which there is no mention by Josephus,
who states that the issue was peaceful, the emperor with-
drawing the edict at the intercession of Herod Agrippa.
So far as one is able to judge in the absence of precise
information the conduct of Petronius reflects great credit
upon his wisdom and humanity. It would seem that
everywhere the power of the imperial system was receiving
the support of religion, a support not demanded of the
people by their rulers nor fostered by any deliberate
policy; but spontaneously granted by grateful men,

---

[1] *Antiq.* xviii. 4 (96 ff.).
[2] *War*, ii. 10 (184 ff.); *Antiq.* xviii. 8 (261 ff.).
[3] Philo, *Legatio ad Gaium.*
[4] *Hist.* v. 8. Tacitus, *Hist.* v. 9: *dein jussi a Gaio Caesare effigiem
eius in templo arma potius sumpsere, quem motum Caesaris mors
diremit.*

who recognised that the peace they enjoyed was due to the orderly government of the world under Roman authority. The provinces were specially indebted to the emperors, and insisted upon thrusting divine honours on them, and on instituting priesthoods in temples dedicated to their Genius. It is little to be wondered at if Caligula, who, either from madness or policy, took his claim to be regarded as a god seriously, resolved that the one nation who refused to admit his statue to their places of worship in the Temple and in their synagogues should be compelled to do so in proof of their loyalty.

Josephus, the only writer except Philo who mentions Petronius, gives a brief narrative in the ' War,' but a far more elaborate and rhetorical one in ' Antiquities,' in which Agrippa plays a conspicuous and heroic part. Petronius was sent with two or three legions to enforce the command of Cæsar but the Jews entreated him to spare their Temple this profanation, refusing to violate the law and offering themselves to be slaughtered. The humane Petronius risked his life to save the nation, but, before he could suffer the penalty of disobedience, news came that Caligula had been killed.

After the accession of Claudius, Petronius wrote a strong letter of rebuke to the people of Doris (Dor) for presuming to set up in a synagogue the image of Caesar.[1] It is remarkable that this most critical episode in the Jewish history of the period is passed over in complete silence in the rabbinical literature. We have hardly any contemporary information concerning Caligula, except in Philo's ' Legatio ad Gaium ' ; and Josephus, who was born the same year in which Caligula was proclaimed, is our earliest authority for his murder.[2]

Marcus or Marsus, A.D. 42.—Marsus, the successor of Petronius,[3] seems to have been extremely suspicious of

---

[1] *Antiq.* xix. 6 (300 f.)

[2] [The attempt of Gaius failed : the image never was set up, so it afforded no legal precedents. The Talmud gives no continuous history of Israel : all we get there as history are isolated tales told for a legal purpose. The silence of Luke in Acts is really *more* remarkable.— F. C. Burkitt.] The story is only told by Josephus. Philo, who lived at the time, makes no allusion to it.

[3] *Antiq.* xix. 7 (326 f.) ; 8 (338 f.).

Herod Agrippa, who under Claudius had been given most of the dominions of his grandfather Herod the Great. Agrippa was very popular with the Jews; and Marsus may well have suspected that he had in his mind a design to set up an independent principality. Finding that Agrippa was fortifying Jerusalem with a wall intended to enclose the growing city on the north side, Marsus procured orders from Rome to prevent its erection [1]; and, when in Galilee Agrippa gave a splendid entertainment to the neighbouring kings of Commagene, Emesa, Lesser Armenia, Pontus and Chalcis, Marsus, suspecting that they were conspiring against Rome, ordered them all to return to their own dominions. In this we recognise the natural antagonism between the Roman authorities and the semi-independent kings in and around the province of Syria.

Cassius Longinus, A.D. 45, and Ummidius Quadratus, A.D. 50.—The next two legates of Syria, Cassius Longinus[2] and Ummidius Quadratus,[3] occupy little space in Josephus save for the fact that the Samaritans appealed against the Jews to Quadratus, who sent Cumanus, the procurator of Judæa, with others to Rome to answer for their conduct—a proof that the procurator was no more than a subordinate.

Cestius Gallus, A.D. 63.—The last ruler of Syria mentioned by Josephus is Cestius Gallus, whose disastrous defeat at Bethhoron was the beginning of the Jewish war in A.D. 66.

Importance of Syria.—The great province of Syria was one of the most important in the entire Roman Empire, and was only entrusted to men of consular rank, who with an army at their disposal ruled the East from its splendid capital at Antioch. From what we can gather from Josephus the attitude of these imperial officers was statesmanlike, and even sympathetic, and the priests of Jerusalem found them desirous of respecting the national religion. On the whole it may be safely assumed that affairs in Judæa would have gone better had Palestine been incorporated in the Syrian province. A strong government

---

[1] *War*, v. 4 (152); *Antiq.* xix. 7 (326 ff.).
[2] *Antiq.* xx. 1. [3] *Antiq.* xx. 6 (125).

which was not antagonistic to the religious aspirations
of Judaism might have pacified the country and solved a
difficult problem. It was quite obvious that the policy of
Pompey and Gabinius, by which the Jews were allowed
self-government and denied the power of tyrannising
over Greeks and Syrians, was right. The mistake of the
Roman government was that it persistently endeavoured
to continue the Asmonaean domination in the person of
the Herods. Yet the Asmonaeans in the days of their
power had not been altogether popular with the Jewish
people. They were no more legitimately High Priests
than the Herods were pure Jews, and both met with violent
opposition from their own countrymen. A great *legatus
Augusti pro praetore* might have ruled the Jews, but as the
above narrative shows he only interfered as a sort of *deus
ex machina* in serious emergencies.[1]

The Procurators.—When the dominions of Archelaus
were placed under the control of the Emperor, Judaea and
Samaria were committed to the charge of an officer termed
a procurator (ἐπίτροπος). The title implies no more
than that of a steward or revenue officer, and is analogous
to that of a ' collector ' in British India, to whom, as to
his Roman predecessor, the duties of a magistrate were
entrusted. In a province under the senate the proconsul's
deputy was the quaestor ; but for those under the
emperor procurators were appointed, who were supposed
to look after the imperial estate. These officials were
always members of the equestrian order, which represented
the middle-class financiers of Rome. When entrusted
with a minor province like Judaea, a procurator had the
command of a small force of soldiery, and had the power
of life and death over all who were not Roman citizens.
Apparently under exceptional circumstances his authority
in the sphere entrusted to him was absolute ; but in
emergencies the *legatus* of Syria, as we have seen, generally
intervened. The headquarters of the procurator were at
Caesarea Stratonis, and it was only occasionally that he
visited Jerusalem. In all probability a region, if it were

[1] See Appendix D.

part of an imperial province, was more likely to find its government less oppressive than if it were placed in charge of a procurator. In the first place, every class of the community would feel the exactions of an official whose power of enriching himself was limited to a narrow area, and in the second the procurator was taken from a class less experienced in the art of government than the men specially selected by emperors like Augustus and Tiberius, who were interested in seeing the dependencies of Rome well administered. Certainly, according to Josephus, the Jewish War was brought about by the misgovernment of the later procurators.

The first procurators : Coponius—Ambivius—Rufus—Gratus, A.D. 4–26.—The silence of Josephus makes it highly probable that the first measures of Varus in suppressing the revolts following upon the death of Herod the Great, if in our eyes horribly cruel, gave Palestine a period of comparative tranquillity. As has been shown, Josephus tells us nothing about the administration of Archelaus as tetrarch of Judaea ; but merely says that Augustus banished him after ten years because of his misgovernment, and put in Coponius as his procurator with power of life and death. After Coponius nothing whatever is told us for a time in the ' War.' In the ' Antiquities ' the names of two procurators, Marcus Ambivius and Annius Rufus, are given ; and the only incident recorded concerning these is that, under Coponius the Samaritans gave some trouble in the Temple. Valerius Gratus, appointed by Tiberius, as has been indicated above, destroyed the most formidable rebels. The last-named procurator changed the office of High Priest several times and finally left it in the hands of Joseph Caiaphas.[1]

Gratus was procurator for eleven years, and in A.D. 26 was succeeded by Pontius Pilate. The silence of Josephus surely allows us to infer that for a considerable time, after some vigorous measures taken by Gratus against some insurgents, there was not much to disturb the peace of Palestine, and, if so, it is a significant proof that even in the most turbulent district in the East comparative

[1] *Antiq.* xviii. 2 (34 ff.).

tranquillity was assured under the excellent provincial administration of Tiberius.

Pilate (1) the Standards.—To Christians the name of Pontius Pilate inevitably suggests the awful crime of the crucifixion of our Saviour. We are consequently liable to put the worst construction on what Josephus has to say of him. But the few brief paragraphs devoted to him in the 'Antiquities' and in the 'War' do not present his conduct in a wholly unfavourable light. Pilate had ordered the Roman standards, which bore the image of Caesar, to be brought into Jerusalem by the troops who were going to winter in the city. It must be remembered that Pilate did not openly defy the prejudices of the people by marching his soldiers into the gates with their ensigns displayed, but the Jews had got wind of the fact that Caesar's images were within the walls, and crowds hastened to Caesarea to petition that they might be withdrawn. For five days they importuned the procurator with all the frenzy of Oriental fanatics, but on the sixth orders were given to the Roman soldiers suddenly to appear in arms. The suppliants bared their necks for the slaughter; Pilate relented, and ordered the standards to be taken back to Caesarea. By so doing he risked his own life; for, as he told the Jews, Tiberius, who was a distinguished soldier and a strict disciplinarian, might consider his procurator guilty of an unpardonable offence in separating the soldiers from the standards which bore the imperial likeness.

(2) the aqueduct.—The second alleged offence of Pilate, as related by Josephus, is just such as to-day a British administrator might be charged with by discontented Hindus, namely, that of insulting their religion on the plea of anxiety for their welfare. The water supply has always been a cause of anxiety to every governor of Jerusalem, and Pilate sought to supply a remedy by making an aqueduct forty miles in length, and taking the cost out of the Temple treasury. A cry of sacrilege was instantly raised, and the mob became at first clamorous and finally insulting. Pilate, who was in Jerusalem, resolved to make his soldiers act as police. He dressed a

number as civilians and armed them with clubs. When the
crowd refused to disperse he gave orders to clear the place.
The soldiers behaved with more violence than Pilate had
intended, and some of the people were killed or wounded.
At any rate, what might have resulted in a serious outbreak
was suppressed without anything approaching a massacre.[1]

(3) the Crucifixion of the Christ.—Even the Gospel story
of the Crucifixion never charges Pilate with worse than
weakness in sacrificing a victim, whom he did his best to
save, to prevent a dangerous outbreak on the part of the
Jews, nor do the Christians seem to have borne him special
ill-will for his share in this great judicial crime. He appears
to have been no heroic figure, but a moderate and cautious
man, very desirous not to proceed to extremities, but on
one occasion ready to brave the wrath of Tiberius rather
than provoke the fatal fanaticism of the Jews.

(4) the Samaritans.—Pilate was finally deprived of his
office in A.D. 37 by Vitellius, who had received a complaint
from the Samaritans that he had used undue violence
in suppressing what he feared might be a treasonable
gathering, due to the promise of an impostor to reveal the
treasures Moses had hidden on Mount Gerizim.[2]

Disorder in Jerusalem.—But with the death of
Tiberius (A.D. 37) peace seems to have departed from
Israel. No longer are two procurators allowed to manage
affairs each for about ten consecutive years. In future
they change repeatedly, generally before they have
time to learn the nature of the problems which confront
them.

Death of St. Stephen.—The martyrdom of Stephen is
thought to belong to the period when there was no regular
procurator, and if this be so, the narrative of his death in
Acts is significant. There is evidently an intentional
parallelism between the death of Jesus and His first

[1] Pilate's administration is described in *War*, ii. 9 (169 ff.) and in
Antiq. xviii. 3 (55 ff.). In the *War* only the affairs of the standards
and the aqueduct are alluded to. In the Slavonic Josephus the episode
of the death of Jesus comes before the story of the aqueduct. In the
Antiquities the disputed passage about Jesus and the Christians comes
after the aqueduct.
[2] *Antiq.* xviii. 4 (85 ff.). With this story, which is not found in
the *War*, *cf.* that of the Galilaeans in Luke xiii. 1.

martyr. Both are said to have foretold the destruction of
the Temple, both are accused by false witnesses, both die
praying for their enemies, both are tried before the High
Priest, both are buried by their followers, in both narratives
the Son of Man is on the right hand of God. But here the
parallel ends. The accusers of Jesus have great difficulty
in getting Him condemned, but there is no such trouble to
obtain a death sentence for Stephen, who is hurried from
the judgment to be stoned. Here we have a confirmation
of the accuracy of Acts as to the general facts. A Roman
procurator like Pilate would not condemn even a criminal,
who was not a citizen, without some show of justice or
formality. A Jewish court had no scruple in hurrying
one of their own race to death as a blasphemer.[1] It was
the same with James, the Lord's brother, when the High
Priest Ananus had him haled before the Sanhedrin and
condemned to death, certainly in this instance during the
absence of the procurator.[2] It is not too much to conjecture that the Jewish priesthood chafed under the
calm inflexibility of a government which had no sort of
sympathy with their enthusiasm in vindicating their
religion.

**Marcellus, Marullus, Cuspius Fadus, and Tiberius
Alexander.**—After Pilate's deposition Vitellius committed
Judaea to a friend named Marcellus, and a little later
Caligula sent Marullus, a knight, as procurator. What
either of these did is not recorded by Josephus ; but
Cuspius Fadus, who suppressed the rebellion of Theudas,
was followed by Tiberius Alexander, a nephew of Philo,
belonging to one of the chief Jewish families in Egypt.
But, to further his worldly interests, this procurator had
renounced his religion, and risen to high rank in the
Roman army. In Judaea he seems to have maintained
order, because both he and his predecessor Fadus did
nothing to shock the susceptibilities of the inhabitants,
whose religion at least Alexander understood. But he
would not tolerate the brigandage, which under the name

---

[1] Acts vi.–vii. See Wilfred L. Knox, *St. Paul and the Church of
Jerusalem*, ch. ii.
[2] *Antiq.* xx. 9 (200).

of patriotism was distracting the country, and executed
the sons of that Judas of Galilee who had raised a rebellion
at the time of the enrolment by Quirinus.[1]

Cumanus.—Under Cumanus the Roman government of
Judaea was evidently in a condition of collapse. The
hatred of the Jews was manifesting itself on every side.
The people of Caesarea had shown indecent joy when
news came of the death of Herod Agrippa. A copy of the
Law was treated with insult. A soldier, guarding the
Temple manifested his contempt of the worshippers by
gross gestures, and provoked a riot. Everywhere the
brigands continued to render life and property unsafe, and
when such a state of affairs prevails, it is almost invariably
with the connivance and sympathy of the inhabitants.
Palestine with its mountains and caverns is peculiarly
suited to an irregular warfare, by which a discontented
population displays its hatred to the ruling caste. Life
was growing generally unsafe, when men suspected of dis-
loyalty or even of lukewarm attachment to the Jewish
nation or religion were assassinated. Things had in fact
been, since the death of Tiberius, hastening to a climax,
every year with increasing speed ; and it is almost impossible to say how the catastrophe could have been averted.
For this the Romans were in part responsible, but even
more so was the intense unpopularity of the Jewish people
among the Greeks and Syrians in Palestine.

Felix.—The procurator Felix's memory labours under
the disadvantage of his being the subject of one of those
brilliantly epigrammatic sentences which condemn a man
to eternal infamy. Because Tacitus has said that in
Judaea he ' exercised the power of a king with the character
of a slave,' it is inferred by most subsequent historians
that he must have been a thoroughly bad man, a judgment
which has the support of the undoubted fact that he was
the brother of Pallas, the wicked counsellor of the Emperor
Claudius. Josephus in his ' Antiquities ' charges him with
being privy to the murder of Jonathan, a virtuous chief
priest. As the record of his long tenure of the government of Judaea throws much light on the condition of the

[1] *Antiq.* xx. 5 (102 f.).

country, and his treatment of St. Paul increases our interest in him, it seems necessary to discuss the value of the testimony of Tacitus by the light of Josephus and the Acts of the Apostles.

The actual facts of the career of Felix are difficult to unravel. Tacitus says that he and Cumanus were joint administrators of Palestine, and that the Jews and Samaritans were assaulting one another. Instead of trying to repress the disorder consequent on this state of affairs, Felix and Cumanus conspired to encourage it, and made large profits out of the anarchy of the country. The governor of Syria, Ummidius Quadratus, intervened and tried the case ; but, to save Felix, he placed him on the bench of judges and Cumanus was found guilty, whereupon Quadratus sent him to Rome to Claudius.[1] In the ' Histories ' Tacitus says that Felix married Drusilla, the granddaughter of Antony and Cleopatra, and thus was related to Claudius, thereby revealing his ignorance of the real fact, for Felix had married, not a Drusilla of Roman stock, but the sister of Agrippa II. It is to be noticed that Josephus' animosity against Felix is much greater in the ' Antiquities ' than in the earlier ' War.' [2] The only facts related about Felix in the ' War ' are a description of the rise of the *sicarii* or dagger men, who resorted to the festivals, stabbed their enemies, and escaped, often with the connivance of the surrounding crowd. Among other victims was Jonathan, son of Ananus.

Felix's administration was disturbed by revolutionaries under the guise of inspired prophets, who led their dupes out of Jerusalem into the wilderness, persuading them that God was about to bring about a great deliverance. The worst of these was an Egyptian who led 30,000 men to the Mount of Olives and threatened to besiege the city. This dangerous army of fanatics was dispersed by Felix, aided on this occasion by the inhabitants of Jerusalem ; and, though the invaders were utterly defeated, the Egyptian escaped, and his followers in

---

[1] This is related in the *Annals*, xii. 54.
[2] Compare *War*, ii. 13 (253 ff.) with *Antiq*. xx. 8 (161 ff.). In the *War* Felix is not made responsible for the death of Jonathan, whose appointment as High Priest is nowhere mentioned.

alliance with the brigands spread terror throughout
Judaea. The Greek population of Caesarea began at this
time to attack the Jewish inhabitants of that city. After
some severe rioting, in which the Jewish faction had the
upper hand, Felix appeared and boldly ordered the mob
to disperse ; and on their continuing contumacious, commanded his soldiers to disperse the crowd. Finally, he
sent the ringleaders on both sides for trial at Rome.
From this we should infer that Felix, as we are informed
by Suetonius,[1] was an energetic military man, who really
made an effort to reduce the distracted country to some
sort of order. The marriage of Felix with Drusilla, who
had been persuaded to desert her husband, the King of
Emesa, points to a design to rule Judaea in the name of the
family of the old priest-kings ; but Felix was recalled,
and a good procurator, named Festus, sent out who did
all in his power to restore order by suppressing brigandage.

Treatment of St. Paul by Felix and Festus.—The arrest
of St. Paul, who was in the hands of both Felix and
Festus, throws some light on the character of the administration of these two procurators, not wholly to
the discredit of either. The Apostle had been accused
of the very serious crime of defiling the Temple by allowing a heathen friend to enter the sacred precincts, and
when we read of the condition of things in Josephus we
can well imagine the scene described in Acts, when a
frenzied mob clamoured for Paul's blood. The tribune in
Jerusalem acted with wise decision; and to save Paul's life
sent him under a strong guard to Caesarea. As a citizen
of Rome he could not be put to death by the procurator,
and the government was answerable for his safety.[2]

Roman method of government.—But the interest here
lies, not so much in the personal character of either
Felix, Festus or Agrippa II, as in the nature of the
government of Judaea by the Roman officials. The
general impression left on the mind by Acts xxi.–xxvi. is
that of an administration in a distracted country trying
to conduct affairs in accordance with Roman legal ideas.
A citizen was to be protected at all costs, a man might

---

[1] *Claudius*, xxviii.   [2] Acts xxi.–xxvi.

be kept in custody to conciliate Jewish prejudices, but could not be surrendered to popular fury and condemned till he had had every chance of defending himself. But the number of troops needed to convey St. Paul from Jerusalem to Caesarea is a proof that the authority of Rome was dependent only on force, and that the least relaxation of its military prestige was certain to be followed by universal anarchy.[1]

Albinus and Gessius Florus.—The death of Festus left Judaea without a procurator, and the opportunity was taken by the High Priest to convoke the Sanhedrin and to compass the judicial murder of James the brother of Jesus. The two last procurators, Albinus and Gessius Florus, are said by Josephus to have been the worst of men; but their misgovernment, especially that of Florus, may well have been the misgovernment of despair and have hastened, rather than rendered inevitable, the great Jewish War.

Picture of state of Palestine in Acts.—Two facts are worth considering. The first is that Josephus gives a complete list of the procurators, who must have been comparatively obscure men in the imperial polity, a proof that he must have had good documentary material and probably free access to the governmental archives. Another, that the very brief record in Acts gives an amazingly correct picture of the state of affairs in Palestine, considering that the ruin of the Jewish nation in torrents of blood must have made events before the war a dim memory to the generation which followed. Of these the Jews have preserved scarcely any Hebrew or Aramaic tradition. One cannot but be struck with astonishment that the obscure sect of the Christians of the first century should have produced a record, which, if it seems unsatisfactory to us by its brevity and absence of information on certain points, should have been as accurate in its general features as that found in the last chapters of the Book of the Acts of the Apostles.[2]

[1] Acts xxiii. 23 ff.
[2] The alleged dependence of Acts on Josephus, with some inevitable repetition of what has been said here, is discussed in chapter xvi.

CHAPTER X

THE JEWS IN PARTHIA

BEFORE he tells the story of the break with Rome and the disastrous war which followed, Josephus interrupts his narrative by relating the doings of the Jews in the remote East beyond the boundaries of the Roman Empire. Among other things, we have the long story of Asineus and Anileus, to be told later in this chapter, which may appear irrelevant when first perused, but is in reality of great significance in accounting for subsequent events.

The known East.—In the days of Josephus the civilised portion of the human race, exclusive of those of the remote and practically unknown East, *i.e.* of Hindustan and China, inhabited a narrow strip of the earth's surface between the river Indus and the shores of the Atlantic. To the north were the nomad barbarians, destined hereafter to play so important a part in history, to the south lay the Indian Ocean and the burning sands of the African deserts. Two organised governments were in rivalry, one European, which here may be styled Graeco-Roman, the other Asiatic, the Perso-Parthian. Speaking generally, the Roman Empire of the East was the successor and representative of that founded by Alexander the Great, whilst the Parthian stood for Cyrus and Darius, and their predecessors in the East who had claimed to be ' Kings of kings.' The external history of Judaism is often explained by the age-long conflict of these successive great monarchies with the Western powers.

Alexander and the Seleucids.—The greatness of Alexander of Macedon is to be measured even more by his aims than by his exploits. His victories were great but his plans were grander. He was the first to realise the importance of linking Europe with India, and of establishing by a chain of Macedonian or Greek cities lines of communication with what was to his world the remote East. He and the Seleucids who immediately succeeded to his eastern dominions were indeed the only European rulers who ever were able to pass through their own dominions from the Tigris to the river Indus. In what is now known as Persia, Afghanistan, and Beluchistan five cities were named after Alexander, the best known being Kandahar, the ancient Alexandropolis ; in addition to which cities arose, bearing such names as Seleucia, Apamaea, and Antioch.

Reasons for the failure of the Macedonians in the East.—But many circumstances made it impossible for the successors of Alexander to hold their Eastern provinces. In the first place, they had ambitions to advance westward. They desired to annex Egypt and Asia Minor. This made them leave Seleucia-on-the-Tigris and establish their capital at Antioch in Syria. Again, they had to administer their more distant provinces by appointing satraps ; and wherever empires are feeble, the viceroys tend to become independent princes. Thus, as early as the middle of the third century B.C., Bactria was lost. Further, the Macedonian Greeks were aliens, and the native Asiatics were sure to combine against them whenever a suitable leader could be found.

The Parthians.—The insignificant province of Parthia supplied the man. Parthia proper was a narrow strip of country on the south-east corner of the Caspian. Its inhabitants were a hardy race. The ancient writers describe them as Scythians ; a word which probably denotes their habits rather than their exact branch of the human family. They seem to have been of the same stock as the Turanian peoples, who have made such formidable invasions of the civilised world. They had received a certain civilisation when under the dominion of the Persians and Macedonians, but retained the courage of barbarians. Their armies of horsemen were the best disciplined and most efficient which the Romans had had to encounter since the days of Hannibal.

Rise of their empire.—About 256 B.C. Arsaces and Tiridates, two Parthian brothers, revolted against the satrap of Antiochus II (Theos, 262–264 B.C.). For a brief period Arsaces enjoyed the title of king. At his death his brother Tiridates took his crown and his name, and from henceforth every king of Parthia was known as Arsaces. Fortunately, however, the classical historians and writers often call them by their original names. Arsaces II reigned about thirty years, and virtually laid the foundation of the Parthian monarchy, which became increasingly formidable ; and, by the time of the appearance of the Romans in the East, had extended its frontier to the Euphrates. At Carrhae, in A.D. 54, Surenas, the general of the Parthian king Orodes, defeated the Roman army of Crassus, the triumvir, who had crossed the Euphrates in order to invade Mesopotamia ; and from that day the two empires, first the Parthian, and later the Persian, waged war for centuries against the Romans with varying fortunes.[1]

The Jews and the Parthians.—The late Dr. Mahaffy has pointed out that Alexander visited Jerusalem and showed so much favour to the Jews because, insignificant as they were in power and number, their constant passing and repassing from Jerusalem to Mesopotamia had made them invaluable as guides to the country he was about to invade.[2] There was a regular route by which the Jews must have travelled ; and we know from the second chapter of Acts that the feasts at Jerusalem were attended by their Oriental brethren. In the days of the Persian domination the Jews had owed much to the favour of the Great King ; and the Parthians were after all the successors to the Persian ascendancy. The Jews therefore may well have regarded the Parthian Empire as far more disposed to be sympathetic with them

---

[1] For the rise of Parthia consult George Rawlinson's *Sixth Great Oriental Monarchy*.

[2] *The Empire of the Ptolemies* (1895), p. 85.

than the Roman; and to have looked for its victory in
Palestine with hope, as likely to leave them greater
freedom to restore the state founded by the priest-kings.
The defeat of Crassus, who had despoiled the Temple,
must have been welcomed; and, when the Parthians,
fourteen years later, burst into Syria, they naturally
endeavoured to win over the Jews by giving them a
representative of the high-priestly line in the person of
Antigonus in place of the pro-Roman family of the
Edomite Antipater who supported Hyrcanus. Both
Herod Antipas and, later, Agrippa I were suspected by
the *legati* of Syria of intrigues which might have led to
seeking the aid of Parthia in the event of a Roman
disaster in the East.[1] Just before the outbreak of war
Agrippa II told the insurgent Jews not to look for help
from the Parthians against the Romans, as the emperor
was now able to demand that their king should send his
sons as hostages to Rome.[2]

Josephus has something to say about the relations
between the Parthians and the Jews in or near his own
day. In the invasion of Syria in 40 B.C. by Pacorus, the
son of King Orodes, and his general Barzapharnes, the
Parthians did not take Jerusalem, but sent a body of

[1] *Vide supra*, chapter viii.
[2] *War*, ii. 16 (245–401). Whether Agrippa made the speech or
Josephus put it into his mouth, it is a very noteworthy production as
a description of the condition of the Roman world at the time. Dr.
Thackeray rightly calls the speech a *tour de force* possessing distinct
historical value. *Josephus the Man and the Historian* Lecture II.

After the death of Josephus, in the days of Trajan (A.D. 98–117),
when Jewish troubles were again distracting the East, one may hazard
the bold suggestion that one of the reasons for sending St. Ignatius
to be devoured by wild beasts in the arena at Rome may possibly
have been that the Emperor, who had shown in his correspondence
with Pliny forbearance in dealing with the Christians at Bithynia,
was resolved to make a fearful example of those who might be suspected of Parthian sympathies. That the Christians were con-
fused with the Jews of Antioch is not unnatural, and this also may
partly explain why the saint warns them against having any dealings
with Judaism. The facts before us about this period are so meagre
that such conjectures may be, if not admissible, excusable.

Bishop Lightfoot has wellnigh exhausted the subject of St. Ignatius
in his *Apostolic Fathers*. But the problem remains unsolved. How
was it that Trajan took such precautions to send the Bishop of Antioch
to be executed publicly in Rome, and yet placed no obstacles in the
way of his receiving delegations from his brother Christians on his long
journey?

cavalry to assist Antigonus against his uncle Hyrcanus; and it is evident that they sought to establish an alliance with Jerusalem by the destruction of Herod, whose brother Pheroras killed himself when he found that he was made a captive by the treachery of the Parthian general. The deposed High Priest Hyrcanus was taken to Babylon, where he was treated with honour by the Jews; but when Herod was king he returned to Palestine at a great age; and is said to have been put to death by the unscrupulous husband of his granddaughter Mariamne. What induced Herod to be guilty of so barbarous and impolitic a crime can never be known, unless Hyrcanus had been sent by the Parthians to disturb the peace of Palestine by his presence in the country.[1]

Jewish intrigues with the Parthians.—In the Eighteenth Book of the 'Antiquities,' Josephus, after relating the removal of Pilate from the procuratorship of Judaea and the visit of Vitellius, the *legatus* of Syria, to Jerusalem, when he restored to the Jews the custody of the high-priestly robes, devotes a section to the story of how Vitellius made peace with Artabanus, King of Parthia. Artabanus III had tried to annex Armenia, and the Emperor had bribed the kings of Albania and Iberia to make war on him, and had encouraged the courtiers of Artabanus to procure his assassination. The kings mentioned did not attack Artabanus themselves, but allowed a barbarian horde to pass through the Caspian gates into Parthia. As Artabanus defeated his enemies, Tiberius resolved to make peace. Antipas was the host at the conference on a bridge over the Euphrates, and reported the issue of the meeting before the letters of Vitellius could reach Tiberius, to the great offence of the *legatus*. The sequel is seen later. No sooner was Tiberius dead than Antipas asked Caligula to grant him the title of King. Herod Agrippa, however, wrote to say that Antipas had been supporting Sejanus, and at this time was plotting against Rome with Artabanus, in proof of which Agrippa declared that Antipas had 70,000 stand of arms in his arsenal at Tiberias.

[1] *Vide supra*, chapter vii.

This Antipas could not deny, and accordingly he was deprived of his tetrarchy and banished.[1]

In the sequel to his account of the conversion of Izates of Adiabene, Josephus relates that the King of Parthia took refuge with that prince, and was received with high honour, in gratitude for which Izates was allowed by Artabanus to enjoy many of the privileges of a Parthian monarch. Izates is mentioned only by Josephus, but he is important, not only for the religious interest of his conversion, but as a proof that the Jews had the support of a powerful vassal of Parthia beyond the Tigris, and consequently far outside the Roman frontier.[2]

Asineus and Anileus.—But the loss of all hope of support from the Parthians in the Jewish struggle with Rome is shown in the long story Josephus tells of the two brothers Asineus and Anileus, in which the weakness of a semi-barbarous Oriental empire is manifest in contrast with the harmony and organisation of that of Rome.

The account of the two brothers [3] is found only in Josephus ; but there is no reason for doubting its substantial accuracy. The only patent mistake is that the two cities Nisibis and Nahardea are both said to have been on the same river (ἔστιν δὲ καὶ Νίσιβις πόλις κατὰ τὸν αὐτὸν τοῦ ποταμοῦ περίρρουν), whereas they are hundreds of miles apart and Nisibis is not on the Euphrates.[4] This seems to prove no more than that Josephus was ignorant of the geography of Mesopotamia. Despite this, however, what he relates bears every other sign of probability.

Nahardea is described as a well-fortified city of Babylonia on the Euphrates, being almost surrounded by the river. Trusting in its strength and that of Nisibis, the Jews banked the money collected for the temple-tax in these cities. Periodically this was remitted to Jerusalem,

---

[1] *Vide supra*, chapter viii.   [2] *Antiq.* xx. 3 (54 ff.).
[3] *Antiq.* xviii. 9 (310–379).
[4] See Neubauer, *La Géographie du Talmud.* Nisibis, a great emporium of trade, was the centre for the Jews in the north of Mesopotamia (p. 370), whereas ' Nehardaea ' was in the south. Nisibis was on a small river, called the Mygdonius.

escorted by many myriads of men. At Nahardea lived two orphaned Jewish boys, whose mother apprenticed them to a weaver, this being considered a highly honourable trade. But they were not suited to make beautiful Persian carpets. Their master, irritated by their clumsiness, beat them; and in revenge they robbed his house, which contained many warlike weapons, and betook themselves to a place where there was excellent pasturage. There they were joined by a crowd of idle youths, and built a robber fortress from which they dominated the neighbourhood, and forced the farmers to pay blackmail, in return for which they protected their herds from all other marauders. In the end they became so wealthy and formidable as to be a menace to the entire province. Thus far their story resembles the old tale of David, when he was rebelling against Saul in the south of Judah.[1]

The local satrap resolved to suppress what appeared to him a very dangerous confederacy. Whilst Asineus and his company were observing the Sabbath by resting on the shores of a lake, he attacked them in the hope that they would not violate the sacred day by their resistance. The sharp ears of the Jewish leader detected the approach of a formidable body of cavalry. ' Men,' said he, ' I hear horses neighing, and not such as are feeding, but horses mounted, and I can also hear the jingling of their bridles.' Scouts were sent to report whether he was right, and announced the approach of an enemy. It was resolved that the emergency justified a breach of the Sabbath, and the Jews gained a decisive victory.

Asineus recognised by Artabanus III.—The next phase would appear somewhat incredible if we were not in possession of some facts related elsewhere. Artabanus III was an unpopular king. He was more than once deposed, though Josephus does not hint at this till he comes to the story of Izates. Any satrap, if allowed too much power, might be a possible rival.

---

[1] Cf. 1 Samuel xxv., where David threatens Nabal for his churlish refusal to supply his troop with provisions, though he has protected Nabal's cattle from marauders.

Accordingly, the Parthian monarch resolved to make terms with Asineus and invited him to a conference. Anileus first went in place of his brother, but after some hesitation Asineus was persuaded to visit the king, who gave him the right hand of fellowship. Though the royal officers advised that he should be killed, Artabanus committed the country of Babylonia to his care, giving him as a charge (παρακαταθήκη) to keep it clear of robbers. What the Parthian king did is exactly analogous to the policy of the later Seleucids, who made robber chiefs, like the brothers of Judas the Maccabee, into princes with legitimate authority. Asineus proved worthy of the confidence reposed in him; for fifteen years he maintained peace and order; but his brother Anileus lacked his discretion, and proved in the end no better than a turbulent bandit.

Murder of Asineus.—A Parthian general had a beautiful wife, of whom Anileus was enamoured. To secure her, he declared war, killed the husband and captured the widow. According to the unchangeable custom of her country, this woman concealed the household gods in her baggage, as Rachel, herself a native of Mesopotamia, had done ages before when Jacob escaped from Laban.[1] At first she worshipped them in private, but gradually grew more bold, and when the companions of Anileus rebuked him for tolerating this idolatry and complained of her conduct to Asineus, she poisoned her husband's brother.

Defeat and death of Anileus.—Anileus, now in supreme command, then attacked Mithradates, a Parthian noble, a son-in-law of Artabanus, took him captive and exposed him to a gross insult by making him ride naked upon an ass. Finally, however, from fear that Artabanus would take vengeance upon all the Jews in Babylonia, Mithradates was liberated and allowed to go to his home. At the instance of his wife he collected a great force of horsemen, marched against Anileus and defeated his army. Anileus, however, collected another force as numerous, if less disciplined, and with this became the

[1] Gen. xxxi. 34.

terror of the district. The inhabitants complained to the Jews in Nahardea and demanded the surrender of Anileus. Finally, the Babylonians were able to surprise the brigand army of Jews, and slay their leader.

Jews unpopular in Seleucia on the Tigris.—Josephus gives no date, but probably the defeat of Anileus and the dispersion of his band must have taken place about A.D. 40. It was followed by a savage attack on the Jews in Babylonia, the centre of which seems to have been the commercial city of Seleucia-on-the-Tigris. The country folk, actuated by a common hostility to the Jews, forced them to take refuge in the great city, which is said to have been one of the largest in the world, and to have once had a population of some 600,000 exclusive of slaves. The inhabitants were a few Macedonians and many Greeks and Syrians, and the two last were constantly at variance. For five years the Jews lived in Seleucia at peace ; and then troubles broke out again of which Josephus gives a disappointingly brief account. Seleucia was the foundation of Seleucus I (Nicator), whose name the city bore. It was more suitable for commerce than Babylon, because there the Tigris and the Euphrates are only twenty-five miles apart. With this in view, Seleucus Nicator selected the site and built a city at the expense of the ancient and more famous Babylon, the materials of which were often used for the new foundation. The people of Babylon gradually abandoned the place for the new city ; and, though forty miles distant, Seleucia henceforward was often spoken of as Babylon.

Parties in Seleucia.—Josephus thus describes the condition of life at Seleucia. Apparently, as at Alexandria, the different races were sharply divided and the Greek and Syrian inhabitants were at constant variance. The large influx of Jews gave the Syrians, who had been hitherto subordinate, the predominance. The Greeks, now the oppressed class, found that their only resource was to make peace with the Syrians, and joined them in an attack on the newcomers. More than 50,000 Jews were massacred, only a few escaping by the connivance of their friends to Ctesiphon on the opposite side of the

river. Ctesiphon, though the winter residence of the
Parthian kings, was mainly Greek ; but even the presence
of the king did not prevent the people from objecting to
the presence of the detested Jews, as formidable fighters
liable to make trouble. There was, in fact, a regular
war between the combined forces of the Greeks and
Syrians against the Jews, who were in the end compelled
to retire, and to entrench themselves in their two strongly
fortified cities of Nahardea and Nisibis.

The events related in this single section of Josephus
must have occupied a considerable time, perhaps some
years. It is evident that, what with the disturbed condition of the Parthian Empire owing to rival claimants
to the throne, as is related by the classical writers, and
the independence of the great cities, no aid could be
expected from that source ; and in the event of a rebellion
against Rome in Judaea the Jews would be left to their
fate.

**The Jews in Parthia bold fighters but bad neigh-
bours.**—But although from the long story which Josephus
tells of the adventures of Asineus and Anileus we can see
how in the Parthian as well as in the Roman Empire in
Syria the Jews were bad neighbours to the people among
whom they dwelt, there is no hint that, in Parthia at any
rate, their religion was the cause of their unpopularity.
Except for their regularity in paying their temple dues,
and the care with which they remitted them to Jerusalem,
we learn nothing of their peculiar customs, save that,
though once they overcame their scruples by defeating
their enemies on the holy day, they hesitated to fight on
the Sabbath, and also that they objected to Anileus
marrying an idolatress. Nor does their aptitude for
business seem to have been a reason for jealousy. The
fame of Asineus and Anileus rests on their skill in war.
The elder brother, an insignificant little man, as Josephus
expressly tells us, was a mighty warrior, and at the same
time a wise and prudent administrator ; the younger was
an unscrupulous ruffian. Strange as it may seem to us,
the Jews were celebrated as among the most formidable
in arms of all the Eastern people. Asineus and Anileus

were of much the same stuff as the soldiers of Alexander Jannaeus, the robbers in the days of Herod and Varus, and the military factions when Jerusalem was besieged by the Romans.

Babylonian schools.—But as in Palestine, so also in Mesopotamia there was a better side of Judaism. Babylonia was destined to become a great centre of learning. The Prince of Captivity, as the Jewish leader was called, became a great potentate under the Parthian and Persian kings. In fact, the Jews appear to have excited less bitter feelings in the Eastern than in the Western world, and though retaining their peculiar religion, to have prospered in many walks of life.

The Parthians in Christian imagination.—As a proof of the impression made by the Parthian invasion one may cite the popular belief about the time of the fall of Jerusalem that Nero was not dead but would be restored by a Parthian army, and also the Christian belief, found in the Apocalypse, that destruction would be wrought by terrible hordes of horsemen coming from the East.[1] The Parthians, in fact, occupied a place in the imagination of the civilised west as did later the Huns, ' the scourges of God,' in the later days of the Empire.

[1] Rev. vi. 1–8.

CHAPTER XI

The Outbreak of the War with Rome

Misgovernment of the Procurators.—For the Jewish war and its terrific consequences Josephus is our only contemporary authority, most of Tacitus' account being hopelessly lost ; and there is no orderly record from any other Jewish source in existence. Our historian lays the blame for the calamity on the misgovernment of the procurators and the excesses of the fanatics. But one has to read between the lines of the extremely unsatisfactory conclusion of the ' Antiquities ' to understand the course of events under the last procurators Fadus, Tiberius Alexander, Cumanus, Felix, Festus and Albinus. These officials, with the possible exception of Festus, may have been as bad as Josephus depicts them ; but nevertheless one can but feel compelled to make some allowance for the almost impossible position in which they were placed. It seems that the conduct of Gessius Florus, the last of the procurators, admits of no excuse whatever, though the explosion of the rebellion which took place under his misgovernment had long been preparing.[1]

Patriotism or brigandage.—The great curse of Palestine for many years had been the prevalence of brigandage. Under the name of patriotism, formidable bands of marauders had taken to the mountains, and waged constant and relentless war with all peaceable persons ; especially those who were not Jews by race or religion. Nothing but a government of relentless severity could cope with the evil. After the death of Herod Agrippa I it broke out worse than ever ; and it may be

[1] *War*, ii. 14 (277 ff.).

inferred that the sons of Judas of Galilee (the sophist or
rabbi) were among the leaders, as Tiberius Alexander
found it advisable to crucify two of them (A.D. 46).   As
a Jew, this procurator perfectly understood the danger
of the mixture of patriotism and religious fanaticism
embodied in the principles which Judas had laid down.
But if he, Felix, and Albinus showed some respect for
justice and were zealous in attempting to check brigandage, Gessius Florus ostentatiously displayed (ἐπόμπευσεν)
his abhorrence of the Jewish people, and deliberately
incited them to rush upon ruin by provoking them to
defy the power of Rome.   Thus, Josephus suggests, he
hoped to conceal his enormous tyranny and brutality in
Judaea from the imperial authorities.

   Jews insulted in Caesarea-by-the-Sea.—The trouble
began at Caesarea.   It has been already indicated how
the Greek inhabitants had shown the hatred in which
they held the Jews by the brutal and indecent demonstra-
tions of joy when they heard of the death of Herod
Agrippa I.[1]   Another opportunity of insulting their
fellow citizens occurred in A.D. 66.   The synagogue stood
near a plot of land which the Jews were ready to
purchase at a fancy price.   The Greek who owned the
land refused to sell, and proceeded to build a factory
which practically blocked any access to the synagogue.
The more impulsive of the young Jews tried to wreck the
new building; but the cooler heads, represented by John,
the publican [2] (τελώνης = tax collector), went to Florus
and offered him eight talents of silver if he would stop
the erection of the proposed edifice.   Florus retired to
Sebaste ; and one of the Greeks of Caesarea insulted the
Jews by placing a pot turned bottom upwards at the
door of the synagogue and sacrificing birds upon it.   This
led to a riot ; and though the Roman Jocundus, a commander of cavalry, removed the obnoxious pot, the Jews

---

[1] See above, chapter viii.   *War*, ii. 14 (285 ff.).   From this point
we are entirely dependent on the *War*.
[2] *War*, ii. 14 (287).   The word publican, so familiar to readers of
the New Testament, means a farmer of the revenue.   The leading
publicani even in Palestine were often rich ; *cf*. Luke xix. 2, Zacchaeus
the publican of Jericho.   For the usual method of farming the revenue
of a province *cf*. the story of the Tobiades, *Antiq*. xii. 4 (160 ff.).

were compelled to quit the city, and retired with their copy of the Law to a place called Narbata.[1]

Florus marches to Jerusalem.—Florus interpreted the action of the Caesarean Jews as one of hostility to Rome and marched his forces into Jerusalem. He took seriously the insults of a few seditious persons, making them an excuse for allowing his soldiers to pillage and massacre in the city. Queen Berenice, who happened to be there, displayed the magnanimity and courage in which none of her family, with all their faults and crimes, seem to have been deficient. She was discharging a vow in the Temple, but directly she heard of the tumult she rushed boldly at the peril of her life among the infuriated soldiery to entreat for the people ; and even came as a suppliant with bare feet into the presence of Florus. Her high rank scarcely saved her from death. As Florus was thought to meditate a raid upon the Temple, the Jews destroyed the portico from the Antonia by which the Roman soldiers could enter the outer court of the Temple. Florus in dismay retired to Caesarea.[2]

Herod Agrippa II tries to pacify the Jews.—Herod Agrippa now made his appearance in Jerusalem. Summoning the people to the Xystus, and placing his sister Berenice on the roof of the palace of the Asmonaeans, where she could be seen by all, he delivered an oration, the report of which may possibly have been a joint composition of Josephus and himself in after days explaining their conduct in adhering to the cause of the Romans. It can hardly be supposed that an infuriated people would have listened to so elaborate and learned a description of the imperial power of the Romans. Nevertheless, some of the arguments advanced are of interest as descriptive of the attitude taken by Josephus.[3]

Herod Agrippa's speech.—Agrippa ascribes the three motives of the war party as due to youthful inexperience, to unreflecting (ἀλόγιστος) hope that war would give independence, and also to a desire on the part of others to make profit by fishing in troubled waters. The crimes

---

[1] *War*, ii. 14 (289 ff.).   [2] *War*, ii. 15 (309 ff.).
[3] See the note on this speech in chapter x. p. 173.

of the procurators are not sufficient excuse ; the emperor may send better men ; and besides, how can the Jews cope with Rome ? They might possibly have done so in Pompey's day when their kingdom was strong—but now ! Where is their fleet ? How much have they in their treasury ? The Romans are not Egyptians and Arabs : their strength has never been subdued. All other nations have submitted to Rome—the intelligent Greeks, the haughty Macedonians, the five hundred cities of Asia. Gaul, rich and populous as it is, is so obedient that only twelve hundred soldiers are needed to maintain order. And so the king goes on to enumerate the Roman provinces, which were so contented and peaceful that a newly conquered island like Britain only required four legions, and a vast country like Spain but one, to keep the peace. As for God helping the Jews, it is evident from the success of the Romans that He is on their side. In addition, if the Jews keep the Sabbath in war time, they will suffer the fate of their ancestors in the days of Pompey ; and if they break it, how can they look for God's support ? The Jews have no allies : even Parthia now sends its princes to Rome as hostages. Let, therefore, the Jews remain at peace, and thereby save their city and their Temple.[1]

The sacrifices for Rome cease in the Temple.— Agrippa's eloquence calmed the people for a while ; they collected forty talents of tribute and rebuilt the porticos connecting the Temple with the Antonia. Then the insurgent party got the upper hand. Agrippa had to leave the city, the rebels captured Masada and slew the Roman garrison, and in the summer of A.D. 66 the captain of the Temple, Eleazar son of the High Priest Ananias, forbade the sacrifices for Rome to be continued. In vain the chiefs of the priesthood and other responsible persons urged the restoration of the sacrifices. The die had been cast and the war with Rome was inevitable.

Massacres and reprisals.—The months of August, September, October, and November in A.D. 66 witnessed a series of massacres followed by hideous reprisals through-

[1] *War*, ii. 16 (345–410).

out Syria and Egypt. It was not merely against Rome that the Jewish fanatics were fighting, but against the civilisation of the world. To make the events of these dreadful days more comprehensible it may be well to abandon the order of Josephus; and to record the happenings in Palestine, Syria, and Egypt before speaking of the progress of the insurrection in Jerusalem.

Caesarea, the storm centre at the beginning of the disturbances, was the first city to inaugurate a massacre of its Jewish inhabitants. If we may trust Josephus, who likes large round numbers, no fewer than twenty thousand were put to the sword.[1] The Jews retaliated by sending a force, apparently from Jerusalem, which at first virtually followed the course of Judas the Maccabee's first victorious campaign outside Judaea. Crossing the Jordan, they sacked the cities of Philadelphia, Heshbon, Gerasa, and Pella. Carrying fire and slaughter wherever they went, the Jews attacked the cities of Gaulonitis, and went as far north as Kadesh of Naphtali. They even burned Sebaste, as Herod had renamed the place when he rebuilt Samaria. Anthedon and Gaza were also razed to the ground. Palestine was one scene of terror and bloodshed; and those peaceful people whom the Gentiles suspected of Jewish sympathies were in hourly peril. In Scythopolis the Jews offered their aid to assist their fellow citizens; but the non-Jewish population, distrusting this profession of amity, persuaded them to assemble in one place and massacred thirteen thousand. A famous Jewish warrior who had done doughty deeds in defence of the city, when he saw the massacre begin, slew his father and mother, his wife and children, and standing over the corpses of his entire family plunged his sword into his throat in the sight of all. The heathen naturally retaliated; but Antioch, Sidon, and Apamea spared the Jews; and the people of Gerasa showed similar humanity. The fortress of Machaerus was taken by the rebels, provoked by the brutality of Herod Agrippa's general Noarus; Masada, which contained the armoury of the Herods, had been captured earlier.[2]

[1] *War*, ii. 18 (457–460).   [2] *War*, ii. 18 (467 ff.).

Alexandria.—In Alexandria there was a terrible massacre, arising out of a riot of Jews and Gentiles in the amphitheatre. Alexander, the imperial viceroy of Egypt, the apostate Jew whom we have met with as procurator of Judaea, allowed the two legions stationed in the city to plunder the Jews of the district called ' Delta.' In the end he ordered the soldiers to desist, and they obeyed ; but the infuriated mob of the city were with the utmost difficulty prevented from venting their fury on the hated Jews. Josephus says that fifty thousand in all were slain.

All this was leading to a catastrophe which made the co-operation of Hellenic Roman civilisation and Judaism impossible for many centuries, to the infinite loss of human society. Yet in reading Josephus it is impossible not to see a certain analogy between the Roman government of Palestine and some of the difficulties the British administration has met with in disaffected portions of the Empire.[1] It is the old story of a revolt provoked by want of tact and judgment, to use no harsher terms, and an attempt to suppress it by some incompetent governor in the end necessitating the despatch of a formidable army commanded by the best available generals. The Romans began by underrating the military qualities of the enemy, and had to learn by bitter experience the terrible consequences of driving a nation of warriors like the Jews to fanatical despair.

Jerusalem at the outbreak of the War, August, A.D. 66.—We must now return to consider the state of affairs in Jerusalem after Agrippa had withdrawn from the city. The more prudent of the priests and the moderate party had obtained reinforcements from the King and occupied the Upper City, whilst the Lower City with the *Acra* and the Temple were in the hands of Eleazar, the son of the High Priest Ananias, the leader of the extremists. Fierce fighting ensued for some days during the month of August, till the Upper City was captured by the aid of the *sicarii*. The High Priest and his brother took refuge in the strong palace of Herod.

---

[1] *Vide supra*, chapter ix.

The insurgents next captured the fortress of Antonia, having found a new leader in Menahem, the last remaining son of Judas of Galilee. The High Priest and his brother, Hezekiah, were murdered, the palace and its strong towers taken ; and soldiers of the Roman garrison, who had surrendered on condition of having their lives spared, were put to the sword. Menahem assumed the ensigns of royalty, but was driven out of the Temple by his rival Eleazar, and finally dragged from his hiding place and killed.

Cestius Gallus marches to Jerusalem. — This had happened in September, A.D. 66, when Cestius Gallus the *legatus* of Syria felt it was time to leave Antioch and take the field in Palestine. With a considerable force at his disposal, he reduced Galilee to temporary quietude, and after taking Lydda, advanced by the pass of Bethhoron on Jerusalem, arriving at Gibeon in October whilst the Feast of Tabernacles was being celebrated. The Jews, aided by the kinsmen of Izates of Adiabene and other friends, made a furious and not altogether unsuccessful attack on the Romans, whilst Simon, the son of Gioras, later so famous a leader in the siege, cut off the rear guard of the Roman army as it toiled up the ascent of Bethhoron. But by November Cestius had occupied Bezetha, the northern suburb of Jerusalem, and almost captured the Temple and the City. Had he persisted Josephus thinks that he could have ended the war.

Rout of the Romans at Bethhoron, November, A.D. 66.—But Cestius, like a weak man, asked the advice of his subordinate officers, who, bribed as Josephus declares by Florus, advised a retreat. The Jews now swarmed around the Roman army. Cestius returned to his camp for a night and then withdrew to Gibeon, where he remained two days. In his subsequent attempt to reach the Philistine plain by the pass of Bethhoron his army lost nearly six thousand men as well as their baggage siege train. The battle of Bethhoron was fought on November 25, A.D. 66, and all hope of peace was at an end. Many distinguished Jews, to quote Josephus,

abandoned the city as if it were a ship which had
foundered.[1] The Jews now prepared formally for war
and selected twelve generals, of whom Josephus was one.

Vespasian given the command by Nero.—Nero received the news of the defeat of Cestius Gallus with a
calmness worthy of Philip II of Spain when he heard of
the loss of the Armada sent against England, or of
Napoleon on receipt of the news of the battle of Trafalgar.
He remarked with haughty indignation that what had
happened was due rather to bad generalship than to the
valour of the enemy. Still, he realised the seriousness of
the situation, and the man he selected for the task of
restoring the Roman prestige was Vespasian. Nor could
he have made a better choice. Sprung from a family of
Sabine farmers and revenue officers, a successful, if not
a brilliant general, a strict martinet, yet loved and
respected by his troops, Vespasian lacked the birth and
prestige to make him appear formidable to Nero as a
rival, and seemed just the man to bring to a successful
issue a campaign of much difficulty, in which little glory
could be acquired. The task was not that of winning
great victories, but of subduing a country full of men who
could be easily defeated in the open, but with a long
training in irregular warfare, knowing every inch of their
country, and capable of making every mountain village
a stronghold difficult to take, and every cave a hiding
place in the event of defeat, men, moreover, inspired by
that religious fanaticism and contempt of death which
has from time to time characterised the warriors of the
East. To subdue such a foe is a tedious and costly
operation, needing infinite patience, and rarely rewarded
by the glory acquired by the more spectacular feats of
warfare. But Vespasian's generalship, if not brilliant,
was just what the situation in Palestine demanded.
Slowly but persistently he subdued the whole country,
rounding up the insurgents till he drove them to take
refuge in their formidable stronghold of Jerusalem.
The very divisions of the Jewish nation added to the

---

[1] The disastrous expedition and defeat of Cestius Gallus occupies
the whole of the nineteenth chapter of the second book of the *War*.

tediousness of his task, since it was impossible to make peace with insurgents agreed only in their hatred of Rome, and consequently incapable of being bound by any common agreement to desist from hostilities. It took two campaigns to concentrate resistance in and around Jerusalem, and wellnigh six months to capture and destroy the city and reduce its Temple to ashes.

Summary of events, A.D. 67-70.—Vespasian's campaigns in Palestine were in the years A.D. 67-68. The first year was occupied by the reduction of Galilee, the second by the subjugation of Peraea, Idumea, and the rest of Palestine. Then followed a year in which nothing was done. The death of Nero, June 9, A.D. 68, was followed by the rise and fall of the three emperors Galba, killed January 3, A.D. 69, Otho April 16, and Vitellius December 22 of the same year. Vespasian was proclaimed Emperor on July 1 at Alexandria, and the war in Palestine was not prosecuted seriously till the spring of A.D. 70, when its conduct was entrusted to Vespasian's son Titus. On September 25, A.D. 70, Jerusalem was taken and all was over.

Digressions by Josephus.—Unless Josephus is relating his personal experience in Galilee, his narrative of the war till the army of Titus appears before Jerusalem is not of great interest ; but he possesses the art of varying the monotonous record of the campaign by several interesting digressions, and with real skill the historian relieves the tedium of the record of the progress of the Romans after the defence of Jotapata, and his own surrender to Vespasian and Titus, related elsewhere, by his descriptions of places of interest in Palestine, and his survey of the city of Jerusalem. He also gives an account of the organisation of the Roman army, which is not only of interest to posterity as showing what it was in the early days of the Empire, but also because it indicates that Josephus considered that many of the readers whom he hoped to attract would be glad to be instructed on the subject, the legions being for the most part stationed on the frontiers, and rarely seen in the peaceful and prosperous districts.

Josephus relates how the Jews commanded by Niger of Peraea, Silas the Babylonian, and John the Essene, three of their most celebrated generals, were attacked by a Roman force near Askelon and utterly defeated. Niger took refuge in a tower, from which, when the Romans set it on fire, he escaped. Vespasian now advanced with his army from Antioch by way of Ptolemais into Galilee. The only city which welcomed him was Sepphoris, one of the largest and strongest places in the district, now entirely pro-Roman in sympathy.[1]

Description of Palestine: (1) Galilee.—Having brought his readers thus far, he proceeds to describe the country, beginning with the province of Upper and Lower Galilee. It will not be forgotten that not so long ago Galilee had been a Gentile land, but now was almost entirely Jewish. Galilee is bounded by Syria and Phoenicia. Its western frontier is the territory of Ptolemais (Acre). Mount Carmel, which used to be part of Galilee, then belonged to Tyre. South of Galilee was Samaria and the territory of Scythopolis. On the East lay the districts of Hippos Gadara and Gaulonitis. On the North the country belonged to Tyre. Upper Galilee was parted from Lower by a line drawn from Tiberias to Chabulon (Cabul), but small as they were the two Galilees were rich and populous districts ; and, being hemmed in by hostile nations, their men were warlike and courageous. The land was extraordinarily fertile, not an inch being uncultivated. There were many towns, as Josephus declares. Perhaps with his usual proneness to exaggeration, he adds that the smallest village contained at least 15,000 inhabitants. That, even with the important city of Sepphoris as his base, it took Vespasian an entire summer campaign to subdue Galilee says much for the valour of the Jews and their capacity for guerilla warfare, and their power to defend their small fortified cities.

(2) Lake of Gennesareth.—This description of Galilee is supplemented at the close of the third book of the

[1] *War*, iii. 2 (9 ff.).

'War' by one of the Lake Gennesar (Γεννησάρ), better known to readers of the New Testament as the Sea of Galilee. The lake takes its name from the district.[1] The water is very pleasant, not the least like marsh or river water. Exposed to the air it becomes as cold as if it had been kept in the snow. The fish in the lake are quite different from those found elsewhere. The Jordan which flows through the lake was supposed to rise in the Grotto of Pan. Josephus says the real source is farther north in a crater called Phiale or the bowl. This was discovered by the tetrarch Philip, who threw chaff into the Phiale and found that it was carried underground to Panion, where was his city of Caesarea Philippi. The Jordan passes the Lake Semechonitis (the waters of Merom) and enters the Lake of Gennesareth near the town of Julias. Josephus dwells with enthusiasm on the excellence of the climate and the fertility of the soil of the country round the Lake, where nature seems to have made peace with all climates by allowing trees like the walnut, which wants a cold climate, to grow side by side with palms and olives. The country is watered by a beautiful spring called Capharnaum, in which Coracin fish are found, a species of eel otherwise supposed to be confined to Lake Mareotis near Alexandria in Egypt.[2]

(3) Peraea.—To return to Josephus' account of Palestine. Peraea was more extensive than Galilee, but the soil is not so good except in patches. Olives, vines, and palms were the chief trees cultivated in the plains. The rivers flow constantly even in summer. The country extended from Machaerus near the Dead Sea to Pella.

---

[1] For Galilee see *War*, iii. 3 (33–43).

A fine testimony to the *Pax Romana*. A superficial view in 1927 of the coast lands of Palestine gave the writer a similar idea of Zionism under the *pax Britannica*.

'Never did the men lack courage nor the country men . . . every inch of soil has been cultivated by the inhabitants ; there is not a parcel of waste land. The towns, too, are thickly distributed, and even the villages, thanks to the fertility of the soil, are all so densely populated, that the smallest of them contains above fifteen thousand inhabitants' (Thackeray's translation of *War*, iii. 3 (42–43)).

[2] *War*, iii. 10 (506–521). The author has discussed the subject of the fish in the Sea of Galilee in his *Peter, Prince of the Apostles*, where he refers his readers to Canon Tristram's *Natural History of the Holy Land* (9th ed. 1898).

Samaria and Judaea.—The countries of Samaria and Judaea are very similar. The rainfall is abundant, and there are no deserts. The running water is remarkably sweet. Owing to the excellent pasturage, the milk is excellent. The population is dense in both provinces.

Vespasian's campaigns.—The army of Vespasian including that of his allies numbered about 60,000 soldiers and a large number of non-combatants, who, however, were well disciplined, and capable of fighting if required. Josephus calls attention to the fact that the Romans utilised as soldiers the very slaves employed by the army.

The Roman army.—Since the days of Marius and Sulla, towards the close of the republic, the Roman army had ceased to be composed of citizens, who after a campaign returned to their lands or civil occupations. It was now a professional army, whose business in peace was to prepare for war. Engineers and artillerymen formed an important part of every legion or army corps. A camp was a regular city which sprang out of the ground as if by magic. Its improvised walls were defended by catapults and other weapons. The four gates were approached from within by roads, each one leading to the centre, where the general's tent stood like a veritable temple. The workmen and engineers had their own quarters as in a city. The breaking up of the camp was a perfect marvel of organisation and discipline. The arms of the infantry and cavalry are described ; and one is amazed at the weight each soldier had to carry, consisting of his weapons and armour, tools, and three days' provisions. Josephus says he was weighed down like a baggage-mule. He adds that this description of the Roman army is not to flatter the victors but to console the vanquished by showing to what a formidable enemy they had exposed themselves.[1]

Vespasian reduces Palestine.—As the personal experiences of Josephus have been already related there is no need to repeat his story of the fall of Jotapata. The chief events of this year (A.D. 67) reveal the quiet persistence with which Vespasian ground down all Jewish

[1] *War*, iii. 5 (70–109).

opposition north of Jerusalem. The chief events are:
(1) the destruction of the pirates of Joppa; (2) rebellion
of Agrippa's Jewish subjects in Tiberias and Tarichaeae,
and the fight on the Lake; (3) the sieges and capture of
the towns of Gamala and Gischala, and the escape of
Josephus' enemy John, the son of Levi, known hereafter
as John of Gischala. With the capture of Gischala all
Galilee was subdued. Gamala fell on November 10,
A.D. 67, Gischala, presumably a few weeks later. The
story of these battles and sieges is well told by Josephus
and displays his powers as a narrator of what he may have
seen himself, though we must not forget that he was at
this time held in honourable captivity by the Roman
generals.

The pirates of Joppa.—(1) Joppa had been sacked
and destroyed by Cestius Gallus; but the fugitives from
devastated districts had occupied and rebuilt the town,
and created a fleet of pirate ships with which they raided
the coasts of Syria and Egypt. Vespasian marched
against this den of marauders, who took to their ships
and remained out of reach of the Roman missiles. But
Joppa, Josephus remarks, has no harbour. The shore is
like a half-moon with cliffs jutting out on each side.
When a north wind blows, the waves render the road-
stead more perilous than the open sea. A wind called
Melamborion [1] burst upon the pirate fleet and drove the
ships ashore. A dreadful scene of massacre followed.
Joppa was again destroyed and a camp established to
prevent its being re-occupied.

Battles on the Lake.—(2) Vespasian, feeling that he
had now pacified Galilee, went to enjoy the hospitality
of Agrippa at Caesarea Philippi. There he was told that
the two great cities on the Lake, Tiberias and Tarichaeae,
were in revolt. Accordingly he sent Titus to bring more
troops from Caesarea-by-the-Sea to Scythopolis, and
when they were assembled he advanced to a place called
Sennabris, about 4 miles from Tiberias, whither he sent

---

[1] Thackeray translates this by ' Black Norther.' *Cf.* the tem-
pestuous wind called Euraquilo or Euroclydon in Acts xxvii. 14 ·
War, iii. 9 (414–431).

an officer named Valerianus with fifty horsemen to exhort
the inhabitants to submit. But Josephus' old enemy
Jesus, the son of Saphat,[1] took a considerable force and
captured the horses of the cavalry, who had been ordered
to dismount in order to show that their intentions were
pacific. Tiberias submitted, but Tarichaeae remained
hostile. Titus was repulsed at first ; at last, however,
he forced his way to the gates of the city and found the
inhabitants divided, the natives being all for peace, and
the crowd of refugee insurgents for war. In the end the
peaceful citizens surrendered the town, and the war
party took refuge on the Lake in boats. Vespasian
ordered rafts to be made and attacked them. Not a
man of the rebels on the boats escaped. The Lake was
red with blood, and the beaches strewn with corpses.
When we remember that the Sea of Galilee is six hundred
feet below the sea level and the climate tropical, the
results must be left to the imagination. Vespasian
decided to spare the natives of Tarichaeae, but not the
insurgent crowd. These he ordered to proceed to
Tiberias and treacherously allowed them to expect his
clemency. Arrived at that place, the general put to
death 1200 of the more feeble in cold blood, and sent
6000 of the strongest to dig the Isthmus of Corinth for
Nero. The remainder he sold as slaves, giving Agrippa
those who were his subjects to dispose of as he willed.
These also were sold into servitude.[2]

Siege of Gamala.—(3) Josephus is at his best when he
relates events in which he himself played no part save
possibly that of an eye-witness. This may be due to the
fact that the reader is neither disgusted nor misled by
his overweening vanity and self-appreciation. But he
is also singularly happy in describing the natural surroundings of the scene ; and his picture of the city of
Gamala is both vivid and convincing. The site of the
place on the east of the Sea of Galilee has only been
vaguely determined ; but Josephus says it was a mountain
ridge which looked like a camel's back, hence its name

[1] He is called Sapphias in the *Life*.
[2] *War*, iii. 9–10 (433–542).

Gamala.[1] The sides of the ridge on which the city was built are precipitous : at ' the tail end ' it was easier of approach ; a deep trench had been dug. The houses were built very close together and the town looked as if suspended in mid-air, and the houses as though they were falling headlong. The city faced south, where owing to its height stood the citadel. Josephus, having himself fortified Gamala, knew its strength, and doubtless was able to give Agrippa and Vespasian valuable advice.

The Romans erected earthworks, applied their battering rams and forced an entry into Gamala, only to meet with disaster. The houses collapsed and fell on the besiegers. Vespasian was nearly overwhelmed ; but he ordered his soldiers to make a *testudo* with their shields, and saved himself and them from the falling debris. Gamala fell in the end, as did Gischala and Mount Tabor, and all resistance in Galilee was at an end. That it had taken so efficient an army, commanded by such experienced generals as Vespasian and Titus, is no small testimony to the warlike qualities of its Jewish inhabitants.

Vespasian at Jericho.—The rest of the campaigns of Vespasian in Palestine may be dismissed in a few words. In A.D. 68 he subdued Peraea and was master of the country east of the Jordan. He then conquered Idumaea and Judaea ; and at last we find him with his army at Jericho. This gives Josephus an opportunity of describing the resources of the country around, and of attributing the source of its prosperity to the miracle of Elisha, who had made the bitter water sweet. At Jericho Vespasian learned that Nero had died on June 9, A.D. 68 ; and though warlike operations continued to the spring of the following year, he withdrew to Alexandria to be in touch with public affairs which were leading to the overthrow of Vitellius and his own accession to the supreme power.

Jerusalem was now left as in the days of Sennacherib or Nebuchadrezzar, as a ' cottage in a vineyard, as a lodge in a garden of cucumbers, as a besieged city.' [2]

---

[1] *War*, iv. 1 (1–10).   [2] Isaiah i. 8.

The prudent Vespasian had refused to advance against it, hoping that Zion's ruin would be consummated by the dissension of her own children, and resolved not to pluck the fruit before it was ripe.   It was left to Titus to complete his father's work ; and the civil war in Italy gave the city a year's respite.   The story of its calamities at the hands of its citizens as well as at those of the Romans may be left for another chapter.

CHAPTER XII

The Siege of Jerusalem

THE story of the fall of Jerusalem and the destruction of
the Temple would be pronounced incredible had we not
the testimony of one who was an eye-witness of the
unparalleled catastrophe. Even then Josephus might be
suspected of invention and gross exaggeration of the
horrors perpetrated, were it not for the fact that the
scene can be so easily realised from pictures and plans,
even by those who have never visited Jerusalem, that
what must have happened cannot fail to appeal to the
imagination. For though the city has been repeatedly
taken since, and practically wiped out so often that the
levels of the ground on which it stands are entirely
changed by the debris and destructions of centuries;
though the comparatively modern walls of Suleiman the
Magnificent do not enclose the same space as those
erected by the Herods; though the exact site, let alone
the appearance, of even the latest temple is a matter for
conjecture, yet nothing can utterly obliterate the physical
features of the land on which the successive cities have
stood from the days of Melchizedek to our own times.

Jerusalem consisted of a Temple and forts.—However
well suited the site of Jerusalem may have been for a
fortress, it is not so for a great city. Remote and inaccessible from the sea, only conveniently approachable
from the north, it lies on no road by which the traffic from
Egypt or Arabia can pass; situated in a comparatively
cold and barren country, it owes its attraction entirely to
the religious association connected with it. The modern
population has been estimated at 85,000, but a great
portion is to be found in the settlements outside the old

walls, which enclose an area of some 216 acres or less than a third of a square mile. If, as Josephus declares, nearly a million and a quarter perished, the horrors of the summer of A.D. 70 can hardly be realised. Allowing for

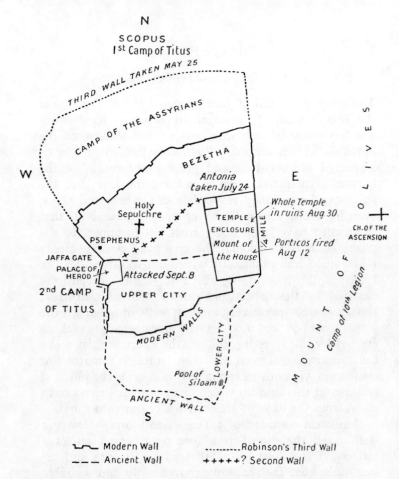

⌐⌐ Modern Wall	.... Robinson's Third Wall
– – – Ancient Wall	+++++? Second Wall

exaggeration, a large population crowded together in so narrow a space must have suffered untold anguish in a siege lasting for five months; and, in addition to this, the miseries inflicted on the Jews by the Romans were hardly greater than those they inflicted on one another.

Factions in Jerusalem.—The Roman army had left

Jerusalem alone from the retirement of Cestius Gallus in November, A.D. 66, to the spring of 70, and the first thing is to see how the respite of three and a half years was employed. As is evident from the records of Josephus in his ' Life,' the city was a scene of constant intrigue between the rival factions. The party of the historian, represented by the more cautious and moderate members of the priesthood, was steadily losing ground, and the control even of the Sanctuary was passing out of the hands of the hierarchy. Jerusalem, in fact, was fast becoming the prey of the military heads of the more fanatical parties, who in the absence of the Roman enemy were devouring one another in civil war. Indeed, one may be permitted to wonder whether, if Vespasian had been content that his army should occupy Palestine and leave Jerusalem alone, the rival factions would not in the end have exterminated each other. Such indeed was the policy of this eminently businesslike emperor; but Jerusalem had necessarily to be besieged, otherwise had its defenders been allowed an egress they would unquestionably have carried fire and sword to every Greek city in Palestine.

Merits and defects of Josephus.—In surveying the horrors of the last days of Jerusalem and the Temple it is necessary to bear in mind that Josephus, our sole authority for all but the fact of the downfall of the city, though here at his best as an historian, cannot always be trusted implicitly. On such matters as the topographical details of the siege, on the general appearance of the city, on the structure of the Temple, he is invaluable. Some of his personal experiences are admirably related; his Greek style is excellent, and based on the best models, and the narrative is eminently readable. But, after justice has been done to his merits, the unsatisfactory features of his account of the capture must be given due consideration. In the first place, his enumeration of the numbers slain on different occasions must be received with much caution. Dean Milman, in his ' History of the Jews,' gives the total of victims slain in the war, from the procuratorship of Florus to the destruction of the city and the final subjugation of Judaea by the capture of Masada, as 1,356,400.

Of these, 1,100,000, according to Josephus, perished in
Jerusalem. These figures are taken from the seven books
of the ' War ' ; and the Dean fully realises the capacity
for exaggeration which impairs the trustworthiness of the
Jewish historian. Taking into account the circuit of the
walls of Jerusalem, Milman pronounces the appalling total
of over a million inconceivable.[1]

Motives actuating Josephus.—It must not be forgotten
that Josephus was writing under imperial patronage to
exalt the exploits of the Flavian house. Full of gratitude
for the favours already bestowed and doubtless with a
lively anticipation of others to come, it was but natural
that he should dwell on the fact that their conquests were
worthy of admiration, especially as there were people who
averred that the triumph of Vespasian and Titus was over
a contemptible foe. To show the groundlessness of such
a calumny, Josephus had to dwell on the formidable
character of the task of subduing the Jewish nation, to
multiply the forces ranged against the Roman People,
and to magnify the victory of the Emperors. He found it
also necessary to dwell at some length on the magnanimity
of Titus, and the wisdom of his friend and patron King
Herod Agrippa II. Nor was he, as a Jew, likely to
minimise the sufferings of his people in their overthrow.

Josephus' admiration for Rome.—The severe judgment
which Josephus passes on the leaders of the Jewish nation
is to be accounted for by the fact that, not only had he
played an unheroic part in the War, but also that he
honestly believed the whole insurrection to have been a
criminal error. Every patriot in his eyes was a robber ;
and indeed it must generally be so when an oppressed
nation rises against its real or fancied tyrants. The main
thesis of the ' War ' is that God had justly punished the
people for opposing themselves to His will ; and, therefore,

[1] *History of the Jews*, Book xvi. In a footnote to vol. ii. p. 379, the
Dean notes Strabo's testimony to the populousness of parts of Palestine
in the fact that 40,000 armed men could be levied from Jamnia and
the adjoining villages. Josephus justifies his estimate of 1,100,000
by saying that the Jews were caught suddenly by Titus and shut
up in the city at the time of the Passover, when it was calculated
that some two and a half millions attended, *War*, vi. 9 (423-426).
But how many Jews could have come up to the Passover of A.D. 70 ?

that those who persisted in the rebellion against Rome were the enemies of Heaven. Josephus is consequently incapable of recognising anything but criminality in the Zealots and fanatics who followed the lead of Eleazar, John of Gischala, or Simon, the son of Gioras. He is merely able to credit them with a sort of diabolical courage combined with ruthless cruelty, not only to the Roman enemy, but to the party of moderation in Jerusalem. All he tells us must be received with caution, whatever our estimate of his character may be.

John of Gischala arrives at Jerusalem.—The capture of Gischala, the last city of Galilee to fall before the Roman arms, was announced by fugitives headed by their leader John of Gischala, who, undaunted by disaster, maintained a bold front, assuring the people that the Romans were already exhausted by their efforts in Galilee, and that with their siege trains worn out by their operations against its cities, they could not possibly take Jerusalem. At first, however, John supported the High Priest Ananus, the leader of the moderates, together with Jesus, the son of Sapphias, the old enemy of Josephus, for whose wise leadership the historian had a real respect. But Eleazar and his party, who had taken upon themselves the honourable name of Zealots,[1] held the Temple ; and John in the end joined them.

Zealots, Idumaeans and Sicarii. — Ananus tried earnestly to bring the people of Jerusalem to resist the new tyranny and addressed them in a long and pathetic appeal, but to no purpose.[2] An Idumaean army approached the city and demanded admittance, which Ananus refused. But the Zealots in the Temple used the sacred saws to cut the bars of the gate, and the fierce soldiery poured in and began to massacre the citizens. A regular inquisition was held and those suspected of favouring the Romans were put to death. Ananus and his colleague in the priesthood, Jesus, the son of Gamalas,

---

[1] Foakes Jackson and Lake, *Beginnings of Christianity*, vol. i, pp. 421 ff. Josephus says : ' Zealots, for so these miscreants called themselves, as though they were zealous in the cause of virtue, but were for vice in its basest forms.' *War*, iv. 3 (161).

[2] *War*, iv. 4 (238–269).

were, as we might expect, murdered, and their bodies refused burial. Yet another able head of a military faction was destined to appear. The *sicarii* during the war had captured the strong fortress of Masada by the Dead Sea,[1] from whence the renowned Simon, the son of Gioras, had wrought havoc and desolation on all sides. People crowded into the city, which might have made a far longer resistance had not the food supply been largely consumed by the multitude of non-combatants, or destroyed by the mad rage of the factions. But perhaps enough has been said to give a partial idea of the condition of a city in the hands of three independent and hostile armies, agreeing only in tyrannising over the defenceless inhabitants. Upon the whole, the Zealots appear to have been the least lawless of the factions, and at one time set up courts to try disloyal persons; and by this means, despite the injustice of the tribunals, to have limited the number of victims by checking indiscriminate massacres. One of the accused, whom Josephus calls Zacharias, the son of Baris,[2] was acquitted by the Sanhedrin, but was set upon by his enemies and murdered in the Temple. It must be remembered that Josephus did not witness the civil war which went on from the autumn of 67 to the spring of 70, when Titus appeared before Jerusalem. He must have heard the story from the few who survived the siege, before the beginning of which he had recovered his personal liberty and was enjoying the full confidence of Titus, whom he accompanied on his march to the city together with two other distinguished Jews, Tiberius Alexander, who had secured the empire for Vespasian in Egypt, and King Agrippa.

Sacrilege of John of Gischala.—Whilst the people in Jerusalem were awaiting the coming of Titus and his army, civil strife was being waged as ferociously as ever. The rival parties were trampling over the unburied corpses in their furious desire to slaughter one another.

---

[1] *War*, ii. 17 (408); *vide supra*, p. 167.
[2] See Thackeray's note on *War*, iv. 5 (334 ff.) in reference to the supposed identity of this man with Zechariah the son of Barachiah. Matt. xxiii. 35.

Then it was that John of Gischala committed a crime which, in the eyes of Josephus, outdid all his murders and cruelties. King Agrippa had at great expense brought huge timbers from the Lebanon to underpin the sanctuary. This sacred wood was utilised by John to make towers to enable him the better to attack his enemies. The approach of Titus made these towers useless; but at the feast of the Passover John managed by craft to oust the Zealots from the Temple, and was then guilty of introducing men who were not ritually pure into the sanctuary. Here we have a curious example of the religious attitude of Josephus, to whom no crime is comparable to a violation of the ritual law. This may be compared with the argument put into the mouth of Agrippa, that if the Jews were compelled by the necessities of war to violate the Sabbath they could not expect the assistance of a God offended by disobedience to His commands.[1]

Advance of Titus.—Titus left Alexandria in the early spring and marched along the coast of Palestine to Caesarea, where he found a sufficient force to complete the subjugation of Judaea, which in the days of Nero's tyranny his father may have hesitated to do thoroughly. Now, however, as masters of the Roman world, the Emperor and his son could employ all the forces of the State to accomplish the task. Titus was in command of four legions and a large auxiliary force when he advanced on Jerusalem. Before, however, entering upon the story of the siege itself it may be well to endeavour to discover from Josephus the difficulties which the Roman army had to encounter.

Jewish preparation for defence.—In all the sieges of the city from the days of Antiochus and onward it is noticeable that the town itself was usually captured with no great difficulty, and that the real task had been to take the Temple. Even before Herod had rebuilt it, the Mountain of the House, as the Temple area is called, was a fortress of extraordinary strength. Since the defeat of Cestius Gallus the Jews had been left by the

[1] *War*, v. i (36).

Romans severely alone; but, despite their internal dissensions, they had been preparing for the inevitable siege for more than two years. They had fortified the northern wall which Agrippa I had tried to build round the suburb of Bezetha, and had amply provisioned the Temple. The defending force, we are surprised to learn from Josephus, was far smaller than might have been expected, numbering 23,400 men.[1] But all of these were reckless soldiers, trained in predatory warfare, burning with fanaticism, and perfectly ready to let the defenceless population starve rather than surrender to the Romans.

The walls of Jerusalem.—Such then was the task before Titus, who appears, for all his popular gifts, to have continued the cautious policy of his father by refusing to waste the lives of his soldiers in spectacular enterprises, being content to wait for the final victory when the enemy was exhausted. Josephus gives a careful description of (1) the walls; (2) the hills and forts of Jerusalem; and (3) of the Temple.

The ' third ' or northern wall.—(1) We may begin with what he calls the ' third wall,' meaning outer wall on the northern side of the city, where Jerusalem was most open to attack, the uneven character of the ground making fortification more simple. Any attempt on the part of the Jews to defend the city on the north was regarded with jealousy from the time when Judah and Israel were rivals. The defeat of King Amaziah by Jehoash, King of Israel, was followed by the destruction of four hundred cubits of wall from ' the gate of Ephraim to the corner gate,' leaving the city at the mercy of the northern kingdom. Isaiah's description of the advance of an Assyrian army almost corresponds to Josephus' account of that of Titus.[2] Pompey attacked the Temple

---

[1] *War*, v. 6 (248–250). Simon, the son of Gioras, commanded 10,000 Jews and 5000 Idumaeans, John of Gischala had 6000, and Eleazar, the chief of the Zealots, 2400. With this number of defenders so strong a place as Jerusalem would be wellnigh invincible, especially if they were well supplied with food and water, and one cannot but suspect that Josephus in multiplying the remaining population has added to the pathos, but not to the credibility, of the events which he relates.

[2] 2 Kings xiv. 13 ; Isaiah x. 28–32 ; with this cf. *War*, v. 2 (50–51).

from the north. No wonder, therefore, that Agrippa I had attempted to surround the suburb of Bezetha by a strong wall; nor can we be surprised at the governor of Syria, Vibius Marsus, ordering the king, high as he was in favour of the Emperor, to desist. But the foundations of Agrippa's wall still remained; and the Jews had raised them high enough to give the army of Titus, efficiently equipped for siege operations as it was, fifteen days' hard work before this defence could be carried.[1]

The second wall.—The second wall is very briefly described by Josephus as beginning at the gate in the first wall called Gennath, and enclosing the northern district of the town, only terminating at the Antonia or Temple fortress.[2]

The first wall.—The first wall began at the tower called Hippicus; and on its north side extended to the Xystus, close by the Temple area. The rest is hard to identify. ' It descended past the place called Bethso to the gate of the Essenes, then turned southwards above the fountain of Siloam; thence again it inclined to the east towards Solomon's pool; and after passing the spot which they call Ophlas, finally joined the eastern portico of the Temple.' Whatever this description may imply —for Bethso, the gate of the Essenes, and Solomon's fountain, have not been identified—it is clear that this wall enclosed the ancient city, which could not have been much more than a mile and a half in circumference.[3]

The hills of the City.—(2) The highest part of the city was Bezetha. The other hills were in the time of Josephus known as the Upper and Lower City. The Upper City was on the north-west side near the present Jaffa gate and was the fortress (φρούριον) of David. The Upper and Lower Cities were divided by the valley of the cheesemongers, in Greek the *Tyropoeon*. Another valley, now filled up, separated the so-called *Acra* from what was once a third hill; and the Lower City was on the hill called ' the *Acra*.' All Josephus' descriptions of

[1] *War*, v. 4 (147–155). For Herod Agrippa I, *vide supra*, chapter viii.
[2] *War*, v. 146. The order of the walls in Josephus has been reversed, because they were taken in the order adopted here.
[3] *War*, v. 4 (142–145).

Jerusalem are hard to understand, partly because the
original form of the hills on which the city was built
has been changed by the many sieges it has since
undergone.[1]

The Towers.—(3) The towers were truly wonderful.
They were twenty cubits or sixty feet high, and twenty
broad, and their stones were not inferior to those of a
temple. The third wall had ninety towers at intervals
of two hundred cubits, the middle wall fourteen ; the
old wall, sixty. The whole circumference of the city
was thirty-three *stadia* (furlongs), *i.e.* less than four miles.
The largest and most famous towers were Psephinus, on
the turn of the western corner of the third wall, and near
it were Herod's three towers of Hippicus, Phasael and
Mariamne. These were to the north of the wonderful
palace built by that king, the gardens of which are carefully described : ' Their open courts (were) all of green-
sward ; there were groves of various trees intersected by
long walks, which were bordered by deep canals, and
ponds everywhere studded with bronze figures, through
which water was discharged, and around the streams
were numerous cotes for tame pigeons.' [2] This confirms
the fact that Jerusalem was remarkable, considering the
aridity of the country around, for its supply of water, a
very important consideration in the event of a siege.[3]

The Antonia.—The strongest of all the fortresses was
the Antonia, built at first by the Asmonaeans, and reconstructed by Herod the Great. Josephus calls it ' the
crowning effort of the innate grandeur of his genius.' It
was built on a rock fifty cubits high, rendered practically
inaccessible by smoothed flagstones. The castle was not
only a stronghold but a palace. It contained broad

---

[1] Josephus says that the Upper City was called by David the
' Stronghold ' (2 Sam. v. 7), and what is now known as David's Tower
is there, near the Jaffa Gate. But the modern view is that David's
' Stronghold ' was on the south-east of the city on the *Acra*. See G. A.
Smith, *Jerusalem*, vol. i. chapter vi.

[2] *War*, v. 4 (180, 181), The translation of χαλκουργημάτων as
' bronze figures ' is, I think, unfortunate, as it might imply human or
animal representations, which would have caused great scandal in
Jerusalem. Perhaps ' bronze ornaments ' would be less misleading.

[3] G. A. Smith, *Jerusalem*, vol. i. chapter v, ' The Waters of
Jerusalem.'

courts, baths, and accommodation for soldiers. It was, in fact, a city in miniature, and a palace in magnificence. The highest tower commanded the Temple, and there was a stairway leading to the porticos and to the outer court. On the north the castle was cut off from the suburbs of Bezetha by an artificial trench. This stupendous fortress had been captured by the insurgent Jews in August, A.D. 66, three months before the disastrous retreat of Cestius Gallus and the discomfiture of his army in the pass of Bethhoron.[1]

Such, therefore, was Jerusalem when Titus arrived in the spring of A.D. 70. If we condemn the Jewish historian for having exaggerated the number of the inhabitants of the city, it must not be forgotten that the smaller the population the harder would be the task of capturing the place, if defended by an intrepid and warlike garrison.

Narrow escape of Titus.—Titus with four legions and numerous auxiliaries advanced on Jerusalem. Arrived at Gabath Saul or the ' hill of Saul,' about thirty furlongs from Jerusalem, he with six hundred cavalry rode unmolested along the western wall till he reached the Tower of Psephinus, when the Jews suddenly sallied forth and nearly cut him off from his main force. Escaping, unarmoured as he was, with difficulty, he encamped his army at Scopus, from which he obtained his first view of the city, and of the grand pile of the Temple with its golden pinnacles. The Tenth Legion which had come from Jericho was encamped on the Mount of Olives.

Desperate sallies of the Jews.—The siege began ingloriously, as far as the Romans were concerned. The Jews, the factions being temporarily at peace, made furious sallies, and drove the Tenth Legion from their works on the Mount of Olives. The soldiers were panic-stricken by the fearless if irregular attacks of the enemy ; for, as Josephus says, and experience has proved in all ages, highly disciplined troops are liable to be thrown into disorder by the attack of a mass of desperate men, each fighting on his own initiative, and accustomed to the use of weapons ; for it must be remembered that the

[1] *War*, ii. 17 (430-432).

troops of John and Simon were drawn, not from the citizens of Jerusalem, but were desert marauders, inured to predatory warfare. Titus had to rally his troops, to set them a personal example of intrepidity and contempt of danger, and to reproach and even inflict severe punishment on his dispirited soldiers. He began his siege works near the tomb of John, the High Priest, probably near the Jaffa gate, with the object of taking the upper town, and thus to capture in succession the fort Antonia and the Temple. His works were repeatedly attacked by Simon, the son of Gioras, but the Jews were much harassed by the *ballistae* which hurled great stones at the defenders of the wall, sometimes killing many at a single shot. When a stone was seen hurtling through the air, there was a cry in Aramaic, ' The son's coming,' and the men would take cover. To prevent the missiles being seen, the Romans had them blackened, and thereby made them more effective. Simon had artillery captured from Cestius Gallus, but his men did not know how to use it. Besieged and besiegers sometimes conversed ; and when thus engaged, John, an Idumean general, was killed by an arrow, generally regretted by all as he was a valiant and sensible man. By means of this and similar digressions does Josephus endeavour to brighten the story of his account of the siege.

Third wall taken May 25.—On the seventh day of the month Artemisius (May 25) the third wall was taken ; and Titus encamped in Bezetha on what was then known as the Camp of the Assyrians.[1] Five days later, at the end of May, the second wall was captured after desperate fighting. Titus, unwilling to proceed to extremities, now hoped the Jews would yield. He was, however, disappointed. The second wall was again taken by the Jews, and retaken by the Romans, and a great part of it was destroyed.

[1] Where this ' Camp ' was is unknown. It is supposed that it was where Sennacherib's army had been stationed when Jerusalem was delivered from it in the days of Hezekiah. But there is no evidence that Sennacherib's army ever came near Jerusalem. Anyhow, the tradition proves that Jerusalem must naturally be first attacked on the north.

Titus parades his troops.—Titus, now that he had
captured the second wall, held a review of his troops and
paraded his army with all the pomp and circumstance of
war with their armour and weapons brightened,[1] so as
to make the display as magnificent as possible.   By this
means he hoped to overawe the inhabitants and induce
them to surrender the city when they saw how irresistible his army was.   It was, however, all in vain ; the
siege continued, and the Romans began to raise their
earthworks at the Jaffa gate and the Antonia.   By this
time the defenders had learned to use the artillery they
had captured, and showers of stones drove the Romans
from their works.

Josephus addresses the Jews.—Josephus was now
ordered by Titus to address the Jews in their own
language ; and did so, if we may trust his own statement,
with customary prolixity, giving detailed accounts of
the sieges of the city from the days of Abraham, whose
wife Sarah was taken prisoner in an invasion of Palestine
by Pharaoh Necho !   The company of the patriarch,
which in Genesis xiv is said to have consisted of three
hundred and eighteen ' trained men born in his house,'
becomes a force under the same number of officers, each
in command of an innumerable army.   The improbability
of Josephus having delivered such a speech on this
occasion, is only matched by the impossibility of the
historical information it contains.   In his address
Josephus repeats his conviction that the Romans were
God's servants appointed to punish the Jews for their
sins.[2]

Titus builds an earthwork around the City.—The
month of June had now advanced, and the horrors of
famine were aggravated by the savagery of John and
Simon and their soldiers.   In order that the combatants
might have sufficient provisions to protract the siege,
the rich were ruthlessly plundered and the most miserable
food torn from the poor.   Titus allowed as many as

---

[1] The country around the city shone as with silver and gold,
the soldiers having uncovered their polished armour, *War*, v. 9 (350 ff.).

[2] *War*, v. 9 (362–419).

were able to get away to desert the city, but only a few were able to do this as the parties in power kept the strictest watch.[1] As the mercy of the general was without effect, Titus tried severity. Prisoners were tortured and crucified in sight of the walls by hundreds ; and the soldiers, maddened by the resistance of the Jews, nailed up their captives .in different grotesque postures. Nothing, however, could deter the defenders, who on one occasion sallied forth, destroyed the earthworks and wellnigh captured the Roman camp. It was now time to resort to the expedient of holding a council of war, after which Titus and his generals decided to abandon active operations, and to build an encircling wall to make egress from the city impossible. The wall was thirty-nine furlongs in length, and included the Mount of Olives. The whole line of circumvallation was less than five miles, the walls of the modern city being under two. It is indeed hard to realise the smallness of Jerusalem at any time, but here the numbers of the dead given by Josephus are appalling. Out of one gate 150,880 corpses were carried between May 1 and July 20, and 600,000 dead bodies of the poor were cast unburied outside the walls. The earthworks were made by the Romans in three days, so great was the efficiency of the engineers of Titus' army.[2]

Country round Jerusalem laid desolate.—Amid all the horrors on which Josephus dwells so minutely there is one thing which cannot fail to strike the imagination, namely, the havoc and desolation around the city wrought by the Roman army. It is impossible for even the most casual visitor to-day not to be struck by the barrenness of the surroundings of Jerusalem. But when the army of Titus arrived, the environs are represented as delightful to the eye. The country was well wooded, and all around were well-watered and highly cultivated gardens. But the necessities of the siege made the army of Titus

---

[1] [It must have been at this time that Johanan ben Zakkai, the founder of rabbinical Judaism, escaped as a dead man in a coffin. He also was of the peace party.—F. C. Burkitt.]

[2] *War*, v. 12 (491–511) ; for the number of those who died see v. 13 (567–569).

destroy every tree for ninety furlongs about the walls; and all was a desolate and treeless waste.

Capture of Antonia by the Romans.—By July 20 the tide was gradually turning in favour of the Romans. John of Gischala plundered the Temple and even drank and allowed others to drink the pure wine which Augustus and Livia had given to the sanctuary, and permitted his men to anoint themselves with the holy oil. This enormity, worse in the eyes of Josephus than all the murders and crimes perpetrated by those he calls ' the robbers,' brought the Divine vengeance upon the devoted city. On July 24 Antonia was taken, and the attack on the Temple commenced early in August.

The daily sacrifices cease.—It was not till after much severe fighting that Titus ordered the demolition of Antonia and the preparation of a road by which his army might enter the Temple area in full force. Titus learned that the daily sacrifice had ceased on August 5 ; and made a last attempt to induce the people to surrender and save their sanctuary. Again the eloquence of Josephus was in demand. Like St. Paul a few years before, he addressed the multitude in ' Hebrew.' His deadly enemy, John of Gischala, declared that the Temple was the Lord's, and He would never leave it to be destroyed. Josephus replied that as a Jew he would never abjure his race or its traditions ; but declared that God was bringing fire upon the Temple to purge the national sin.

Attacks on the Temple repulsed.—Many of the better class Jews now surrendered themselves to Titus, who received them kindly and assigned to them a residence at a place called Gophna. Then the Romans attacked the Temple enclosure in earnest, but the desperation and valour of the Jews repeatedly drove them back. On August 12 the porticos around the court were set on fire, first by the Jews, and later by the Romans. Three days later the troops of Titus suffered a disaster by the enemy retiring from a portico, under which they had secretly placed inflammable materials, in order to induce the soldiers to invade it, whereupon many perished in the flames. Again and again the Romans were repulsed, yet the famine grew more and more terrible, and Josephus tells the dreadful story of Mary, the daughter of Eleazar, devouring her own child. At last Titus ordered the gates of the Temple to be set on fire.

The Temple burned.—Titus now held a second council of war to debate whether the Temple should be destroyed. The commanders of the five legions, the procurator of Judaea, Marcus Antonius Julianus, and Tiberius Alexander, Caesar's chief of staff, were invited. The opinions of these generals differed as to the fate of the sanctuary. Some advised its destruction; others were prepared to preserve it if only the Jews would not use it as a fortress. Titus was for sparing, if it were possible, so splendid an edifice. Apparently Alexander, though a Jew by birth, was ready to sacrifice the Temple; but in the end, he and two of his colleagues agreed with Titus.[1] But God, says Josephus, had already sentenced the Temple to be burned. A soldier, moved by divine impulse (δαιμονίῳ . . . ὁρμῇ) cast a brand into the sanctuary or into one of its chambers; a flame shot up and a tragic cry went up from the agonised Jewish spectators.

Titus was resting in his tent when he heard the news. He rushed to the scene and tried to get the flames under. A soldier, however, threw another firebrand and the gate was aflame. Nothing could now save the Temple, the soldiers exasperated by the long resistance of the Jews, slew without mercy, and plundered the burning edifice. All was over; the whole of the Mountain of the House was destroyed. This happened on August 30, A.D. 70.[2]

[1] According to the fourth-century historian Sulpicius Severus, Titus advised the destruction of the Temple in order to suppress the Christian as well as the Jewish religion. Some suppose that this writer may have depended on a lost work of Tacitus. Thackeray, *Jewish War* (Loeb series), vol. ii. p. xxiv.

[2] *War*, vi. 4 (249 ff.). The Temple was set on fire on 'the tenth day of the month Lous, the day on which of old it had been burned by the king of Babylon.' This would be on August 29 or 30. Dean Milman's words are : ' It was on the 10th day of August, a day already darkened by the destruction by the king of Babylon.' According to Jeremiah lii. 12, 13, the Temple was burned by Nebuzar-adan, the general of Nebuchadrezzar, on the 10th day of the 5th month. In 2 Kings xxv. 8 it was on the 7th day. The Jews keep in memory the

Soldiers massacre the Jews. — The soldiers, now gathered in the temple court, and setting up their standards by the eastern gate, hailed Titus as 'imperator,' thereby acknowledging that his triumph was complete. Simon and John now begged the victor to grant them terms; and Josephus eagerly seizes the opportunity of putting a long oration into the mouth of Titus, laying the blame of all the calamities of the people on the shoulders of their leaders, and refusing the request to spare the city. On September 8 the Upper City was attacked; by the 25th the end had come. Even at the end of the siege the Caesar pardoned some who surrendered; but the terrors of the last days of Jerusalem, the wholesale murders, and the barbarities of soldiers, equally inspired by greed and thirst for vengeance, must have been altogether unspeakable.

Portents.—Many portents had foretold the impending calamity. A star like a sword had been seen over the city and a comet had been visible for a year. A brilliant light at Passover had shone over the altar. A cow brought for sacrifice gave birth to a lamb. The great bronze gate, which twenty men could scarcely move, opened of its own accord. Celestial chariots and armies appeared in the sky. At Pentecost a voice was heard from the Temple crying 'We are departing hence.' Tacitus mentions some of these prodigies and especially the oracle—found as Josephus says in the Jewish Scriptures—that one from Palestine would rule the world, who was declared by the two historians to be Vespasian.[1]

Jesus, the son of Ananias.—But far more striking than any of these portentous signs is what Josephus tells about the unlettered peasant Jesus, the son of Ananias. He appeared four years before the war, when all was peace, and the feast of Tabernacles was being celebrated.

destruction of the Temple on the 9th of the month Ab. But the porticos were only burned on Aug. 15–16. Dr. Thackeray suggests that a fictitious symmetry between the destruction of the two Temples has been at work.

[1] *War*, vi. (388–316); Tacitus, *Hist.* v. 13; Suetonus *Vesp.* 4.

Standing in the Temple, he cried :

> ' A voice from the East, a voice from the West,
> A voice from the four winds.
> A voice against the bridegroom and the bride,
> A voice against all the people.'

For seven years and five months he continued this mournful cry. He spoke no other words save ' Woe, woe to Jerusalem.' He neither cursed those who beat him, nor blessed those who gave him food. During the siege he cried from the walls :

> ' Woe to the people, and to the Temple.'

At last a stone from a ballista struck him as he exclaimed ' Woe, woe to me also,' and died on the spot.

Josephus concludes his sixth book with these tragic words · ' Nevertheless, neither the antiquity (of the city) nor its great wealth, nor its people who had gone forth to the uttermost parts of the earth, nor the glory of its worship availed anything to avert its ruin. And thus ended the siege of Jerusalem.'

Supplementary Note

Josephus states, to take two examples : (1) that 20,000 Jews were massacred at Caesarea Stratonis by the Greek inhabitants in a single hour ; that 40,000 perished, when he as the sole survivor escaped from Jotapata ; (2) that the people of Scythopolis rounded up 13,000 Jews and put them all to death. It is difficult to credit these enormous totals. If the Jews numbered but one in five of the population of Caesarea, for example, it would be a difficult task for 80,000 fellow citizens to kill so large a number, especially as the Jew of that period in Palestine was not the man to die without resistance. No doubt Caesarea was a great city ; but it is almost impossible to guess the number of inhabitants even approximately ; nevertheless, in the ancient Roman Empire cities of a hundred thousand inhabitants must

---

[1] Josephus says the massacre lasted only *one* hour ! *War*, ii. 18 (457).

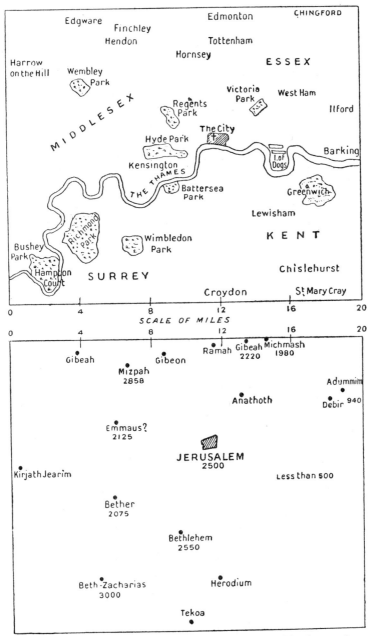

Environs of LONDON and JERUSALEM on same scale. The figures show the levels of the ground around Jerusalem and indicate the extremely uneven nature of the country; much land, especially S.E. of Jerusalem, is wilderness.

have been few. Nor is it easy even for those actually present to calculate exactly how many have been killed in a riotous outbreak, or even the number of dead on a battlefield. Massacres on the scale of those at Caesarea or Scythopolis implying myriads of unburied corpses would be certain to breed pestilence in walled towns with restricted areas, by which the slain would be more than avenged. But, when the figures of Josephus have been fully discounted, our sympathy for the suffering of the insurgent Jews in the ' War ' remains almost undiminished. If a million people were shut up in Jerusalem when the Roman army invested the city and the compass of the walls had been four miles—it was much less—by a very rough calculation it would be as if the entire population of England was crowded into a space not as large as the city of New York on the Island of Manhattan from 110th Street to the Battery. The whole of the city of Jerusalem could be reconstructed in one of the smaller parks of London.

PART V

AFTER THE FALL OF JERUSALEM

CHAPTER XIII

THE LESSON TO BE LEARNED FROM JOSEPHUS

Jerusalem, a small but important city.—Jerusalem was in ashes; and it is time to see what Titus had actually accomplished. Josephus leaves us to imagine that the Romans had with incredible severity wiped out a great and populous city. But a glance at the measurements of the walls of Jerusalem, when the third or northern wall, which included the district of Bezetha, had been carried, gives an enclosed space so small that the buildings, Temple forts and everything else would, as has been already remarked, hardly have occupied one of the parks in a city like London. As a matter of fact, Jerusalem must have been less of a city than a group of fortresses. Its population must always have been small; and, as we learn from Nehemiah, the inhabitants of Judaea preferred to live on their farms than to dwell within the walls.[1] But as a stronghold Jerusalem was a most valuable possession. Its prince could go forth and raid the neighbourhood, and retire, safe in the impregnability of his fortress city. To the people of the coast and the south of Palestine Jerusalem must always have been a dangerous spot, and its strong Temple sometimes dreaded as a veritable ' den of robbers,' to adopt the words of Jesus,[2] or at best of marauding armies, such as those which the priest-kings, notably Alexander Jannaeus, led forth to conquer and devastate the cities of Palestine.

Opposition to building of Jerusalem at the Return.— From the quotations of the correspondence preserved in the book of Ezra we should gather that the heathen of Palestine, the Samaritans, and their Persian governors,

[1] Neh. xi. 1-2.   [2] Matt. xxi. 13 ; Mark xi. 17 ; Luke xix. 46.

had no objection to the exiles from Babylon settling in their old homes ; but, directly the idea of rebuilding Jerusalem or restoring the Temple was mooted, they were up in arms. The Samaritans offered a compromise. ' Let us,' they said in effect, ' join you as worshippers of the same God in rebuilding the Temple.'[1] It was probably something more than religious exclusiveness that actuated the Jews in their refusal. They had the permission of Cyrus to rebuild their Temple ; and they did not wish to allow any stranger to claim a right to interfere. Nor must it be forgotten that this was before the adoption of the Priestly Code two generations later in the days of Ezra ; consequently, the exiled Judaeans on their return may have thought as much of the independence of their ancient kingdom as of the unique character of their Temple. From the books of Ezra and Nehemiah, whatever their date, it is evident that the rebuilding of Jerusalem or its Temple was regarded with great apprehension by the people of Palestine and their Persian rulers ; and it was only with much difficulty that Nehemiah, though a Persian governor, was allowed to wall in the city.[2] It was not, therefore, in order to suppress the Jewish religion, which had been recognised by Roman law, but in the interests of the peace of Palestine that Titus demolished the fortresses of Jerusalem, and especially that of the Temple. Only the three towers of Phasael, Hippicus, and Mariamne were left as memorials of the powerful defences of Jerusalem ; and the Tenth Legion was stationed to guard the spot.

Simon, the son of Gioras, taken.—But, even when the city was taken and its houses demolished, all was not over. Jerusalem is honeycombed by subterraneous caverns ; and the more desperate patriots still occupied them. Simon, the son of Gioras, was one of these ; and, when his situation appeared to be desperate, he boldly resolved to play upon the superstitions of the soldiers by appearing in a white garment, over which he had thrown a purple mantle. But all to no purpose ; the men stood their ground and Simon ordered them to

---

[1] Ezra iv. 1–3.   [2] Ezra iv. 1 ff. ; Neh. ii. 19 ; iv. 1 ff.

summon Terentius Rufus their general. Rufus put him in chains and sent him to Titus at Caesarea. The underground passages were explored, and the remainder of the patriots taken.[1]

Triumphant return of Titus.—We have now reached the most painful part of the narrative of Josephus, which gives us the worst opinion of his character. Titus returned in triumph to Rome and Josephus was apparently his honoured companion. The route of the conqueror was marked by sumptuous festivals. On October 24, the birthday of Domitian, the brother of Titus, was celebrated with great pomp at Caesarea ; and the crowd was indulged in an exhibition of 2500 Jewish captives compelled to contend with wild beasts, or to kill one another in sham fights. An even more splendid show, with doubtless a larger massacre of captives, was held at Berytus on the birthday of Vespasian in November.[2] Titus then went to Antioch, where there occurred an event which at any rate illustrates the justice of the Romans, as well as the suppression of the rebellion in Judaea does their relentless cruelty.

Titus and the Jews of Antioch.—Antioch had suffered from a serious fire, and an apostate Jew, named Antiochus, accused his countrymen of having caused the conflagration. The Jewish community was wealthy and not unpopular, as many Greeks attended its synagogues. Antiochus was a malignant apostate : he even denounced his own father, and roused the mob to attack and persecute his countrymen. With the aid of troops lent by the Roman governor, he forced the Jews to violate the Sabbath and procured the abolition of the weekly day of rest in other cities. Another fire broke out, and the Jews were in a worst plight than ever. People began to declare that they had seen Jews firing the town in places. The *legatus* of Syria sent out by Vespasian had not arrived, but his deputy ($\pi\rho\epsilon\sigma\beta\epsilon\nu\tau\eta$s) managed to allay the popular resentment ; and it was discovered that the real criminals were not Jews at all. When Titus reached Antioch, he was met by throngs enthusiastic

---

[1] *War*, vii. 1 (26 ff.).　　　[2] *War*, vii. 3 (37–40).

to greet him, and by petitions that the privileges of the Jews should be revoked and even that they should be expelled. Titus refused to listen to such requests, and left the Jews of Antioch in the position they had formerly occupied, a sure proof that Rome had warred not against Judaism as a religion, but against the rebel Jews in Palestine. When the people of Antioch invited Titus to visit their theatre, and asked him to banish the Jews, he replied : ' Their own country, to which as Jews they ought to be banished, has been destroyed, and no other place could now receive them.'[1]

Titus revisits Jerusalem.—From Antioch Titus went as far as the Euphrates, whence, after receiving an embassy from the King of Parthia, he returned to the coast, and journeyed to Egypt, revisiting Jerusalem on his way, viewing its ruins, says Josephus, not with the exultation of a conqueror, but with profound sorrow. There he found people searching everywhere in the debris for hidden treasure. From Alexandria he sailed to Italy with his captives, the two generals Simon and John, and seven hundred of the finest-looking prisoners to grace his triumph.

The Triumph.—Arriving home, he was greeted with the greatest enthusiasm by the people, by his father Vespasian, and by his brother Domitian. The three *Imperatores*,[2] for so the victorious generals Vespasian, Titus, and Domitian were styled, had each of them been decreed triumphs by the Senate, and it was decided that the father and his sons should combine in one of exceptional magnificence. Josephus describes this triumph with much detail, though even to him it must have

---

[1] *War*, vii. 3 (41–62) and 4 (100–111). These sections are especially interesting as revealing the condition of the Jewish community at Antioch, and the attraction their religion had among the heathen population. The fire in Antioch, attributed to the Jews, reminds us of that in Rome under Nero, the blame of which was laid on the Christians.

[2] It may not be out of place to recall to the readers the well-known fact that Imperator (Emperor) was not the title by which the Caesars ruled the Roman world, nor was Imperium (Empire) used in the modern sense. A victorious general was hailed as Titus had been (*vide supra*) as Imperator, and the Imperium signified the right of a Roman to rule his province. Domitian had been proclaimed Imperator for his successes in Germany.

caused a pang to recollect and record as well as to witness the humiliation of his race and the ruin of his native city. His account of the ceremonies is extremely interesting, as that of an eye-witness explaining the scene without technicalities to strangers.[1]

The *Imperatores* did not sleep in their palace on the Palatine but in the Campus Martius near the Temple of Isis. At daybreak Vespasian and Titus went to the Portico of Octavian and met the Senate. The soldiers were dismissed to a breakfast given by the *Imperatores*, after prayers had been uttered by Vespasian and Titus; they then withdrew to outside the Porta Triumphalis, by which they would have to enter the city. They sacrificed to the gods at this gate before the triumphal procession went on its way. Every soul in Rome had left home to see the show; and only with difficulty was there room for the *cortège* to make its way to the Capitol. Almost everything which ministers to human luxury was carried as part of the spoils. The silver and gold, the ivory, Babylonian embroideries, precious gems seemed to flow like a stream; and it appeared incredible to the beholders that such things were really rare. Then came every sort of wild animal, led by servants in gorgeous liveries. Even the captives, carefully selected for their beauty, were richly adorned, and any wound or disfigurement was scrupulously concealed by their sumptuous garments.

All the chief events of the war were represented on stages (πήγματα) in tiers, some three or four stories high. There were portrayals of devastation of fair countrysides, of houses in flames, of engines demolishing great walls, and troops pouring in through the ruins. Art was lavishly bestowed on making these warlike operations as vivid as possible. On each stage stood a representation of the general of the captive city, just as he appeared when taken prisoner. At the end of the procession the treasures of the Temple were carried; the golden table many talents in weight, the seven-branched candlestick. The copy of the Jewish Law was borne last of

[1] *War*, vii. 4 (123 ff.).

all the spoils.   Images of victory all made of ivory and gold followed, and at the end of all came Vespasian and Titus in their chariots, the youthful Domitian riding by them on a splendid charger.

Simon, son of Gioras, executed.—It was the brutal custom of the Romans at the conclusion of the triumph to execute the general who had commanded the enemy, and Simon, the son of Gioras, was selected, to his own honour and to the disgrace of his conquerors, for a cruel death.   Having been made to walk in the procession, he was scourged and led by a halter to his doom.   When the joyful news that this brave if cruel general was no more was proclaimed there were shouts of applause. All Rome kept festival, the people were entertained lavishly by Vespasian ; and one can but wonder whether Josephus had much appetite for these sumptuous festivities.   Suetonius records that Vespasian himself was thoroughly bored by the tedious proceedings of this eventful day.[1]   In A.D. 75 the Emperor erected the Temple of Peace, where he deposited the vessels of the House of the Lord.   The copy of the Law and the purple curtains he kept in his palace.

Masada captured.—After the triumph at Rome there remained only the aftermath of the war.   Three fortresses held out : two on the western side of the Dead Sea, Herodium and Masada, and Machaerus on the eastern. Herodium soon fell, Machaerus resisted awhile ; and Josephus tells a story of a young man, named Eleazar, who was captured by a gigantic Roman soldier, and threatened with such tortures that his relatives were induced to surrender the place to save him.   The siege of Masada is more vividly described.   Here another Eleazar, the last of the sons of Judas of Galilee, induced all the garrison to commit suicide, so that the Romans found no living creature when they entered the fortress.[2]

The *sicarii* in Egypt.—Temple at Leontopolis destroyed. —A remnant of the *sicarii* escaped to Egypt and began

[1] Vespasian, xii.: *Triumphi die fatigatus tarditate et taedio pompae.*
[2] *War*, vii. 8 (252 ff.).   A visit to Masada is vividly described by my friend and colleague Professor Fosdick in his *Pilgrimage to Palestine.*

to make trouble. In vain did the elders of the people endeavour to calm the ardour of the fugitives, and persuade the native Jews of Alexandria to oppose the movement. These *sicarii* were evidently Zealots of an extreme type, with their cry ' No king but God.' Six hundred of them were taken prisoner, and those who had escaped into Upper Egypt were rounded up and brought to Alexandria, where they endured unheard-of tortures rather than acknowledge Caesar. Josephus is divided between admiration of their constancy and condemnation of their folly.[1] Lupus, the governor of Alexandria, on receipt of orders from Vespasian, now closed the temple of Onias at Leontopolis; and his successor Paulinus completed the work by confiscating the property, leaving no trace of the worship of God on the spot. Onias had made his temple a strong fortress, and its appearance was that of a tower ninety feet in height. From this time sacrifice ceased to be part of the Jewish religion. The Roman authorities tolerated the synagogue services, but would have no more Jewish temples, which might again become centres for insurrection.[2]

Josephus accused.—At the same time trouble broke out in Cyrene; and a certain Jonathan, with the connivance of the governor Catullus, tried to implicate Josephus. However, when Jonathan was sent to Rome, Vespasian found him guilty and, Josephus adds, inflicted on him the punishment he deserved. The wretch was tortured and then burnt alive. Catullus was not punished by the Emperor; but God smote him, and he died in great agony. With this Josephus ends his history of the ' War,' modestly leaving to the judgment of his readers his literary style.[3]

Limitations of Josephus.—The story of the Jewish people from the restoration of the second Temple to their

---

[1] *War*, vii. 10 (407 ff.). [2] *War*, vii. 10 (420 ff.).
[3] The concluding words of the *War* are : ' Here we close our history which we promised to relate with perfect accuracy for the information of those who wish to learn how this war was waged by the Romans against the Jews. Let the manner in which it has been interpreted (καὶ πῶς μὲν ἡρμήνευται) be left to the reader to judge ; but as concerning truth, I would not hesitate boldly to assert that throughout the entire narrative this has been my single aim.'

complete subjugation by the power of the Roman Empire as Josephus relates it is now before us. What he tells us is really the account of his people in Palestine ; yet, with all his pious reflections and commendation of the Law of Moses and the sacred literature of the Hebrews, it is secular history, told by a sagacious man of the world, who seems incapable of recognising wherein the true greatness of Israel consists. Josephus is able to tell a story with power and animation, and often to select his material with judgment. But he seems to be at times singularly lacking in perception of character. Scarcely anyone whom he depicts stands out unforgettably on his canvas. Perhaps the only figure who seems to live and move is that of Herod the Great ; and this may be due to Josephus' authority, Nicolaus of Damascus. An exception may be made of the portraiture of Herod Agrippa I drawn by the historian himself, though he knew that monarch only by hearsay, and seems unconscious that he really is sketching the character of an unscrupulous adventurer, whose patriotism and piety was little more than a cloak for ambition. Josephus, indeed, appears incapable of appreciating what is really admirable in Judaism. Of the better side of Pharisaism he has little to say. Of Gamaliel the elder, Hillel, and Johanan ben Zakkai, he has nothing to tell us ; nor does he so much as hint that it was the ethical principles of the great rabbis which preserved Judaism.[1] To understand his position a recapitulation of the story as he tells it, even at the risk of some repetition, may be desirable.

Summary of Jewish history.—The Jews who returned from Babylon with the decree of Cyrus permitting them to rebuild the Temple established an aristocratical government under their high priests. When the story as told in the Scriptures fails him, our historian has nothing to relate except a few isolated incidents—the visit of Alexander the Great, Ptolemy Philadelphus and the translation of the Law, stories about the Tobiades. All we can say for certain is that the high-priestly rulers during

---

[1] This being the case, why should we wonder if Josephus is silent about Jesus of Nazareth ?

this period became gradually richer, more enterprising, and more worldly. With the appearance of Antiochus Epiphanes, the hierarchy had degenerated so greatly in their lust for wealth and influence that they were ready to co-operate with the Macedonian rulers of Syria in their efforts to accommodate their religion to the prevailing Hellenism of the age. But these apostate priests had not reckoned with the religious zeal of the common people, who revolted against the kings of Syria, and became independent under the leadership of the priests of the family of Asmon. For nearly a century, from 168 B.C. onwards, the new leaders increased in power, till, as Kings of the Jews, they almost dominated all Palestine.

Then, as was usual with all Eastern monarchies, rival claimants arose, and the Romans appeared on the scene as arbiters. Upon the whole, the new rulers of the Near East desired to leave the Jews alone. They respected their peculiar institutions, and apparently demanded no more than that they should live at peace with their neighbours. At first the Jews were allowed self-government under five separate councils, but when a really capable ruler was found in the Idumaean prince Herod, the kingdom was restored. But, with the extension of his dominions, Herod found it was necessary to conciliate his Greek as well as his Hebrew subjects, which naturally displeased the Jews; but he was so powerful that they dared not rebel and assuredly profited by the tranquillity of his reign. At his death, the country relapsed into an anarchy which was only repressed by the strong hand of Varus as governor of Syria. Order was restored, and Judaea with all southern Palestine placed under imperial procurators. These Roman officials possibly did their best to conciliate the people, but even apparently harmless acts were regarded as outrages on the peculiar customs of the Jews. Still, till the death of Tiberius, A.D. 37, some sort of peace was maintained; and after the administration of his successor, Caligula, a new expedient was tried. That Emperor's folly in insisting on the introduction of his image into the Temple had driven the people to exasperation; and at his death it was resolved to settle the Jewish question by giving Palestine a king, who on his grandmother's side represented the royal priests. Agrippa I might have averted the catastrophe, for he alone was popular with the Jewish people. But his reign was too short, and the Romans once more resorted to appointing procurators as governors of Judaea. Again disorders broke out, at first sporadically, gradually with more organised deliberation.

Demand for political independence.—Availing themselves of the weakness or indecision of Roman authority, the Jews began to make it a religious duty to demand political independence. In vain the more moderate men, the priests and rulers, including Agrippa II, advised submission. They were not listened to, and war became inevitable. Even then things need not have proceeded to extremities. Vespasian and Titus would gladly have come to some arrangement. During the siege of Jerusalem Titus was badly needed at Rome, and was only too anxious to arrive at an accommodation. But the Jews were involved, not so much in a war as in a revolution, with the object of overthrowing all government. Their leaders were idealists inspired by religious aspirations, hoping for a new order which was to come suddenly, violently, and probably by some miraculously divine intervention. Men in this frame of mind are impervious to prudential considerations ; and, because they consider their object to be all important, reckless of danger for themselves and ruthless in regard to the sufferings of others. As in other revolutions, the extremists seized the reins of power, and among these there were assuredly some men of genuine devotion, but not a few unscrupulous adventurers.

Josephus and the Law.—A man of such studied moderation as Josephus cannot escape the censure of posterity, though the events proved that he was right after all. The providential purpose of the revelation of God to Israel has been to train the nation in His service in order to bring mankind to acknowledge, not merely His sovereignty, but His moral demands. Beginning with a form of worship which differed but little from that of other nations, the Chosen People were taught by their prophets that it was not sufficient to adore One God, but necessary also to fulfil His will by justice and mercy to one another and to their fellow men.   Josephus fully recognised that the Law of Moses, properly obeyed, would bring about a reign of peace and righteousness on earth. He also believed that such an ideal could not be secured by the display of warlike patriotism.   A turbulent nation, fighting for earthly independence, could not be as pleasing to God as one which patiently sought to live in accordance to His will, and accept those whom He had appointed to rule over them.   Resistance to Antiochus Epiphanes, who sought to make the Jews violate the Law, might be allowable ; but the Romans had never attempted to imitate his policy.   On the contrary, their legislation had been markedly in favour of permitting the Jews to live in accordance with their peculiar customs.   It is further evident that Josephus, who recognised that the empire of Rome meant the peace of the world, also believed it to have been established by divine Providence.   Josephus regarded Jerusalem and the Temple as the sacred posses- sion of his nation, and the Law as a philosophy destined to be adopted by the human race ; and if the Roman Empire allowed these to exist, he was content to await God's good time, especially as he had no fervid convictions to make him personally impatient. A mistaken patriotism proved the ruin of the nation, which had incurred God's displeasure by refusing to wait till He should be pleased to deliver Israel in His own good time.   Judaism's fall was due to its ambition to secure worldly independence and ultimately predominance by force.   As we have had occasion to remark, Israel was saved by men more truly religious than Josephus, but practically in accord with him in this matter.

Judaism becomes isolated.—These views can hardly commend themselves to the more ardent Jews of to-day, notably to those who hope for a predominant Zionism. But it is the business of the historian of the past to dis- cover and relate what actually happened and to form judgments on events, rather than speculate on what might have resulted had things happened otherwise. The secular ambitions of the Jewish patriots ruined the political development of the nation. They forced Titus to destroy Jerusalem, and compelled Hadrian to complete the work of A.D. 70. The religious aspirations persisted in two forms—the Rabbinic and the Christian. The Judaism of the schools withdrew from the life of the Western world. It busied itself with the Law and the Tradition, and no longer interested itself in Hellenic art, culture, or philosophy. It refused either to be amalgamated with the Hellenic Roman world or to be effaced. It triumphed by its isolation.

Christianity becomes world-wide.—The religion of Jesus Christ, on the other hand, was from the rabbinic standpoint a heresy, but in its origin it was fundamentally Judaic. Jesus lived and taught as a Jew. The first three Gospels are Hebrew documents. The theology of the Fourth Gospel is an echo of the Alexandrian teaching of Philo, the Jewish Platonist. Even Paul could never divest himself of his ancestral traditions. At first hesitatingly, and finally with enthusiasm, the Christian preachers turned to the Gentile world, and not only sought converts, but adopted much of its philosophy and outlook on life. The rabbis rejected the Greek language and taught in Hebrew and Aramaic ; the Christians made Greek, and later Latin, the vehicles for their instruction and for the expression of their doctrines. This species of Judaism conquered the Roman Empire, which had tolerated the older faith of Israel but had waged relentless war against the form it assumed in Christianity because it appeared to be an insidious and aggressive attempt to undermine the institutions and culture of the civilized world. In the end the Empire had to acknowledge its defeat ; and scarcely more than three centuries after the destruction of the Temple it proclaimed Christianity, which included the God, the Scriptures, and much of the worship of ancient Israel, as the official religion.

It will always be a matter for debate whether this astonishing triumph was a blessing to the world or the reverse. Can Christians to-day look back with complacency on the day when Constantine adopted Christ as his ally and routed his enemies with the Cross as his ensign ? In other words, can the methods of this world, the courage of the warrior, the dexterity of the politician, the adaptability of the demagogue, preserve the true religion ? Does not this belong to the province of an all-ruling God ? The lesson we may learn from the record of Josephus is that the marvellous continuance of his ancestral faith could not have been due to the men who played a conspicuous part in the tragedy of Judah from the days of Antiochus Epiphanes to those of Titus. God indeed has worked something by means of those who, in the words of the son of Sirach, ' have left a name behind them, to declare their praises ' ; but even more by an obscure majority ' which have no memorial; who are perished as though they had not been ; and are become as though they had not been born ; and their children after them.' [1] Such were the unknown seers, prophets, and teachers of Israel, whose names have found no place in the pages of Flavius Josephus.

[1] Ecclesiasticus xliv. 9–10.

CHAPTER XIV

Josephus and the History of Israel : The 'Antiquities' or Archaeology

Josephus' account of his literary education. — The 'Jewish War' is Josephus' masterpiece. Before, however, we pass from it to the 'Antiquities,' it is advisable to see what he says of himself as a man of letters. He implies at the end of this work that his pronunciation of Greek was never quite satisfactory, although he had studied carefully the literature and construction of the language ; and he attributes his failure to attain perfection to the fact that Jewish priests of his class did not trouble themselves about foreign tongues in their zeal to attain a thorough knowledge of the Law. Yet it seems certain that he must have been able to speak Greek from his youth up, as is evidenced by his success as an emissary to Rome before the outbreak of the War. One must always discount what Josephus says, even in depreciation of himself. However produced, some of the Greek writings which appeared under his name are praiseworthy; and when he says : ' Those of my own nation freely acknowledge that I far exceed them in the learning belonging to the Jews,' it is certainly permissible to indulge in some scepticism in regard to the accuracy of this remark. In his Prologue to the ' War ' he says that the original of this work was written in Aramaean or Hebrew for the benefit of the ' Barbarians up country ' (τοῖς ἄνω βαρβάροις), that is to the Parthians, Babylonians, Arabs, Jews beyond the Euphrates, and the people of Adiabene, none of whom spoke Greek. He declares he translated the ' War ' into Greek, but the general excellence of the language of the book forbids us to accept the

statement literally. From Josephus' latest work, the
' Apion,' we have a hint of how he came at times to write
such good Greek. He tells us that he employed assistants
to revise his language in order to enable him to produce
work which could be read with pleasure by his Greek-
speaking patrons. But that he should have selected
his advisers so judiciously is no small testimony to his
literary ability.[1]

Josephus attempts to popularise the Old Testament.—
We now turn to the first part of his ' Antiquities,' in
which he makes an effort to render the history of Israel
as told in the Hebrew Scriptures of interest to Gentile
readers. One may safely say that no one can possibly do
justice to Josephus' endeavour to take the Bible and
adapt its contents to modern readers in an historical
form, unless he has himself made a similar attempt.
Otherwise the reader is almost bound to criticise the work
of the Jewish historian unjustly, because, until he has
tried himself, it is difficult fairly to appreciate the nature
of the task. It must be confessed that Josephus' Bible
story is not particularly interesting to read. It is turgid
and declamatory, illuminating mainly where it illustrates
some rabbinic traditional amplifications, and in addition
it is marred by the author's inveterate habit of putting
speeches into the mouths of scriptural characters, not
excluding the Deity Himself. But let any author make
a similar experiment, and when he peruses his own work
he will not be over ready to condemn the attempt of
Flavius Josephus.

Preface to the ' Antiquities.'—In his Preface to the
' Antiquities,' Josephus explains why so much stress has
to be laid upon the origin of mankind. ' Why,' he asks,
' did Moses devote so much space to enquiring into the
origin of things (φυσιολογία) ? ' Then in a really fine
passage he declares that the lawgiver fully realises that
to order his life aright a man must have a true notion of
the nature of God. Other legislators have recourse to

[1] *Antiq.* xx. 2 (263) ; *War*, Preface (3 and 6) ; *Apion*, i (50) ; see
also *Life*, 65 (361 ff.). The reader is referred to Dr. Thackeray's
admirable introductions to his volumes in the Loeb series.

fables, which attribute acts of folly to their gods, and give the wicked an excuse for their misdeeds; but Moses, sometimes plainly, and elsewhere allegorically, shows the nature of God, in the hope that those who read may strive to imitate the perfection of the Ruler and Father of all.[1]

Josephus on Genesis.—Many of the additions of Josephus to the story of the Creation, the Fall and the Flood are to be found in the Rabbinic literature, Philo, and various Apocryphal writings, and here there is little to merit our attention. The rationalism inherent in our author is evident in his attempt to account for the great ages of the early patriarchs, where he explains that they were permitted to live so long in order to perfect the arts necessary to existence, astronomy, geometry, etc. Besides, they had to be on earth 600 years, the space of time in which the ' Great Year ' (*i.e.* the Pythagorean Cycle) was completed, in order to be able to predict the course of the heavenly bodies.[2] Josephus naturally brings forward the testimony of various ancient writers to confirm the primitive story of Genesis, and mentions certain objects still standing to prove the truth of his narrative—an inscribed stone in the land of Syria, set up by Adam, who foresaw the Deluge and wished to preserve the memory of the knowledge man had already acquired, and the relics of the ark in Armenia. Unlike Philo, he makes no serious attempt to indulge in allegory on the mysterious subject of Creation.

Pompous language of Josephus.—The perusal of Josephus' treatment of a story so pathetic in its simplicity as that of the sacrifice of Isaac, is a revelation of his historic method as well as of his complete inability to appreciate what is to us the extreme beauty of the language of Scripture. ' And Isaac spake unto Abraham his father, and said, My father ; and he said, Here I am, my son. And he said, Behold, the fire and the wood : but where is the lamb for a burnt offering ? And Abraham said, My son, God will provide himself a lamb for a burnt offering ; so they went both of them

---

[1] Preface to *Antiquities* (18–26).   [2] *Antiq.* i. 3 (106).

together . . . and Abraham stretched forth his hand, and took the knife to slay his son.' [1] Josephus develops the narrative by putting this speech into the mouth of the patriarch :

> ' My child in a thousand prayers I asked God for thy birth ; after thou didst come into the world, there is no trouble I have not bestowed upon thy education, and nothing would have appeared to me happier than to see thee come to man's estate, and when I died to leave thee heir to my power. But since it is the will of God who made me thy father, and that it pleases him that I should lose thee, bear the sacrifice valiantly,' etc.

I have made this rendering from the excellent French translation of M. Jules Weil, which has reproduced the pompous Greek in which his imaginary oration is cast, not unlike in style to that of a religious tragedy in the days of Louis XIV. It is but just to say that centuries after Josephus the simplicity of the Hebrew story was, even by earnest believers, long regarded as one of its chief defects.[2]

Josephus and Moses.—When we reach the early days of Moses, Josephus has much to tell of him which is not to be found in the Bible. The daughter of Pharaoh was named Thermuthis ; the future lawgiver conducted an expedition against Ethiopia, and married the king's daughter, Tharbis. The passage of the Red Sea is said to have been similar to an experience of Alexander the Great, who led his soldiers through the Sea of Pamphylia, which opened a path for them when God was pleased to destroy the power of Persia.[3] This is characteristic of Josephus, who has a truly modern dislike of relating miracles as historical events, and constantly seeks to explain them away. This does not, however, prevent his indulging in superstitions of his own, dreams, portents, and the like. As regards the legislation of Moses, Josephus

[1] Gen. xxii. 7 ff.
[2] *Antiq.* i. 12 (227 ff.). St. Augustine found the simplicity and barbarism of the biblical language a difficulty till he heard St. Ambrose allegorise it. Admiration of the Bible as literature is very modern.
[3] *Antiq.* ii. 16 (347–348).

constantly refers us to a book he proposed to write on the subject, but apparently never finished.

The Tabernacle.—He is more diffuse when he comes to the making of the Tabernacle, and describes the priestly vestments, especially those of the High Priest. It may be superfluous, and would certainly be tedious, to enter fully into all the details of the construction of the Tabernacle, and to note where Josephus departs from the account in Exodus. Here one may quote but a single sentence as illustrative of his method of making the matter more intelligible to his Gentile readers :

> ' Within the shrine (Moses) set up a table like those at Delphi, two cubits long and one broad, and three spans high. And it had feet the lower half of which were fashioned like those which the Dorians add to their couches, but the upper part of them up to the table is square.'

The seven lamps on the branched candlestick are said to indicate the seven planets ; and this cosmic significance of the decoration of both Tabernacle and Temple is constantly insisted upon. Thus, the twelve loaves of the shew-bread represent the months of the year ; the ephod represents all nature, because God has willed it to be made of four substances, etc. All the vestments of the High Priest, who is called the arabarch,[1] are similarly explained.

Purpose of Josephus in explaining the Tabernacle.— These details on which Josephus lays so much stress are in themselves important as revealing his attitude to his religion. He selects his materials, not unskilfully, in order to persuade his readers that there was nothing in Judaism to excite ridicule or contempt, but that it was an eminently reasonable form of worship, embodying many views held by educated men who would find its philosophic teaching acceptable. In this Josephus finds

---

[1] *Antiq.* iii. 7 (151). The head of the Alexandrian Jews was called the *arabarch* or *alabarch*. Reinach thinks it is a scribal corruption of the Aramaic *kahana rabba* = chief priest. One is reminded of Juvenal's

> *Atque triumphales, inter quos ausus habere*
> *Nescio quis titulos Ægyptius, atque arabarches*
> (*Sat.* i. 129–30).

imitators in the Christian apologists, who labour to show that the Faith is after all the natural religion of the human race and in accordance with all true philosophy. But one finds it hard to shake off the conviction that there is a coldness in the historian which contrasts with the enthusiasm of both Christian and Rabbinical teachers ; and that he is commending a religion valuable chiefly for its antiquity and its instructive ceremonial.

Omissions in account of the Pentateuch.—The first four books of the ' Antiquities ' are occupied by a discussion of the Pentateuch, the omissions being as significant as the additions to the narrative. Such a difficult passage as the circumcision of the son of Moses by Zipporah is passed over in silence ; the scandal of the making of the golden calf by Aaron is not mentioned.[1] Josephus is evidently perplexed by the presence of the winged Cherubim in the Tabernacle. He discreetly ignores the fact that they were to be represented on the veils, as does also the Latin Vulgate ; and, when he speaks of them as overshadowing the Ark of the Covenant, he says that they resembled no creature beneath the heavens. Moses, he adds, had seen such figures sculptured (in low relief) on the throne of God. The debt of Josephus to the traditional Aramaic translation of the Scriptures, to the Septuagint and to Rabbinic tradition is a perplexing question, as is, despite his protestations, his knowledge of the original Hebrew.[2]

The historical books of the Bible.—Throughout the fifth and sixth books the story from Joshua to the end of Samuel is related ; and it is interesting to compare the text used by Josephus with that of our MSS. of the Septuagint and the present Hebrew text, especially as regards the spelling of the different names of places and of persons. But on the whole the narrative is much as we have it despite the alterations and ornamentations of style customary to Josephus, who perhaps rightly feels

[1] Exodus iv. 24 ff. ; xxxii. *passim.*
[2] *Antiq.* iii. 6 (126–127). See Reinach's note *in loco* : ' Notons encore, pour le present passage, que la Vulgate ne parle pas non plus d'êtres ailés, de cherubim : elle traduit le mot *keroubim* (Ex. xxvi. 1 et 31) par [*cortinas*] *variatas opere plumario et* [*velum*] *opere plumario et pulchra varietate contextum.*

that a reproduction of a literal Greek translation would have been unpalatable if not unintelligible to his public. Once, however, he indulges in his propensity to moralise in rather a remarkable fashion. He has related the story of Saul's visit to the Witch of Endor, and his return to his army knowing that he must die in battle next day. This is followed by a eulogy of the witch which is not wholly undeserved. She knew Saul was her enemy, since he had determined to put down her illegal art. But when she saw him oppressed with grief, she hastened to console the miserable king and, poor as she was, offered him the refreshment from no hope of reward, though she was assured that Saul's days were numbered. This, says Josephus, is an example for us all, because nothing can win the favour of God more surely than the conduct displayed by this woman. This is followed by a panegyric on the courage with which Saul went forth to certain death to fight the Philistines.[1]

David.—The reign of David is related in the seventh book at much greater length than are the events recorded in the two earlier ones. The narrative of 2 Samuel, supplemented by that of Chronicles, is followed closely, but, except for some details of interest to the textual critic and the exegete, there is little of importance. In reference to David's victory over the Syrians Josephus quotes Nicolaus of Damascus. He somewhat spoils the beautiful story Nathan told to David before he rebuked the king for his sin in the matter of Uriah, by ascribing diplomatic sagacity to the prophet, whose courtly training had taught him to approach a king by a parable rather than directly. David, we are told, wrote his songs in trimeters and pentameters ; but, although scholars are agreed that there is metre in the Psalter, it is doubtful whether Josephus is a competent judge, especially as he declares elsewhere that Moses after crossing the Red Sea wrote a song in hexameters ![2] Josephus adds that the

---

[1] *Antiq.* vi. 14 (340 ff.).   J. H. Newman has happily used this digression of Josephus in one of his sermons.

[2] *Antiq.* vii. 12 (305): ' When David was freed from war and danger and for the rest of his life was enjoying profound peace, he composed songs to God and hymns in different metres,' etc.   For Moses, *Antiq.* ii. 16 (346).

wealth concealed in the tomb of David was so artfully
hidden that it was not discovered till the time of John
Hyrcanus, 134 B.C., who opened one chamber in which
he found three thousand talents wherewith to bribe
Antiochus VII to abandon the siege of Jerusalem. Subsequently Herod the Great opened another room.[1]

Solomon.—In the account of Solomon, Josephus lays
especial stress on the work preliminary to the building
of the Temple, and he is careful to declare here that the
correspondence between the kings had been preserved,
quoting from Menander and Dios ; but there is nothing
in the ' Antiquities ' which he does not repeat in his
so-called book ' Against Apion.' In the bulls made by
Solomon to support the brazen ' sea ' in the Temple and
the sculptured lions about his throne, Josephus sees the
influence of the heathen wives whom the king had
married. It may further be interesting to note that
Josephus gives an example of Solomon's power over
demons. The king's wisdom was manifested in his
knowledge of incantations, which retained their efficacy
down to the days of Josephus.

' He (Solomon) left incantations to help the sick,
and forms of adjuration to drive out demons so that
they should not return any more. And this sort of
remedy has remained efficacious to our day. For I
witnessed how a countryman of mine named Eleazar
in the presence of Vespasian, his sons, his tribunes
and his military escort, free those who were
possessed by demons from them. For his method
of healing was this : he applied a ring, the signet
of which contained a root of some plant Solomon
had indicated, to the patient's nose, and as the man
sniffed he drew out the demon through his nostrils.
And straightway the man fell down, and Eleazar in
the name of Solomon adjured the demon not to come
back into the man, reciting the incantations which
he had prepared. And Eleazar wishing to prove to
the bystanders that he possessed this power placed
before him a little vessel or foot-bath full of water,
and told the demon as he came out of the man to

[1] *Antiq.* vii. 15 (394).

upset it, and thereby make known to those present
that he had left the man.' [1]

This is enough to show that, if Josephus has a propensity to rationalise the biblical miracles, he certainly
shared in the belief in magic common to the age of the
Flavian emperors.

Elijah.—In relating the history of the kings of Israel
and Judah, Josephus follows the Bible with prosaic con-
scientiousness, supplementing the narrative of Kings by
that of the Chronicles. He seems quite blind to the finer
qualities of the Hebrew narrators, and relates the invasion of Judah by Shishak in the reign of Rehoboam
with no more enthusiasm than he bestows on the magnificently told episodes in the life of Elijah; two specimens
may suffice.

(1) Elijah's visit to Horeb, the mount of God:

' And having eaten and received power from this
food, he comes to Mount Sinai, where Moses is said
to have received the laws from God. And finding
there a hollow cave he went in and stayed making
his sojourn there. And a voice from the void (ἐξ
ἀδήλου) asked him why he had left the city and
come there, because he had killed the prophets of
the alien gods, and persuaded the people that He
whom they had worshipped from the first was the
one God. And he replied that he was sought after
for punishment by the king's wife. And when he
heard the voice again telling him to come into the
open air the next day, and it would be told him
what he should do, he came forth from the cave.
And when he came forth he heard the earth tremble,
and saw a bright light. And when there was silence
a divine voice ordered him not to disquiet himself,'
etc.[2]

Contrast this with the narrative of 1 Kings, and one
can understand how uninteresting Hebrew poetic prose
can become under the heavy hand of a man trying to write
elegant Greek. Well may M. Théodore Reinach say in a
footnote: ' *Remarquer avec quelle platitude Josephe écourte
ici la magnifique récit de la Bible* (1 Kings xix. 11–13).'

---

[1] *Antiq.* viii. 2 (45–48).   [2] *Antiq.* viii. 13 (349–352).

(2) The second instance is the ascension of Elijah. Here the author of Kings rises to great heights of descriptive writing, and Josephus descends to the depths of platitude:

> ' Joram (of Israel) was in other respects an enterprising prince. At the same time Elijah disappeared among men, and no one to this day knows what his end was. He left as his disciple Elisha, as we have previously shown. As to Elijah, and Enoch who lived before the Flood, it is written in the Holy Scriptures that they became invisible and no one had knowledge of their death.' [1]

The motive of Josephus in minimising the wonder of the ascension of Elijah is apparently his sense that the biblical narrative was ill suited to a Greek audience. ' The chariot of fire and the horses of fire,' the mantle of Elijah falling on Elisha, and the rest would savour too much of the miraculous to be acceptable, and his readers might reject the book of Kings as mythology instead of accepting it as history. His object is to show that Israel was a very ancient nation, whose story was told by official historians ; and he must, like many a modern writer on the Bible, have felt that by making his narrative prosaic he rendered it credible. At the same time, even when there is no danger of introducing the supernatural, Josephus shows himself blind to the poetic element of scriptural history. The story of Jehu's accession to the throne, and the murder of Jezebel, contains nothing miraculous, yet it is told in the Bible with inimitable vividness : in the ' Antiquities ' it is made as prosaic as possible. In short, the ' Antiquities ' proves the fact that the historian of the People of God has before him a hopeless task, unless he realises that it can only be told in the spirit of the Hebrew narrators.

Josephus quotes heathen authorities.—The Assyrian invasion as recorded by Josephus contains some interesting features. There is a quotation from Menander about Shalmanezer's invasion of Syria and Phoenicia in the

---

[1] *Antiq.* ix. 2 (28).

days of Elulaeus, King of Tyre. As to the Samaritan settlers he says that five nations were brought to Palestine from the East. In 2 Kings xvii. they came from Babylon, Cuthah, Ava, Hamath and Sepharvaim ; but only Cuthah is mentioned, though Josephus evidently had the chapter before him. Cuthah is the name of a river and district in Persia, from whence the Samaritan people are called Cuthaeans. The new settlers were troubled, not by lions, but by a plague. They consulted an oracle, and learned that they must apply to the King of Assyria for priests to learn how to worship the God of the land. They asserted that they were the sons of Joseph ; and when the Jews prospered they claimed to be their kinsfolk, but repudiated all association when things went ill with Judah. As might be expected, Josephus quotes from Herodotus about the destruction of Sennacherib's army, and from Berosus for Berodach-Baladan of Babylon, who sent an embassy to Hezekiah.

Silence concerning the prophets except Daniel.—It is worth noting that Josephus has little or nothing to say about the prophets either of Israel or Judah. Isaiah and Jeremiah are rarely mentioned, and Josephus makes little allusion to what is of the most interest to us in their books as we have them. Of the teaching or social and moral influence of the prophets he says nothing. Daniel is the only prophet on whom Josephus bestows much attention, and his use of the book is interesting. The stories of Daniel and the Three Children are related without any of the apocryphal additions in our Greek Daniel. Josephus, however, says that, when Daniel was delivered from the lions, the jealous princes declared that they had been fed before the prophet had been cast into the den, and had to prove in their own persons that it was not so. Also we are told that Daniel built a splendid tower at Ecbatana, where the Median, Persian, and Parthian kings were buried. He adds that the custody of the tower was always given to a Jewish priest.[1] The dream of Nebuchadrezzar is explained. The head of gold, as in the book of Daniel, is the king, the arms and shoulders

---

[1] *Antiq.* x. 11 (264).

of silver mean the twofold kingdom, Medes and Persians, which will follow. The kingdom of brass will come from the West and will be destroyed by one of iron—nothing is said of the iron mixed with clay in the feet of the image seen by Nebuchadrezzar, by which the Romans are probably meant. Josephus adroitly avoids any interpretation of the stone which destroyed the image. It is his business to relate the past, not to comment on what has not yet happened. In this way he avoids hinting at any final triumph of the People of God foretold by Daniel.

The Return from the Captivity.—It is difficult to say definitely that in his account of the Return Josephus follows not the Hebrew but the Greek version of the book of Ezra. The only material found in our so-called Apocrypha which he introduces is the story of the Three Youths and their contest before Darius as to the strongest thing on earth. The victory is adjudged to Zerubbabel, who obtains leave to build the Temple. To all appearance Josephus was not acquainted with the last part of our book of Nehemiah. The story of Esther is given at some length, the Ahasuerus of the Bible being Artaxerxes, the son of Xerxes. As has been already indicated, Sanballat, who plays so prominent a part as the enemy of Nehemiah, appears in Josephus as building the Temple on Gerizim more than a century later, in the days of Alexander the Great.

Estimate of Josephus' interpretation of the Bible.— The perusal of the biblical ' Antiquities' of Josephus is certainly weary work. It is a diffuse and yet commonplace *résumé* of Hebrew history. At the same time, it must be admitted that the writer is successful in proving his point by establishing the fact that his people were not upstarts, as the Greeks maintained, but had all the prestige of a respectable antiquity stretching back into a remote past. Like all similar apologetic works, it has become out of date. The contemporary readers of Josephus might be obliged to recognise that the Jews were an ancient people and had a great tradition at the back of their peculiar religion. Whether anyone would be converted to Judaism as a reward for his labour in reading Josephus' story of its origin is another question. But the ' Antiquities ' may remind some who are advanced in life of more recent attempts to teach the Bible, from which they suffered in their youth, when they were compelled to learn the names and exploits of the Judges and to memorise lists of the Kings of Israel and Judah.   These may be desirable for the young to master, but they are, after all, the dry bones of the sacred story.   The Bible makes these to live by showing that, underlying the recorded facts, there are a moral purpose, men of heroic character, and a sense that God is present, directing for His own purpose the destinies of the nation.   Otherwise it is scarcely possible from the bare records to account for the influence of the history of Israel on the world. To us the Bible story is that of a nation, which, with all its admitted errors, was ever striving after a high ideal. The clue to its significance is found in the teaching of the prophets of Israel, and concerning these Josephus is uniformly silent.   Judaism, with the religions which have sprung from it, has always been idealistic.   Whilst revering the past, it has ever looked forward to the future.   Josephus, on the other hand, seems to have lived for the present, satisfied with the respectable antiquity of his nation to account for its religious peculiarities.

Josephus compared with Philo.—It is noteworthy that Josephus makes but one mention of Philo of Alexandria, the famous philosopher, a generation before Josephus, who made a similar attempt to commend Judaism to Greek readers.   Yet it may be instructive to make a brief comparison and contrast between their respective treatments of the story of the patriarchs and the Law of Moses.

Josephus approaches the record of his nation in the spirit of an historian.   His object is to set before the Greek-speaking world the same sort of history as they were accustomed to read.   His patrons were Roman Emperors, who read Greek as a matter of course, and were accustomed to writers like Polybius.   Philo, on the other hand, is a philosopher, and he makes Plato his master, whereas Josephus studied Thucydides. In the spirit of an historian Josephus takes the Scriptures and constructs his story out of them, relating events with ornamental additions adapted to the taste of his age. Philo, on the other hand, regards facts not as things to be recorded, but to be moralised upon, as having a deeper meaning and a lesson for the wise man.

Thus, to Philo the patriarchs are not only examples of virtue in general but of the sort of virtue which is natural to all mankind, inculcated by unwritten law long before the promulgation of any code. Each several patriarch is really not simply a character in history, but a symbol. Each one of them acquires virtue in a different way, Abraham and Jacob progressively, but Isaac spontaneously, whilst Joseph's more practical mind places him on a lower level. All history, in fact, in Philo is allegory with a moral purpose.

It is much the same with the Law. We have seen how Josephus regards its precepts as calculated to create a community in which justice and temperance prevail, and that the ornaments of worship and prescribed ordinances are reasonably explained by the component parts of the universe. But Philo is intent on the moral purpose of the legislation. To him those laws which appear trivial or even absurd have a spiritual significance. Everything Moses ordains is directed to encourage virtue, and to make mankind follow the law of nature implanted in humanity by God. To enlarge on this subject would here be out of place ; it is here sufficient to contrast the profundity of the aims of Philo as a philosopher with the superficiality of Josephus as an historian. Yet it should never be forgotten that, with all his allegorism, Philo allows no excuse for those Jews who consider that a symbolical interpretation of the Law can be made a pretext for a lax observance of its commands.

CHAPTER XV

A Review of the 'Antiquities' and its Sources

Points of contact between the Jew and the Roman.—
Josephus did not inaugurate a new idea when he compiled his 'Antiquities.' His great work was designed to appeal to Roman readers; and was qualified to do so since the Romans as a practical people had an interest in their past. Although, therefore, the Jews in the days of Josephus were bitterly opposed to Rome, hating its methods of administration, which restrained their ambition, and contending against its armies with all the fury of fanaticism and despair, yet in some respects the two peoples were in sympathy, and even displayed a certain mutual respect for one another. One reason for this lies in the fact that the Roman, like the Jew, has always been temperamentally a legalist; and the tendency of the lawyer is to seek for precedent in the past, and to look upon the institutions of his country with respect. To him, what is ancient is not only honourable but of practical importance, because it is the foundation of the law under which he lives. It is true the Jew believed he possessed an unchangeable law, given by God Himself; but even herein he did not differ materially from the Roman, who looked on ancestral custom with religious veneration. The Romans also had a certain respect for Judaism as an institution based on law; and, if they hated the Jews, even the provocation of the war did not prevent them recognising the legal rights of Judaism. Subsequently, the Church in Rome so far carried on the traditions of the Empire, that at least

in the papal city the Jews had the right to worship God
in their own way.[1]

Dionysius of Halicarnassus and Livy.—The Roman
was, therefore, naturally interested in the origin and early
history of his nation ; and before Josephus there were
two great works concerning the beginnings of the city,
one by Dionysius of Halicarnassus in Greek, and the
other by Livy in Latin. Josephus gave to Rome the
story of the Hebrew nation to show that it was in all respects worthy to be compared with that of the Roman
people, and also that its records were more ancient and
better authenticated. According to his own statement,
Dionysius of Halicarnassus came to Rome about 29 B.C.,
just after the conclusion of the Civil War, and remained
there for twenty-two years, completing his historical work
by 7 B.C. He wrote in Greek ; but says that he took
pains to study Latin and to consult the best historical
works in that language. He had probably been a teacher
of rhetoric at his native city, and his chief title to fame
is as a critic and man of letters. To the student of
Josephus, Dionysius is of peculiar interest in that his
book is entitled ' Roman Archaeology, or Antiquity,'
whilst Josephus' work bears the same heading with
' Jewish ' substituted for ' Roman.' The object of both
writers is the same, namely, to show that Romans and
Jews alike owe their fame to the excellence of their
institutions. Both Dionysius and Josephus divide their
work into twenty books, indulge in rhetorical disquisitions, and put imaginary speeches into the mouths of
their leading characters. In fact, these ' Archaeologies '
are written for cultured Romans to whom Greek was a
second language, with a view of providing reading
adapted to the taste of the public of the day. Another
point in common to the themes of these two writers is
that the founders of both Rome and Israel are represented primarily as legislators. Romulus, like Moses,

[1] In the Middle Ages the Jews were rarely molested in Rome.
The *schola Judaeorum* was recognised by the Popes, and more than
once the pontiffs protested against the cruelty with which they were
treated in Europe. I have dealt with this subject in my *Peter, Prince
of Apostles.*

is admitted to be the wisest of political leaders, whose institutions secured civil harmony, at least till the tribunate of Tiberius Gracchus. The religion and polity of the Greeks are unfavourably contrasted with those of Rome. Josephus naturally makes no mention of Dionysius, because his history only takes us as far as the beginning of the first Punic War, 264 B.C., and therefore could not be consulted for the later history of the Jews. But whether Josephus read Dionysius or not is immaterial ; the important fact is that the design of their ' Antiquities ' is similar, the one to show that the civil constitution of Rome, and the other the religious ordinances of the Jews, were destined to endure because of their inherent excellence.[1]

Dislike of the miraculous.—A tendency to rationalise the miracles recorded in primitive history has already been noticed in the ' Antiquities ' of Josephus ; and the same is apparent in those of Dionysius. We have seen how careful Josephus is to call as little attention as possible to the miraculous ascension of Elijah ; and Dionysius is equally solicitous to show that the legend that Romulus was carried up by his father Mars in the midst of a violent storm is capable of a perfectly natural explanation. Some, he tells us, say that the founder of Rome became in his later days a ferocious tyrant, punishing even patricians for robbery by hurling them down the Rock, and that they conspired and killed him, dismembering the body so that it could not be found, while some give another story. Others account for the tale of the mysterious disappearance of Romulus by the fact that both his birth and his death occurred during an eclipse of the sun. It, however, seems clear that there was a strong feeling that the credibility of early history was lessened by any record of miracles which might tend to reduce it to the level of myth. Thus, although both Dionysius and Josephus are by no means free from superstition, yet both, having a common object of proving

---

[1] The titles of the books of Josephus and Dionysius are *Roman Archaeology*, and *Jewish Archaeology* respectively, 'Αρχαιολογία meaning Ancient History.

the respective claims of Romans and Jews to great antiquity, desire to make the early story of these nations as
free from the supernatural as possible.

Popular history.—The late Professor Bury in his
' Harvard lectures on the Greek historians ' has some very
suggestive remarks on the prevailing taste in historical
literature, which throw light on the method of Josephus
when treating the Hebrew Bible as his source.   The orator
Isocrates, the rival of Demosthenes in the fourth century
B.C., had an immense influence on historical composition.
Thucydides, the master historian of Greece, wrote with
the object of recording such facts as came under his
personal knowledge, or were based on the best information
he could procure.   His genius has rescued his history
from the charge of dullness ; but it cannot be said that
he wrote to satisfy the taste of a large circle of readers.
But those who studied under, or were influenced by,
Isocrates deliberately strove to popularise their subject
by employing the art of rhetoric, and indulging in philo-
sophical disquisitions,[1] both of which people demanded
to satisfy their passion for eloquence and style, requiring
to be charmed by the language of what they read rather
than be instructed as to the facts.

Did Josephus read Latin ?—It is doubtful whether
Josephus had, like Dionysius, attempted to learn Latin.
Probably the circle in which he moved in Rome was
entirely Greek speaking ; and, as he confesses, it took
him no little trouble to acquire that language.   He may,
of course, have read the ' Commentaries ' of Vespasian
and Titus in Latin, but it is quite conceivable that these
emperors wrote in Greek, or, if not, that Josephus employed translators.[2]   At any rate we look in vain for
references to Latin authors.   Even the voluminous
history of Livy is not mentioned by him except in one
passage about Pompey's siege of Jerusalem in the Fourteenth Book of the ' Antiquities ' to confirm statements
possibly derived from Nicolaus of Damascus.

[1] *The Ancient Greek Historians*, by J. B. Bury (Macmillan Co.),
a most important and suggestive book.
[2] Josephus alludes to these Commentaries in *Life*, (342 and 358),
and in *Apion*, i. (56).

Josephus and the Greek historians.—It may safely be assumed that Josephus had made a careful study of the history of the Greeks, from the earliest prose sources. At the beginning of his treatise ' Against Apion,' for example, he gives indications that he has studied historical works written before the Persian expeditions against Greece. He declares that the historian Acusilaus corrects the statements of the poet Hesiod ; and that he disagrees with Hellanicus of Lesbos on the subject of genealogies. Josephus also mentions Cadmus of Miletus and Pherecydes of Syros, who with the others wrote before Herodotus. In the ' Antiquities ' he gives extracts from several very early historians, as supporting the biblical statement that in ancient times men lived for a thousand years. How far he was acquainted with the works he cites we are unable to decide, but that he knew of them is certain.

The later books of the ' Antiquities.'—Hitherto we have considered Josephus and primitive history, where we are on the confines of myth, fable, and uncertain tradition, at any rate so far as the history of the Greeks is concerned. In the last books of the ' Antiquities,' when the Hebrew Scriptures cease to supply information Josephus enters upon what was to him modern history and treats of events after Alexander the Great, the authorities for which stand in much the same relation to him as those of the seventeenth century and onward do to us. Here it must be borne in mind that Josephus has received less justice than he deserves from some modern scholars. Because he is a semi-ecclesiastical writer his testimony is regarded as of less value than that of certain so-called ' classical ' authorities who in some instances lived centuries later than when he wrote his authorities.

Long period of silence in Jewish history.—One cannot but be struck with the fact that from the time of Nehemiah to the persecution of Antiochus Epiphanes, Josephus has virtually nothing to relate. He tells us of the rivalry about the Jewish High Priesthood, and of the visit of Alexander the Great to Jerusalem. Of the first Ptolemy

(Soter, d. 283) he records nothing save that he captured Jerusalem on the Sabbath, and made a settlement of Jews and Samaritans in Egypt. Of the second Ptolemy (Philadelphus, 283–247) we have the long account of the translation of the Septuagint taken from the letter of Aristeas. In the days of Ptolemy III (Euergetes 247–221) Josephus tells about the rise of the Tobiades, who became the tax gatherers of Coele-Syria, and continued their activities down to the death of his successor Ptolemy IV (Philometer) in 205. In 198 the Ptolemies lost Syria, which came under the dominion of Antiochus III. In 190 the Romans defeated Antiochus III at Magnesia, and from that time became the real, if not the nominal, rulers of Asia. Of these important events—the loss of Syria to Egypt, and the coming of the Romans—Josephus has little or nothing to say. When we reach the days of Antiochus Epiphanes and his attempt to coerce the Jews, the history for many years seems to be entirely derived from our First Book of the Maccabees.

Materials for history of Egypt and Syria covered in the 'Antiquities.'—We have not to enquire what the materials for the history of the great days of the Ptolemies and Seleucidae really are, since the Hellenistic period is one of the most important in antiquity ; for, not only did the East and West come into contact and mutually influence one another as they have scarcely ever done before or since, but, in the eventful years which followed the break-up of the empire of Alexander the Great, a bridge was built to unite Greece and Rome. Greek civilisation also pushed its way into what was then the remote East ; and Indian and Persian ideas, especially in the sphere of religion, found their way into the West. Then it was that Rome appeared as the future mistress of the known world, and in the hour of victory yielded to the culture of the vanquished Greeks. The strange cults of Egypt alternately repelled and fascinated the Western world, and the influence of Judaism began to be felt far beyond the bounds of Palestine. The various races of mankind began to mingle ; and common languages, like Greek, Aramaic, and Latin, tended to unite them. As a time of transition the third century B.C. is alike interesting and eventful, and yet we have scarcely any definite information about it, which is the more remarkable because the Hellenistic period was not like those in which our historical knowledge is ordinarily at fault. At Alexandria, at any rate, it was an age of intense mental activity. The first of the Ptolemies was the author of an account of the campaigns of Alexander in which he had himself taken part. Most of his successors, whether they ruled well or ill, took an interest in literature and science, and attracted men of learning to their court. Alexandria was the seat of a species of university, and scholars, critics, men of letters, antiquaries, mathematicians (in our sense of the word), abounded. Nor was this all : the social conditions of Greek life in Hellenistic Egypt are known better to us than they are in any other part of the ancient world. The papyri reveal how men bought and sold, paid their taxes, and wrote to their friends and relatives. The age so far resembled our own that in it, if culture was deficient, education was widespread.[1] This makes us regret the more that in the days of the early Ptolemies there is no contemporary historian. The best authority whose works have survived is Polybius,[2] a very honest and able writer belonging to the next century, having been born about 204 B.C. But even of the memorable expedition and career of Alexander the Great no account by anyone who took part in it has survived, except the narrative of Ptolemy I, which would have perished but for it having been utilised by Arrian, who lived towards the close of the second century A.D. It is the same throughout the period. Of the writers mentioned by Josephus or quoted by modern historians of the period between Alexander the Great and Antiochus Epiphanes, none records contemporary events, and many lived centuries after the Christian era. It is hardly too much to say that to-day we, who have access to the papyri and other documents to which so much modern informa-

---

[1] See W. W. Tarn's *Hellenistic Civilisation.*
[2] See T. R. Glover's chapter on Polybius in the *Cambridge Ancient History.*

tion is due, have more knowledge about Ptolemaic Egypt and Seleucid Syria than Josephus.

Authors mentioned by Josephus.—The first author mentioned by Josephus is Agatharchides of Cnidus, who relates how Ptolemy I took Jerusalem on the Sabbath day owing to the ' superstitious ' fears of the Jews, who refused to violate it by fighting. Agatharchides lived at the court of the later Ptolemies, i.e. after 146 B.C., and was a geographer interested in the natural sciences, especially zoology and botany. He is chiefly known to us from that indefatigable bibliophile Photius, Patriarch of Constantinople (A.D. 858, died c. 891), and he is mentioned by Athenaeus, a great collector of miscellaneous information who lived late in the second century of our era. It is a remarkable example of the unjust contempt for Josephus as an ' ecclesiastical ' writer, that though he is eight centuries earlier than Photius, and lived a century before Athenaeus, the information he gives in the ' Apion ' and ' Antiquities ' is often ignored by the writers of most of the articles in the ' Dictionary of Greek and Roman Biography ' which appeared in 1844. In his allusion to the transference of Palestine from the control of Egypt to that of Syria (203–198 B.C.), Josephus quotes the sixteenth book of the historian Polybius, who was born late in the third century B.C. and died B.C. 128.[1] Only the first five books of this author have survived in their integrity; the rest has been collected from a variety of sources. Diodorus Siculus is constantly referred to as an important authority on the history of Egypt, but strangely enough he is never mentioned by Josephus, although there are allusions to the Jews and Palestine in his writings, and a considerable portion of his works have survived. His contributions to history are said to be a compilation of other writers, and chiefly valuable for that reason. The other authors from whom historians have had to draw their information are all later than Josephus, with the exception of Livy who flourished in the days of Augustus, and, as we have seen, is only once mentioned by our author. The geographer Strabo, who

[1] *Antiq.* xii. 3 (135–136).

wrote in Greek, is freely used ; but, as Dr. Thackeray remarks : ' Beyond these authors it cannot be said that he has used others except at second hand.' [1]

Writers later than Josephus.—Of the later writers those most frequently referred to by modern scholars are Justin, who apparently flourished in the fourth century and made an epitome of an earlier writer, Trogus Pompeianus, a man of Gallic origin who had acted as secretary to Julius Caesar and wrote a universal history in forty-four books ; Plutarch at the end of the first century ; Appian who flourished under Hadrian (A.D. 117–135) ; Dexippus late in the third century, fragments of whom are preserved by Photius ; Orosius, a Christian writer belonging to the early part of the fifth century ; and St. Jerome who commented on the Book of Daniel about the same time. But special reliance is rightly placed on Dio Cassius, a great Roman official at the close of the second century.

Josephus and 1 Maccabees.—Enough, however, has been said to explain the comparative silence of Josephus except for his long extract about the translation of the Scriptures in the days of Ptolemy Philadelphus as told in the letter of Aristeas, which, though obviously fictitious, was probably composed as early as 100 B.C. When we reach the persecution of Antiochus Epiphanes, Josephus follows the Jewish narrative of 1 Maccabees, which he treats in much the same fashion as he does the Scriptural history. This takes us down to the death of Simon the last of the heroic Maccabees in 139 B.C., before which event, however, Josephus ceases to use it. It is remarkable that Josephus evidently knew nothing about the Second Book of the Maccabees, nor of the history of the Jews by Jason of Cyrene of which it purports to be an epitome. In telling the story covered by 1 Maccabees, Josephus at times abandons this source in order to relate incidents not contained in it. Thus, in the third chapter of his Thirteenth Book he introduces an account of how, in the days of Ptolemy Philometer and his wife Cleopatra, Onias, the son of the High Priest Onias, petitioned the

---

[1] *Josephus, the Man and the Historian* (New York, 1929), p. 61.

sovereigns of Egypt for leave to build a temple at Leontopolis, and he gives the letter of Onias, and the reply of Ptolemy and Cleopatra authorising its erection. He then relates a dispute between two representatives of the Samaritans, Sabbaeus and Theodosius, and the Jew Andronicus on the relative merits of the rival témples of Gerizim and Jerusalem in which the Jew is naturally victorious, and the Samaritans pay for their defeat, as had been previously agreed, with their lives.

Nicolaus of Damascus.—When we reach the days of John Hyrcanus we are able to check what Josephus has previously related in his ' War ' by comparing it with the account in the ' Antiquities,' and to note where the two narratives of the same period differ. In the ' War,' no sources are mentioned, and rarely any in the ' Antiquities '; but in the section comprising Books XIV–XVII, Josephus has fuller information and almost certainly follows Nicolaus of Damascus, the partial friend and historian of Herod the Great.

In his preface to the Fourteenth Book Josephus evidently realises that he has come to the most interesting part of his narrative, which demands an opening worthy of the events he is about to describe :

> ' In our previous book we have related the reign of Queen Alexandra, and how she died. Now we will tell of the events which followed and their connection with our story, making it our principal object to omit nothing owing to ignorance or defective memory. For we are relating the history and explanation of facts which because of their remoteness are unknown to most people. And although these demand to be told in an attractive way in well chosen language, so as to please our readers, in order that they may peruse our narrative with enjoyment, we must before all things aim at relating the exact truth for the benefit of those who are ignorant of our subject, and therefore must trust to what we are going to state to them.' [1]

Nicolaus of Damascus was indeed a remarkable man,

[1] *Antiq.* xiv. 1 (1–3).

and is mentioned by Plutarch and many later writers. The work Josephus had before him was his Life of Herod, which is the basis of this part of the 'Antiquities.' It is generally agreed that the most brilliant historical work in the 'Antiquities' is taken from Nicolaus.

Josephus on Christian times.—When he loses the guidance of Nicolaus and approaches the period of greatest interest to the Christian reader, Josephus as an historian becomes frequently unsatisfactory. Like many people to-day, Josephus knew little about what happened just before his own birth. In the Eighteenth Book he has nothing to say about the early procurators ; even Pontius Pilate, as has been noted, is dismissed in a few paragraphs. Then follows some objectionable Roman gossip, an excellent account of the not too reputable youth of Herod Agrippa I, and the attempt of Caligula to place his statue in the Temple. Most of this information Josephus may have obtained from Agrippa II. There is no hint as to whence the historian derived the adventures of the Babylonian Jews Asineus and Anileus, which occupy a large part of this book. Book Nineteen is devoted to Roman history, the murder of Caligula, the accession of Claudius, and the rise, reign, and death of Agrippa I. The Twentieth Book is a summary of the history of the Jews from the death of Agrippa to the outbreak of the 'War' (A.D. 44–66). Two out of eleven chapters are given up to the story of the conversion of Izates of Adiabene. Evidently Josephus was tired of his task and anxious to bring the 'Antiquities' to a close ; or, if he had more to say, he does not wish to say it.

Josephus and official documents.—Josephus is careful to insert into his history several documents bearing on Jewish affairs, treaties, rescripts, concessions to his nation by Macedonian kings, Greek cities, and the Roman people. The genuineness of some of these, or, at any rate, their absolute integrity, may be open to suspicion, but they are of importance as showing the extent of the Dispersion and the legal position of the Jews in the Roman world.

Our debt to Josephus.—The debt the world owes to Josephus cannot be overlooked. But for him the bridge between the Old and New Testament, broken as it is, would be almost annihilated, and the life of Christ and His Apostles would have no background. To discover what Judaism actually was in the days of His ministry would have been wellnigh an insoluble problem. The books of the Maccabees would have given us some notion of the national uprising in defence of the Law, but very little idea of its results. Even secular history would have been the poorer had the works of Josephus perished. The Herods would have been mere names. Among other things we should not have known how Caligula died and how Claudius became Emperor, and the events of the Wars of Titus and Vespasian would have been forgotten. We may criticise Josephus but we cannot ignore him.

Josephus as a *raconteur*.—The 'Antiquities' is a compilation, and perhaps inevitably an uneven work, nor is it always easy to say how much is actually due to the author. It is perhaps justifiable to surmise that, as he approached his own time, Josephus, if he fails as an historian, excels as a *raconteur*. His intimacy with Herod Agrippa II, with whom he could claim remote relationship, may have furnished him with material for the very vivid description of how the Emperor Tiberius commanded the arrest of Agrippa I. In the story of the Parthian Jews, Asineus and Anileus, there appear to be signs that Josephus had heard of their adventures by word of mouth. But our author, even as a compiler, cannot be called in modern parlance a 'paste and scissors man.' As we saw in his treatment of biblical sources, his individuality, for both good and ill, appears in everything he touches ; and in this he follows the tradition of Greek historical writing established by Isocrates. Indeed, unless one is permitted to question Josephus' statement that his education was Rabbinic rather than Hellenistic, the 'Antiquities' is a remarkable example of his literary adaptability and versatility. Without doubt he possesses the Oriental gift of brilliant narration, in which imagination plays no small part. Most critics seem agreed that Josephus copied Nicolaus of Damascus in his dramatic account of Herod the Great ; but from what we know of his use of the Bible and 1 Maccabees, we may legitimately assume that in some parts, at least, in this narrative, there may be additions and perhaps improvements by Josephus.

Josephus' lack of patriotism.—Mr. H. G. Wells in his brilliant ' Outline of History ' calls Josephus ' a maddeningly patriotic writer.' An even superficial perusal of his works will reveal that, unless patriotism consist in an interest in the past history, and an admiration for the institutions of one's nation, Josephus was conspicuously lacking in that quality. To a Jew he must always be painful reading. Hardly anything he relates justifies the assumption that the Judaism of Palestine in its death struggle with Rome deserved to succeed. The only good qualities he seems to credit his countrymen with are a readiness to die for the Law, and desperate courage against overwhelming odds in warfare. Even, however, the bravery of the Jews enhances the credit of Vespasian and Titus in subduing them. Of the better side of Judaism, except in the reply to ' Apion,' Josephus has little to say. At any rate, the last part of the ' Antiquities ' is invaluable for the history of an obscure period of the history of Israel ; but for all our gratitude due to Josephus for composing it, it is hard to feel admiration for the man himself.

CHAPTER XVI

Josephus and the New Testament

Did 'Luke' borrow from Josephus?—It is somewhat rashly assumed that, until the books of Josephus appeared, a Christian writer could have had little or no records of the events of his time, and must have owed his information to the Jewish historian. Consequently it is confidently maintained that the Third Gospel and the Acts must be later than the writings of Josephus ; and imaginary scenes have been depicted of Josephus reading his productions at Rome with the Evangelist as an interested auditor.[1] But generally Josephus seems to have been, like other historians, original as far as his personal experience went, but otherwise a most industrious compiler and copyist of earlier works. It is not unreasonable to suppose that others had access to the same books as Josephus has employed. The assumption that ' Luke ' came after Josephus, whom he used as an authority, may be justifiable on other grounds, but it is legitimately open to question if the view is meant wholly to depend on the necessity of the ' War ' and ' Antiquities ' being anterior to the Gospels and Acts. The New Testament is singularly reticent as to contemporary history. But for the mention of Herod the Great, Archelaus, Herod Antipas, and Pontius Pilate, no names of public characters are found in Matthew, Mark or John's Gospels, and very few names of places mentioned by Josephus. In all the Pauline epistles there is no single

[1] See B. H. Streeter, *The Four Gospels* (1925), p. 557. This writer is correct in stating that Luke may have heard Josephus read his works aloud in Rome. But his verdict is : ' I am quite unconvinced that there is dependence of any kind.'

name of any historical personage by which the letters
could be dated.[1] We are thus reduced to the Third Gospel
and Acts as the only documents which bring us in touch
with contemporary history, and are the only subject for
our consideration.

The Enrolment.—The first passage in Josephus in
which he touches on the story as related in the New
Testament, is about the taxing or enrolment. The Gospel
relates that Caesar Augustus decreed that the whole
Empire should be assessed, and that the assessment
was first made when Cyrenius was governor of Syria.
Josephus, on the other hand, says that, when Archelaus
was deposed for his misgovernment as tetrarch of Judaea,
Augustus ordered Cyrenius (Quirinus) to assess his
property,[2] and, as Judaea was now Roman, to make
a general valuation of the country. According to
Josephus, therefore, the taxation was only a local matter,
confined to the province of Judaea ; for nothing is said
by him of Quirinus having included the dominions of
Philip and Antipas in his survey.[3] The governorship,
moreover, of Quirinus occurred about A.D. 6, whereas, if
our Lord was born before the death of Herod, the first
enrolment must have been about 5 B.C. Much ingenuity
has been displayed by scholars in their endeavour to
defend the accuracy of the Gospels in this matter ; but
here it is not necessary to enter the controversy as the
question before us is merely the dependence of Luke

---

[1] ' Aretas the king ' (2 Cor. xi. 32) helps us little, as it was common
to most of the Arabian sovereigns of the time.

[2] Quirinus was sent by Augustus to Syria ' to take account of
people's effects in Syria and to sell the house of Archelaus ' (*Antiq.*
xvii. 13 (355)). In the next chapter, xviii. 1 (2), Coponius is sent, but
Quirinus also came to Judaea. Despite the rather vague statements
of Josephus, I propose hereafter to assume that, by Syria, the dominion
of Archelaus was meant.

[3] Sir William Ramsay, in his *Was Christ Born at Bethlehem ?* argues
that a general assessment like that ascribed by Luke to Quirinus
was quite possible. He quotes the papyri to prove that there were
such enrolments in Egypt. But Egypt was governed not by a proconsul
or a *legatus* but by a *praefectus*. Did Augustus regard Judaea as his
own estate and send his *procurator* Coponius to value and administer
it ?   *Praefectus* and *procurator* were interchangeable titles in some
connections under Augustus for non-senatorial governors of imperial
provinces, like Egypt, Judaea, or the Alpine districts. See Hirschfeldt,
Kaiserliche Verwaltungsbeamten.

upon Josephus, which in this instance is scarcely conceivable.

Rebellion of Judas of Galilee.—In connection with Quirinus and the enrolment is a rebellion by Judas of Galilee, alluded to in Acts in the advice given by Gamaliel to leave the Christians alone :

> ' For before these days rose up Theudas, giving himself out to be somebody ; to whom a number of men, about four hundred, joined themselves : who was slain ; and all, as many as obeyed him, were dispersed and came to nought. After this man rose up Judas of Galilee in the days of the enrolment, and drew away some of the people after him ; he also perished ; and all, even as many as obeyed him, were scattered abroad.' [1]

Nothing can save these words, put into the mouth of Gamaliel, from an obvious anachronism. In the very early days of the Church of Jerusalem the apostles are accused of inciting the people to sedition against the unpopular priests by declaring them responsible for the death of Jesus. The Sadducean party, represented by the High Priest, are all for enforcing the penalty of death. Before pronouncing sentence, a highly respected rabbi named Gamaliel ordered the Apostles to retire while he addressed the Sanhedrin. He advises that the case should be allowed to drop and they are dismissed with a caution and the comparatively mild penalty of a Jewish, as contrasted with the terrible Roman, scourging.

So far the proceedings are in accord with what Josephus consistently tells us in regard to the two great Jewish sects, the Sadducees being generally on the side of severity, and the Pharisees on that of leniency.[2] As for the speech it was delivered in a private session, and the author of Acts, who wrote many years later, may well have recorded what he considers Gamaliel ought to have said rather than his actual words. In this he follows

[1] Acts v. 36 ff. The theory of two Theudases must be mentioned, but the main argument here is that the allusion in Gamaliel's speech is an anachronism.
[2] See *Antiq.* xiii. 10 (294) and xx. 9 (200), alluding to the condemnation of James, the brother of Jesus who was called Christ.

the example of many ancient historians ; and, except that he avoids his occasional prolixity, of Josephus himself.

Theudas.—The examples of the abortive disturbances of Theudas and Judas of Galilee are almost certainly anachronistic ; as, according to Josephus, Theudas caused a fanatical outburst in the days of Cuspius Fadus, the procurator, in A.D. 44–46, at least ten years after the trial of the Apostles. But, as has been acutely observed, these instances are chosen with no little skill. Theudas had pretended to be a miraculous deliverer ; and Judas of Galilee was the founder of a sect which was already giving trouble. Of course ' the days of the taxing ' were long before Theudas, but the sons of Judas of Galilee were executed after his outbreak. The argument put into the mouth of Gamaliel is briefly this. Two other pretenders to a sort of Messiahship were put to death, and their followers came to nothing. Jesus had, in like manner, been executed ; and why should not His few disciples similarly disappear ? [1]

The chapter in Josephus' ' Antiquities ' in which mention is made of Theudas and the sons of Judas is one of those summaries of a period on which the historian had obviously little material to work upon, though the events are near his own lifetime. He has related at some length the story of Izates, King of Adiabene, and his conversion to Judaism, in company with that of his mother Queen Helena. In some seventy lines he then proceeds to record the following :

> ' Fadus became procurator of Judaea ; and in his time a deceiver ($\gamma \acute{o}\eta \varsigma$), named Theudas, persuaded a considerable multitude to follow him across the Jordan—for he declared himself a prophet. He promised, like Joshua, to stay the course of the river that the people might cross on dry land. Fadus sent a troop of cavalry and killed and captured many ; and the head of Theudas was brought to Jerusalem.

[1] Loisy, *Les Actes des Apôtres*, on Acts v. 40. Gamaliel may, of course, be comparing Theudas and Judas, not with Jesus, but with Peter and John.

' The next procurator was Tiberius Alexander, son of the pious alabarch of Alexandria, but an apostate. In his days there was a great scarcity in Judaea, relieved by the liberality of Queen Helena. At the same time James and Simon, the sons of Judas of Galilee, were captured and crucified by order of Tiberius Alexander. Judas of Galilee had withdrawn the people from their allegiance to Rome (τὸν λαὸν ἀπὸ 'Ρωμαίων ἀποστήσαντος) in the days of Quirinus, " as we related above." The King of Chalcis changed the High Priest. Cumanus succeeded Tiberius Alexander. Herod the brother of Agrippa the Great died in the eighth year of Claudius (A.D. 48) and Claudius gave his government to Agrippa II.' [1]

It is quite possible that the compiler of Acts may have composed Gamaliel's speech after reading this unsatisfactorily brief chapter of Josephus ; but surely he might have heard of Theudas and Judas of Galilee and his sons long before Josephus' book appeared. It is worth noting that neither rebellion alluded to in Acts seems to have been of importance. As a matter of fact, every procurator had been constantly engaged suppressing petty insurrections, which were of almost everyday occurrence and so numerous that it would have been tedious to record them. Josephus says nothing of Pilate ' mingling the blood of the Galileans with their sacrifices,' mentioned by Luke,[2] nor of the rebellion of Barabbas, which, if we may trust Mark, was a formidable one,[3] and not unattended by bloodshed.

Was there a rebellion under Judas of Galilee ?—But was the rebellion of Judas of Galilee in itself a serious outbreak ? Here we must consider the statements of Josephus.

---

[1] *Antiq.* xx. 5 (97–102). It would, of course, be quite possible, as has been suggested by Professor Burkitt, to read this summary account and place Theudas before Judas. But is it necessary to assume this carelessness on the part of St. Luke ?

[2] Luke xiii. 1.

[3] ' There was among the rebels [μετὰ τῶν στασιαστῶν, a favourite word with Josephus, cf. *War*, ii. 15 (330) *et passim*] who had committed murder in the insurrection, the so-called Barabbas a prisoner' (Mark xv. 7). In some texts of the parallel passage in Matt. xxvi. he bore the not uncommon name of Jesus.

The chief passage in reference to this Judas is in
' Antiquities,' xviii. 1, where the property of Archelaus
was assessed by order of Augustus, when he was banished
by the emperor for his misgovernment of Judaea.
Archelaus had been given Idumaea, Judaea, the country
of Samaria, and the towns of Strato's Tower (Caesarea),
Sebaste, Joppa, and Jerusalem. This part of Palestine
was subject to the assessment ; but not the dominions
of Archelaus' brothers, Antipas of Galilee and Philip of
Ituraea. Therefore, if there was a rebellion about the
assessment it must have been confined to the Jewish
parts of Archelaus' inheritance ; presumably Judaea and
Idumaea. And though Judas is described as a Gaulonite,
and is elsewhere called ' of Galilee,' his activities seem to
to have been confined to Judaea, as were the rebellions
of his sons. Of this assessment of the domain of Archelaus,
Josephus says that the Jews were horrified at the report
that they were about to be taxed, and were persuaded
by Joazar, the son of Boethus, who was High Priest, to
submit ; and they gave an account of their estates. But
one Judas, a Gaulonite, of a city called Gamala associated
himself with a Pharisee, named Sadduc, and tried to make
the people revolt. In this they failed, but Judas founded
a fourth sect of Judaism, professing the doctrines of the
Pharisees, and in addition he displayed a readiness to
suffer anything sooner than surrender the civil liberty of
Israel.[1] But the principles of this new sect did not
become really dangerous till the very end of the Jewish
state, when the Jews revolted in the days of Gessius
Florus.[2] In the twentieth book of the ' Antiquities '
Josephus says that he has elsewhere related how Judas of
Galilee raised a rebellion against Rome, but his words
may only imply that some of the people were persuaded
to withdraw their allegiance.[3] In the ' War ' Josephus
states much the same. Dr. Thackeray rightly renders
the words ' incited his countrymen to revolt,' as Josephus

---

[1] *Antiq.* xviii. 1 (4 ff.).

[2] *Beginnings of Christianity*, vol. i. ; *War*, vii. 8 (253). The Appendix
with the acute suggestion about the Zealots was the work of my friend
Dr. Lake.

[3] *Antiq.* xviii. 1 (4–10).

at the conclusion of his brief remarks says that Judas was not a warrior but a sophist.[1] At the beginning of the outbreak against Rome, Menahem, the son of Judas the sophist, seized Masada.[2]

The general conclusion to be drawn from what has been said above is that there never was a rebellion of Judas of Galilee, though it is generally assumed that shortly after the birth of the Christ Galilee was distracted by civil war. Josephus never calls Judas of Galilee a λῃστής or a brigand, but a σοφιστής, i.e. a philosopher, or rabbi. He was one of those dangerous persons who use their position as teachers to incite discontent and revolution. Himself probably a rabbi in Jerusalem, known as ' the Galilean,' he preached a dangerous nationalism which led to the rebellion long after his death. In his own days his efforts seem to have been practically abortive, in so far as there was no great rebellion ; but he sowed the seeds of the ruin of his people in their two great wars with the Romans.

There does not, to return to the subject under discussion, appear any reason for supposing that the Acts of the Apostles in this instance need have borrowed from Josephus or that the author or compilers of the book necessarily waited for the appearance of the ' Antiquities ' or even of the ' War.' Everybody must have heard of Judas of Galilee, whose sons were certainly leaders of the revolutionary party, and the little outbreak of Theudas may have been connected with it.

Chronological notice of the Baptist.—We now come to the elaborate chronological note by which the Evangelist dates the beginning of the preaching of John the Baptist.

' Now in the fifteenth year of the reign of Tiberius Caesar, Pontius Pilate being governor of Judaea, and Herod being tetrarch of Galilee, and his brother Philip tetrarch of the region of Ituraea and Trachonitis, and Lysanias tetrarch of Abilene, in the high

---

[1] *War*, ii. 8 (118). There is no reason for identifying this Judas with Judas the son of the brigand Hezekiah (*War*, ii. 4 (56)), who broke into the arsenal of Sepphoris just after the death of Herod.

[2] *War*, vii. 8 (253).

priesthood of Annas and Caiaphas, the word of God came to John the son of Zacharias in the wilderness' (Luke iii. 1–2).

This is a curious geographical description of Palestine, and would appear to be taken from some document which relates the preaching of the Baptist, with the same sort of introduction as we find at the head of some of the prophets of the Old Testament. Amos, for example, is dated ' In the days of Uzziah, King of Judah, and of Jeroboam son of Joash, king of Israel, two years before the earthquake.' The four governments mentioned by Luke are Judaea, including Samaria and Idumaea, Galilee, Ituraea and Trachonitis, and also Abilene, which lay quite outside the territory of Israel. ' Lysanias the tetrarch of Abilene' presents a perfectly insoluble problem if the historical accuracy of Luke has at all costs to be saved.[1]

Josephus and the political divisions of Palestine.— The first subject for enquiry concerns what Josephus relates of these districts.

Pontius Pilate administered the domain which had been assigned by Augustus to Herod's son Archelaus. In the New Testament Pilate is always called as in Luke by the general term ἡγεμών (governor), whereas Josephus more correctly styles him ἐπίτροπος (steward or *procurator*).[2] Herod, never called Antipas in the New Testament, had for his tetrarchy Peraea and Galilee. To Philip were assigned Batanaea, Auranitis and Trachonitis, with a portion of the domain of Zeno ('War,' elsewhere Zenodorus), in the neighbourhood of Caesarea Philippi.[3]

Lysanias of Abilene.—This brings us to Lysanias and Abilene. Lysanias was the son of Ptolemy, son of Mennaeus, and when Palestine was invaded by Pacorus

---

[1] There is evidence for two rulers called Lysanias. But this does not seem to affect my point, which is that Luke iii. 1 is taken by the Evangelist from an account of the preaching of the Baptist, cast in the prophetic form of the Old Testament.

[2] Codex Bezae has ἐπιτροπεύοντος for ἡγεμονεύοντος in Luke iii. 1 as applied to Pilate.

[3] *Antiq.* xvii. 2 (23). According to *Antiq.* xviii. 4 (106), Philip's domain was Gaulonitis and the country of the Batanaeans.

and the Parthians (40 B.C.) espoused the cause of Antigonus the pretender to the Jewish throne.[1] This Lysanias
was later put to death by Antony at the instigation of
Cleopatra. In the enumeration of the grants made to
Herod the Great, Philip, and Agrippa II, Abila of Lysanias
or ' the kingdom of Lysanias ' occurs.[2] It was, therefore,
customary to call the district by the name of Lysanias ;
and the statement Lysanias, tetrarch of Abilene, is a
pardonable error. Neither he nor his kingdom occurs
again in St. Luke's narratives in the Gospels and Acts.

Annas and Caiaphas.—That the statement in the
chronological note could be taken from the extant works
of Josephus is hard to believe. The Lucan and Johannine
writings are in agreement that Annas was intimately
associated with Caiaphas, the High Priest. Mark mentions neither, but Luke couples them twice together ;
and once calls Annas, and not Caiaphas, the High Priest.
John says that Jesus was sent first to Annas and then to
Caiaphas, and calls Annas ' the father-in-law of Caiaphas.'
This evangelist speaks of Caiaphas as High Priest for the
year of the Passion. Matthew speaks of Caiaphas only.[3]

It is hard to imagine that, if the Evangelist had read
Josephus, he would have described Annas and Caiaphas
as joint High Priests. Annas or Ananus was deprived of
the High-Priesthood by Valerius Gratus in A.D. 14.
He was succeeded by Ishmael-ben-Phabi, then came
Annas' son Eleazar, who was followed by Simon, son of
Camithus. Finally, Joseph Caiaphas was appointed under
Gratus, and held office during the procuratorship of Pilate.
Yet Josephus says later that ' the elder Ananus was a
most fortunate man ; for he had five sons, who had all

---

[1] *Antiq.* xiv. 13 (330 ff.).

[2] *War*, ii. 9 (215): Agrippa I is given ' another kingdom ' called
' of Lysanias.' *War*, ii. 12 (247): Agrippa II receives ' the Kingdom
of Lysanias.' For Herod the Great, see *War*, i. 20 (400) ; see also
Antiq. xviii. 6 (237) and xx. 7 (138). An inscription of another
Lysanias of Abila about A.D. 14 has been found. See Easton, *St. Luke*
(1926).

[3] Luke iii. 2. John xi. 49 ; xviii. 13, 14, 24, 28. Matt. xxvi. 3, 57.
In Acts iv. 6 ' Annas the high priest.' In Acts v. 17 Blass suggests
' Annas ' for the participle. See Foakes Jackson and Lake, *Beginnings
of Christianity*, vol. iii. (J. H. Ropes), p. cviii, on the Perpignan MS.
Ropes says that the reading ἀναστάς for *Ἄννας is ' clearly primitive, but
wrong.'

performed the office of high priest to God, and he himself
had enjoyed that dignity a long time formerly. . . .'[1]
The usual explanation of the association of Annas and
Caiaphas, that Annas was *de jure* High Priest, would
not assist the theory that Luke and John had read
Josephus.

Herod the tetrarch and the death of the Baptist.—
' Herod the tetrarch ' is only mentioned by Matthew and
Mark in connection with the death of the Baptist ; but
Luke has allusions to him and his household.   It is quite
obvious that the story of the feast, the dancing of Herodias
and the beheading of John is not derived from Josephus.
But Luke, though markedly interested in the Baptist,
omits entirely the narrative in the two first Gospels,
giving at the same time a fuller account of John's prophetic address and advice to the people.   All he says
afterwards is as follows :

> ' But Herod the tetrarch, being reproved by him
> for Herodias his brother Philip's wife, and for all the
> evil things which Herod had done, added yet this
> above all that he shut up John in prison.' [2]

That Herod put John to death is naturally known to
Luke.

> ' Now Herod the tetrarch heard of all that was
> done (by Jesus) : and he was much perplexed
> (ἠπόρει), because it was said by some, that John
> was risen from the dead . . . and Herod said, John
> I beheaded : but who is this of whom I hear such
> things ?   And he sought to see him.' [3]

Josephus says nothing about the death of the Baptist
in the ' War ' ; but in the ' Antiquities ' he connects it
with the war with Aretas, king of Arabia, which seems to
be his reason for introducing the subject.[4]   The famous
passage informs us :

---

[1] *Antiq.* xviii. 2 (35) ; *Antiq.* xx. 9 (198).   [2] Luke iii. 19–20.
[3] Luke ix. 7 and 9 ; *cf.* xxiii. 8.   The same word ἠπόρει is used in
a different connection to describe the condition of Herod's mind in
regard to the Baptist.   Mark vi. 20 (πολλὰ ἠπόρει not πολλὰ ἐποίει).
[4] The cause of the wars was Herod's treatment of the daughter of
Aretas, but there was an ancient feud between the Herods and the
family of Aretas (*War*, i. 29 (574) ; ii. 5 (68)).

'But to some of the Jews it appeared that Herod's army was destroyed, and that he received a just penalty for his treatment of John called " the Baptist." For Herod killed him, though he was a good man and used to exhort the Jews to display justice to one another and piety towards God, and to unite (συνιέναι) in baptism. For this washing appeared to be acceptable to God, not if used with a view of obtaining pardon for sins ; but to purify the body, if the soul were already cleansed by righteousness. And when the rest of the people were assembling (for they were greatly pleased to hear John), Herod was afraid that his persuasive eloquence might lead people to revolt, as they seemed to do whatever he advised. And therefore Herod considered it best to take time by the forelock and put John to death, before he could cause a revolution which might be regretted when it was too late. So John was sent by the suspicious Herod to Machaerus, the castle I mentioned before, and there killed. Now the Jews thought that Herod had provoked God to punish him by the destruction of his army for the death of John.' [1]

There appear, therefore, to have been several versions of the death of John, two, or perhaps three, of which have survived. The first is that of Mark abbreviated by Matthew.

The Baptist is imprisoned because he has told Herod that his marriage with Herodias, his brother Philip's wife, was contrary to the Law. Herodias resolves to kill John, who nevertheless obtains an influence over Herod, owing to frequent interviews in which Herod is at a loss to decide what it is best for him to do (πολλὰ ἠπόρει), i.e. whether or not to put away Herodias. At a birthday dinner Herodias' daughter dances, and pleases Herod. Instigated by her mother, she asks the head of John. Herod is grieved at her request ; nevertheless he sends his executioner and beheads John. The scene of the

---

[1] *Antiq.* xviii. 5 (166 ff.). A paraphrase rather than a translation. Dr. Thackeray says that βαπτισμῷ συνιέναι is only an affectation of a scribe employed by Josephus for ' to be baptized.' This scribe was an affected imitator of the style of Thucydides.

imprisonment is evidently Galilee, and Herod is represented as feasting in the palace or castle where John was.
The only obvious historic blunder in this account is that
Mark calls Herod a king.[1] Luke's account is in some
respects more like that of Josephus. Certainly there is
an agreement between the two writers as to the character
of Herod Antipas, whom Jesus calls ' a fox.'[2] Josephus
regards the motive for John's execution, which he does
not connect with the affair of Herodias, as a precautionary
measure. Luke represents Herod fearing the influence
of Jesus, as of a ' John risen from the dead.' At one time
he wishes to kill Him, at another to see Him ; and Herod
was evidently not desirous, when the opportunity occurred,
to be responsible for the death of Jesus. His long tenure
of his tetrarchy, and the regard of Tiberius for him, prove
that Antipas was considered what we should now term
a *safe* man. But this agreement as to Herod's character
does not necessitate dependence of one writer upon the
other. Further, it may be urged that Josephus does
relate a story of a Herod being rebuked for marrying his
brother's widow. He tells earlier how Archelaus married
Glaphyra, the wife of his brother Alexander.[3] It might
also be maintained that Josephus knew the Gospel view
that the baptism of John was for remission of sin ; and
that he tried to refute this. Luke seems also to have had
some information about Herod the tetrarch which cannot
be derived from Josephus. Joanna, the wife of Chuza,
Herod's steward, was one of the women who ministered
to the Lord ;[4] and Manaen or Menahem, foster brother
of Herod the tetrarch, was one of the five Christian
prophets at Antioch.[5] The mention of these persons may

---

[1] But it is quite possible that Herod was called ' King Herod ' in the
popular language of Galilee. It is certain from Josephus that Antipas
coveted the royal title and was ultimately ruined by seeking to obtain it.

[2] Luke xiii. 31 ; xxiii. 7 ff. The fact that Herod believed that John
the Baptist might have risen from the dead shows that the resurrection
of a great prophet was not at the time unthinkable.

[3] *Antiq.* xvii. 13 (339 ff.).

[4] Luke viii. 3 ; xxiv. 10. Josephus tells us of two stewards of
Herod Agrippa. One was Thaumastus, who had given Agrippa water
to drink when Tiberius had put him in bonds, and was rewarded later
(*Antiq.* xviii. 6 (193)). Another was Ptolemy, whose wife was robbed
by brigands (*Vita* (128)). [5] Acts xiii. 1.

explain the anxiety of Herod to see Jesus, as has been indicated above in Chapter VIII.

Herod Agrippa I.—Herod Agrippa I, the ' Herod the king ' of Acts, occupies much space in the ' Antiquities,' and in Acts appears as the first royal persecutor of the Christian Church. By Josephus he is said to have been in the days of his prosperity a most devout observer of the Law, and a strenuous upholder of the religion of his people. The words of Acts, ' When he saw it pleased the Jews,' might be taken as the motto of his brief reign. His death is told at some length in both Josephus and Acts and there is a certain similarity in the broad outlines of the story.

> Josephus says : ' Herod Agrippa came to Caesarea, and exhibited shows in honour of Caesar's (Claudius) birthday. On the second day he put on a garment made wholly of silver, and came into the theatre early in the morning. As the sun shone upon the king's garment it made him look so resplendent that his flatterers cried " Be thou merciful to us ; for although we have hitherto reverenced thee only as man, yet we shall henceforth own thee as superior to mortal nature." He did not rebuke this flattery ; and seeing an owl perched on a rope he regarded it as an omen of death. He was seized with violent pains and exclaimed " I, whom you call a god am commanded presently to depart this life." Five days later he expired in great agony.' [1]

When we remember that Herod Agrippa was the one Herod, perhaps the one Asmonaean also, who was really beloved by the entire Jewish people, and that under him the nation had enjoyed a brief spell of liberty and prosperity, it did not need the appearance of Josephus' ' Antiquities ' to make an evangelist aware of the fact of his sudden seizure and death. That the famous Jewish King who had slain one of the close companions of Jesus, and had intended to kill His chief apostle, should be stricken down in the midst of his glory was not likely

---

[1] *Antiq.* xix. 8 (343 ff.).

to be overlooked. In language more Hebraic and in accordance with the literary tradition of the Old Testament, Luke, or his source, informs us that Herod had quarrelled with Tyre and Sidon, whose inhabitants, as in the days of Solomon, looked for their supply of wheat to the fertile lands of Galilee.[1] On the occasion of a reconciliation, due to Blastus the royal chamberlain, Herod addressed the delegates of the two cities. He had arrayed himself in royal apparel, and his flatterers shouted when he began to speak, ' 'Tis a god's voice, not a man's.' For accepting such adulation unreproved an angel smote him and he died. Curiously enough the additional information that the assembly was occasioned by the composure of a dispute with the people on the seacoast, and that Caesarea was the place chosen to confirm the treaty, supplements the information, given elsewhere, both by Josephus and Philo, that Agrippa was exceedingly unpopular with the Greeks of both Syria and Egypt. Yet so determined are the scholars of to-day to make Luke dependent upon Josephus that the very ' royal robe ' in which Herod is made to appear in Acts has to be substituted for the robe of silver of the ' Antiquities.' [2]

The Egyptian and the *sicarii*.—There is one passage in Acts which at first appears a reminiscence of Josephus. When St. Paul was rescued from the furious mob in the Temple courts, he asked the chief captain for permission to address the people. The reply was :

> ' Dost thou know Greek ? Art thou not then that Egyptian, which before these days stirred up to sedition and led out into the wilderness the four thousand men of the Assassins (*sicarii*) ? ' [3]

In the ' War ' Josephus says that an Egyptian false prophet got together thirty thousand deluded men and led them from the wilderness to the Mount of Olives,

---

[1] 1 Kings v. 9–11.

[2] Loisy in his *Actes*, on Herod's royal robes says : ' En costume royal—remarque banale—mais qui accuse plutôt une dependance de Josephe (*Antiq.* xix. 8 (2)), ou le costume d'Agrippa provoque les flatteries impies. . . .' But on a state occasion Agrippa would dress as a king.

[3] Acts xxi. 37–38.

from whence he threatened to break into Jerusalem. However, Felix, aided by the inhabitants, prepared to resist. A battle was fought, and many were slain ; but the Egyptian managed to escape. The story in the ' Antiquities ' is virtually the same, only the killed and captured do not seem sufficient for the defeat of the 30,000 men in the account in the ' War.' [1]

Acts does not seem to owe information to Josephus.—A plausible case could be made out for the Acts here being dependent on Josephus. It would be very natural for the chief captain to suppose that the infuriated mob had captured the Egyptian who had caused such trouble, and was presumably being eagerly sought. But one instance of this description is not sufficient to prove that the author of the Acts drew upon the historian. Standing as it does by itself the remark about the revolt of the Egyptian might be used as evidence in favour of Josephus having derived his information from Acts.[2]

It is not necessary to assume that the writer of Acts knew the long histories of Josephus because he represents Agrippa II being accompanied by Berenice, or Porcius Festus being the successor of Felix. It is, however, worth noticing that Luke says that Felix sent for Paul, and he allowed the Apostle to address him and his wife Drusilla, ' who was a Jewess.' Josephus relates that Drusilla, the sister of Agrippa II and Berenice, had married Aziz, king of Emesa. She was very beautiful and Felix desired her as his wife. He used as an intermediary a Jewish sorcerer (*Magus*) of Cyprus called Simon, who persuaded Drusilla to leave her husband for Felix.[3] It may be said in conclusion that the correspondences between Josephus and the last chapters of Acts is due to the fact that both writers were actually in Judaea during the procuratorship of Felix.

On the whole it is difficult to see what the New

---

[1] *War*, ii. 13 (261 ff.) ; *Antiq*. xx. 8 (169 ff.).

[2] The use of the word *sicarii* in Acts shows a correspondence between Josephus and the New Testament. The arrest of St. Paul at Jerusalem took place when Felix was procurator ; and Josephus declares that in the time of Felix the *sicarii* began their baneful practices.

[3] *Antiq*. xx. 7 (141 ff.).

Testament owes to Josephus as an historian unless we
assume that, as in our own day, he was then the only
source of information ; and also that a man like the
author of the Third Gospel and Acts was ignorant of all
that was going on in the world outside. Whoever wrote the
' Travel Diary ' or ' We sections ' had visited Jerusalem,
spent some time in Palestine and shared in the Roman
captivity of Paul, whose companion he was on the voyage.
He must, therefore, have had as good opportunity as
Josephus himself of knowing about Felix and Festus,
Herod Agrippa II, Berenice, and Drusilla, or for that
matter such events as the census in the days of Quirinus or
the various rebellions in Judaea. The author of the Lucan
documents may have made mistakes, as when he speaks of
Lysanias as a tetrarch when Christ began his ministry, or
places Theudas before Judas of Galilee. But he never
committed a blunder comparable to that of Tacitus, who
makes out that the procurator Felix married Drusilla, the
granddaughter of Antony and Cleopatra, the more so that
the Roman historian makes this statement in order to
asperse the memory of the Emperor Claudius.[1] Luke's
mistake about Lysanias, if he consulted Josephus, would
have implied that the evangelist had turned over many
pages of his authority to obtain the information he had
misunderstood.

[1] *Hist.* v. 9.   ' Ut eiusdem Antonii Felix progener Claudius nepos
esset.' The great historian evidently knew very little about Felix,
except that he was the brother of Pallas, and therefore was capable of
any misdoing. The orator Tertullus in Acts may have given a juster
estimate of his work as a procurator (Acts xxiv. 2). Felix, according
to Suetonius (*Claudius*, xxviii.) married three queens. Two of them
were named Drusilla, daughters of Herod Agrippa and of Juba II of
Mauretania respectively. The third is unknown.

APPENDICES

APPENDIX A

The High Priesthood

IN any description of the polity of Israel the highest importance would naturally be assigned to the chief minister of the religion, who was known as the High Priest. Great as the Lawgiver was, his brother Aaron was recognised as head of the family, if not of the whole tribe of Levi ; for God, when He entrusted Moses with the commission to deliver Israel, gave as an earnest of success that Aaron, his brother, would come forth to greet him, and would be his spokesman to the people (Ex. iv. 14-16). The Tabernacle was entrusted to the care of Aaron, and the conduct of the worship was to become hereditary in his family, and despite the leadership of Moses in the wilderness, and the fact that God spoke face to face with him, Aaron and his sons represented the religion of Israel as a nation, and the descendants of Moses soon sank into obscurity. In theory, at least, there was always a High Priest, who was the head of the house of Aaron and the official head of the national worship, presiding at the one and only sanctuary allowed by the law of Moses. He was supposed to be set apart from the rest of the people. The garments in which he officiated were regal. His sanctity was protected by rigorous laws. At his death even murderers were set free from the cities of refuge, where alone they could have resided. He was the authorised medium by whom God could be approached, and he alone could enter into the Most Holy Place. In fact, the proper worship of the God of Israel was inseparably bound up with his person.

It may, however, be safely assumed that the sort of worship contemplated in the above sketch of the religion of the chosen people was unheard of even in Jerusalem before the return from the Captivity, and that, therefore, a High-Priestly office such as Aaron's probably never existed. It was only during

perhaps the late Persian period that the leader of the priests
of the Temple began to be regarded as the head of the nation,
and even then the dignity did not pass from father to son.
So far from being automatic, the succession was usually
disputed by two brothers, who bid for the support of the
temporal ruler, whether Persian or Macedonian. Thus, in
the days of the last kings of Persia, Johanan and Jesus, two
brothers, strove for the dignity, and Jesus was murdered.
Just before the visit of Alexander the Great to Jerusalem,
332 B.C., Jaddua and his brother Manasseh were rivals, and
their dispute is said to have caused the Samaritan schism.
In the ensuing period the brother, or even the uncle—sometimes the son—succeeds his predecessor, and when we come
to the evil days of Antiochus Epiphanes the highest bidder
is temporarily awarded the right to officiate. It is remarkable how frequently the chiefs of the priesthood, like the great
Rabbis, are mentioned in pairs. Aaron's sons, Nadab and
Abihu, were succeeded by their brothers, Eleazar and Ithamar.
Eli's sons were Hophni and Phinehas ; David's priests were
Zadok and Abiathar ; Seraiah and Zephaniah are mentioned
together in the days of Jeremiah. In later days we have
Jason and Menelaus, Hyrcanus and Aristobulus, and so on to
the Annas and Caiaphas of Luke.

There was only one duty which the High Priest alone could
perform, that of officiating on the Day of Atonement. That
even this could be done by deputy is abundantly evident
from Josephus, and is also mentioned in the Rabbinic treatise
Yoma (" the Day," *i.e.* of Atonement). It really comes to
this, that any priest might act as High Priest on that sacred
day, and was not regarded as an interloper, if only he was
ritually pure and wore the holy garments.

Of the twenty-eight High Priests from the days of Herod
the Great, say 32 B.C., six were appointed by Herod himself,
two by his son Archelaus, one by Quirinus, the *legatus* of
Syria, four by the procurator Gratus, two by Vitellius the
legatus of Syria, three by Agrippa I (king A.D. 38–44), two by
Herod, King of Chalcis, six by Agrippa II, and one was elected
irregularly by lot.

Although Pontius Pilate, who was procurator for ten years,
kept Caiaphas in office all the time, the average tenure of the
so-called High Priesthood was a little more than three years ;
and one may suspect that in the first century of our era the
High Priesthood meant little more than the right to wear the
vestments and to officiate on the Day of Atonement.

The Temple at Jerusalem was in the hands of a few power-ful families ; and, for the last century at least of its existence, some member of this aristocracy was recognised by the govern-ment as the official head. Even the title 'high priest' (ἀρχιερεύς) was applied to men who never held the office as belonging to a leading priestly family. A distinction may be drawn between Ananias, the cruel and violent High Priest who condemned James the brother of Jesus, and the blame-less 'high priest' Ananus, whose murder brought God's wrath on Jerusalem. It is quite probable that he and Jesus, the son of Gamalas, whom Josephus describes as the most eminent of the 'high priests,'[1] were merely leading members of the Temple priesthood. After all, the exorcists at Ephesus are described in Acts xix. 14 as sons of a Jewish 'high priest,' Sceva.

The High Priests from Herod the Great

High Priest.	Reference in Josephus.	Appointed by
Ananelus	*Antiq.* xv. 2	Herod the Great.
Aristobulus	*Antiq.* xv. 3	,, ,,
Ananelus (again)	*Antiq.* xv. 3	,, ,,
Jesus, son of Fabi	*Antiq.* xv. 9	,, ,,
Simon Boethus	*Antiq.* xv. 9	,, ,,
Matthias, son of Theophilus [2]	*Antiq.* xvii. 6	,, ,,
Joazar Boethus	*Antiq.* xvii. 6	,, ,,
Eleazar Boethus	*Antiq.* xvii. 13	Archelaus.
Jesus, son of Sie	*Antiq.* xvii. 13	,,
Joazar (again)	*Antiq.* xviii. 2	the people.
Ananus, son of Seth [3]	*Antiq.* xviii. 2	Quirinus.
Ishmael, son of Fabi	*Antiq.* xviii. 2	Gratus.
Eleazar, son of Ananus	*Antiq.* xviii. 2	,,
Simon, son of Camithus	*Antiq.* xviii. 2	,,
Caiaphas	*Antiq.* xviii. 2	,,
Jonathan, son of Ananus	*Antiq.* xviii. 4	Vitellius.
Theophilus, son of Ananus	*Antiq.* xviii. 5	,,
Simon Boethus (Cantheras)	*Antiq.* xix. 6	Agrippa I.
Matthias, son of Ananus	*Antiq.* xix. 6	,,
Elioneus, son of Cantheras	*Antiq.* xix. 8	,,
Joseph, son of Camus	*Antiq.* xx. 1	Herod of Chalcis.
Ananias, son of Nebedaeus	*Antiq.* xx. 5	,, ,,
Jonathan	*Antiq.* xx. 8	,, ,,

[1] οἱ δοκιμώτατοι τῶν ἀρχιερέων, *War*, iv. 3 (160 *et passim*). The murder of Ananus, as asserted by Josephus, was the cause of the beginning of the fall of Jerusalem, *War*, iv. 5 (319). The distinction between a 'high priest' and 'chief priest' cannot be pressed, for both are in Greek called ἀρχιερεύς.

[2] His brother Joseph acted as High Priest on the Day of Atonement because Matthias was ceremonially impure.

[3] ? The Annas of the Gospels.

High Priest.	Reference in Josephus.	Appointed by
Ishmael, son of Fabi [1]	*Antiq.* xx. 8	Agrippa II.
Joseph, son of Simon	*Antiq.* xx. 8	,,
Ananus, son of Ananus	*Antiq.* xx. 9	,,
Jesus, son of Damnaeus	*Antiq.* xx. 9	,,
Jesus, son of Gamaliel	*Antiq.* xx. 9	,,
Matthias, son of Theophilus	*Antiq.* xx. 9	,,
Phannias,[2] son of Samuel	*War*, iv. 3	by lot.

[1] Killed at the instigation of Felix. Appointment not mentioned. The High Priests Jonathan and Ananias were sent by Felix to Rome, *War*, ii. 12 (243).

[2] Phannias is the last High Priest mentioned.

APPENDIX B

The Mention of Christ and the Slavonic Additions

The disputed passage in ' Antiq.' xviii. about Jesus Christ, known as the *testimonium Flavianum*, has been a fruitful cause of difference among scholars. At one time there seemed unanimous agreement that it was spurious ; now opinion seems to favour its retention, allowing, however, for possible Christian interpolations. It is one of those open questions which can never be settled. All that we can be certain of is that Origen (*d.* A.D. 252) appears to be ignorant of the fact that Josephus had called Jesus ' the Christ,' and that Eusebius, who wrote about a century later, twice quotes the disputed passage in full.[1] Whether it was inserted in the interval is a matter for conjecture. That it is in every manuscript of Josephus is no argument in its favour, because none are earlier than the eleventh century, and all are of Christian origin.

The opinion of the present writer has been given as to the meaning Josephus attached to the word *Christ*, as well as that author's disregard of all religious movements except those of the three leading sects. His view is that Josephus would naturally be expected to say nothing about Jesus ; but that he might well have inserted the *testimonium* in the awkward form in which it appears in the ' Antiquities ' to oblige some friend or patron who was interested in Christianity.[2] At the same time he desires to call attention to Dr. Thackeray's interesting discussion of the language employed to be found in his Hilda Stich Stroock Lecture No. VI, entitled ' Josephus and

[1] Origen, *Contra Celsum*, i. 47, ii. 13 ; *Commentary on Matt.* xiii. 55 (book x. 17), Eusebius, *H.E.*, i. 11 *ad fin.* ; *Dem. Evang.* (S.P.C.K. Transl. p. 143).

[2] Burkitt, *Theol. Tijdschrift*, Leiden, 1913. Whiston's first dissertation, appended to his translation of Josephus, deserves careful attention. One section (III) of the *Observations from the foregoing Evidence and Citations* may be quoted : ' The famous clause in this testimony of Josephus, *this was Christ* or *the Christ* . . . but that Jesus was distinguished by all others of that name, of which there were not a few as mentioned by Josephus, &c.'

Christianity' (New York: Jewish Institute of Religion Press, 1929).

There remain the passages in the Slavonic version of the 'War' relating to Jesus and John the Baptist. These are quoted in German by Berendts–Gass in their books on 'The Jewish War, according to the Slavonic translation' (two vols., Dorpat, 1924–27). As the subject is being treated of by Dr. Eisler with scholarly ingenuity, it seems sufficient to quote these extracts as they appear in Dr. Thackeray's vol. iii. of Loeb edition of Josephus, in the Appendix entitled ' The Principal Additional Passages in the Slavonic Version.' The first two, numbered 9 and 11, refer to the Baptist. No. 12 is about Jesus.

(9) *John the Forerunner*

Now at that time there walked among the Jews a man in wondrous garb, for he had put animals' hair upon his body wherever it was not covered by his (own) hair ; and in countenance he was like a savage. He came to the Jews and summoned them to freedom, saying : ' God hath sent me to show you the way of the Law, whereby ye may free yourselves from many masters ; and there shall be no mortal ruling over you, but only the Highest, who hath sent me.' And when the people heard that, they were glad ; (and there went after him all Judaea and the (region) around Jerusalem). And he did nothing else to them, save that he dipped them into the stream of the Jordan and let (them) go, admonishing them to desist from evil works ; (for) so would they be given a king who would set them free and subject all (the) insubordinate, but he himself would be subject to no one—(he) of whom we speak. Some mocked, but others put faith (in him).

And when he was brought to Archelaus and the doctors of the Law had assembled, they asked him who he was and where he had been until then. And he answered and spake : ' I am a man and hither the spirit of God hath called me, and I live on cane and roots and fruits of the tree.' But when they threatened to torture him if he did not desist from these words and deeds, he spake nevertheless : ' It is meet rather for *you* to desist from your shameful works and to submit to the Lord your God.'

And Simon, of Essene extraction, a scribe, arose in wrath and spake : ' We read the divine books every day ; but thou, but now come forth from the wood like a wild beast, dost thou dare to teach us and to seduce the multitudes with thy cursed speeches ? ' And he rushed (upon him) to rend his body. But he spake in reproach to them : ' I will not disclose to you the secret that is among you, because ye desired it not. Therefore has unspeakable misfortune come upon you and through your own doing.' And after he had thus spoken, he went forth to the other side of the Jordan ; and since no man durst hinder him, he did what (he had done) before.

(11) ' The Wild Man ' (John), Herod Philip's Dream and the Second Marriage of Herodias

Philip, during his government, saw a dream, to wit that an eagle plucked out both his eyes ; and he called all his wise men together. When some explained the dream in this manner and others in that, there came to him suddenly, without being called, that man of whom we have previously written, that he went about in animals' hair and cleansed the people in the waters of the Jordan. And he spake : ' Hear the word of the Lord— the dream that thou hast seen. The eagle is thy venality, for that bird is violent and rapacious. And this sin will take away thine eyes, which are thy dominion and thy wife.' And when he had thus spoken, Philip expired before evening, and his dominion was given to Agrippa.

And his wife (Herodias) was taken by Herod his brother. Because of her all law-abiding people abhorred him, but durst not accuse (him) to his face. But only this man, whom we called a savage, came to him in wrath and spake : ' Forasmuch as thou hast taken thy brother's wife, thou transgressor of the law, even as thy brother has died a merciless death, so wilt thou too be cut off by the heavenly sickle. For the divine decree will not be silenced, but will destroy thee through evil afflictions in other lands ; because thou dost not raise up seed unto thy brother, but gratifiest (thy) fleshly lusts and committest adultery, seeing that he has left four children.' But Herod, when he had heard (that), was wroth and commanded that they should beat him and drive him out. But he incessantly accused Herod, wherever he found him, until he (Herod) grew furious and gave orders to slay him.

Now this nature was marvellous and his ways not human. For even as a fleshless spirit, so he lived. His mouth knew no bread, nor even at the passover feast did he taste of unleavened bread, saying : ' In remembrance of God, who redeemed the people from bondage, is (this) given to eat, and for the flight (only) since the journey was in haste.' But wine and strong drink he would not so much as allow to be brought nigh him, and every beast he abhorred (for food) ; and every injustice he exposed ; and fruits of the trees served him for (his) needs.'

(12) *The Ministry, Trial and Crucifixion of ' The Wonder Worker.'*

At that time there appeared a man, if it is permissible to call him a man. His nature (and form) were human, but his appearance (was something) more than (that) of a man ; (notwithstanding his works were divine). He worked miracles wonderful and mighty. (Therefore it is impossible for me to call him a man) ; but again, if I look at the nature which he shared with all, I will not call him an angel. And everything whatsoever he wrought through an invisible power, he wrought by word and command. Some said of him, ' Our first lawgiver is risen from the dead and hath performed many healings and arts,' while others thought he was sent from God. Howbeit in many things he disobeyed the law and kept not the Sabbath according to (our) fathers' customs. Yet, on the other hand, he did nothing shameful ; nor (did he do anything) with aid of hands, but by word alone did he provide everything.

And many of the multitude followed after him and hearkened to his teaching ; and many souls were in commotion, thinking that thereby the Jewish tribes might free themselves from Roman hands. Now it was his custom in general to sojourn over against the city upon the Mount of Olives, and there, too, he bestowed his healings upon the people.

And there assembled unto him of ministers one hundred and fifty, and a multitude of the people. Now when they saw his power, that he accomplished whatsoever he would by (a) word, and when they had made known to him their will, that he should enter into the city and cut down the Roman troops and Pilate and rule over us, he disdained us not.

And when thereafter knowledge of it came to the Jewish leaders, they assembled together with the High Priest and spake : ' We are powerless and (too) weak to withstand the Romans. Seeing, moreover, that the bow is bent, we will go and communicate to Pilate what we have heard, and we shall be clear of trouble, lest he hear (it) from others, and we be robbed of our substance and ourselves slaughtered and our children scattered.' And they went and communicated (it) to Pilate. And he sent and had many of the multitude slain. And he had that wonder-worker brought up, and after instituting an

inquiry concerning him, he pronounced judgement:
' He is (a benefactor, not) a malefactor, (nor) a rebel,
(nor) covetous of kingship.' (And he let him go ; for he
had healed his dying wife.)

And he went to his wonted place and did his wonted
works. And when more people again assembled round
him, he glorified himself through his actions more than
all. The teachers of the Law were overcome with envy,
and gave thirty talents to Pilate, in order that he should
put him to death. And he took (it) and gave them
liberty to execute their will themselves. And they laid
hands on him and crucified him contrary to the law of
(their) fathers.

APPENDIX C

THE PTOLEMIES AND THE SELEUCIDAE IN JOSEPHUS

WHEN we realise that there were no less than sixteen Macedonian kings of Egypt and that for more than a century Judaea was ruled from Alexandria, it is remarkable how little Josephus has to relate concerning these monarchs. As all took the name of Ptolemy, these are better differentiated by the titles they assumed than by numerals, especially as there is a different reckoning as to their number.

After the death of Alexander the Great, Ptolemy, one of his generals, secured Egypt, which he held as satrap or king from 322 to 285 B.C. All Josephus tells us is that this Ptolemy I (Soter) took Jerusalem on the Sabbath, and settled many Jews in Egypt ('Antiq.' xii. 1, 'Apion,' i. 22 (183), 'Apion,' ii. 4 (37 and 44)).

Of the second Ptolemy (Philadelphus), 285–247 B.C., we have no information save the long letter of Aristeas about the translation of the Law by the LXX ('Antiq.' xii. 2; 'Apion,' ii. 4 (45)).

In the days of Ptolemy III (Euergetes I), 247–222 B.C., we read of the refusal of the High Priest Onias to pay tribute, and of the rise of the family of Tobias—Joseph and his son Hyrcanus—who farmed the revenues of Coele-Syria ('Antiq.' xii. 4). This king's consort is called Cleopatra, whereas the first queen of that name was the wife of his successor. In 'Apion,' ii. 5 (48), this king is said to have visited Jerusalem.

Ptolemy IV (Philopator), 222–205 B.C., is mentioned in 'Antiq.' xii. chaps. 3 and 4. According to III Maccabees this Philopator persecuted the Jews.

Ptolemy V (Epiphanes) is mentioned in 'Antiq.' xii. 3 and 4, as having been defeated by Antiochus the Great and thereby losing Syria.

Of Ptolemy VI or VII[1] (Philometor), 181–146 B.C., Josephus has more to tell. His kingdom was invaded by Antiochus

---

[1] This discrepancy is due to the omission of Ptolemies who were proclaimed but instantly put to death.

Epiphanes, and he was made prisoner ('Antiq.' xii. 5). In book xiii. 3, Philometor received the fugitive High Priest Onias, and gave him the temple of Leontopolis. He invaded Palestine in the days of the usurper Alexander Balas ('Antiq.' xiii. 4). Under Philometor two Jews, Onias and Dositheus, are said to have administered Egypt ('Apion,' ii. 5 (49)).

Ptolemy VII or IX took the name of Euergetes, but was popularly known as Physcon, 146–117 B.C. The only thing we find about him in the 'Antiquities' is that he sent the pretender Alexander Zebina to claim the crown of the Seleucidae. In 'Apion,' ii. 5 (55) (here the Latin version only is preserved), the persecution of the Jews and their deliverance as related in III Maccabees is said to have taken place.

Ptolemy VIII or X (Soter), 117–81 B.C., whom Josephus called *Lathyrus*, sent 6000 men to ravage Palestine in the days of the High Priest Hyrcanus ('Antiq.' xiii. 10). In the time of Alexander Jannaeus this king overran Palestine, and there is a story that he ordered a very Massacre of the Innocents in the cities of Judah to terrify the inhabitants. He is mentioned in 'War,' i. 4.

No other Ptolemies are to be found in Josephus till the famous Cleopatra, in the days of Julius Caesar and Mark Antony.

The Seleucidae and Judaea

The rise of the Jewish nation from a position of insignificance to one of predominance in Palestine is, humanly speaking, due to the gradual decay of the Seleucid empire, which may be dated from the Roman victory over Antiochus the Great at Magnesia in 190 B.C. The Republic exacted an enormous indemnity as the price of peace, and Antiochus and his successors were put to every sort of shift to raise the money. The rich temples in their dominions were subject to pillage, and both Antiochus III (the Great) and Antiochus IV (Epiphanes) lost their lives in their attempt to rob the temple at Elymais in Susiana. The attack and spoliation of their temple exasperated the Jews and largely contributed to the revolt of the Maccabees.

According to II Maccabees iii., Heliodorus, the treasurer of Seleucus IV (Nicator), 187–175 B.C., was told by Simon the Benjaminite, the overseer (προστάτης) of the Temple, about the wealth in the treasury; but when he attempted to despoil it, Heliodorus was driven out by a celestial warrior on horse-

back.   The story as related has the appearance of a legend ;
but that some attempt was made to despoil the sanctuary is
not improbable.   How Antiochus IV (Epiphanes) took away
all the gold to be found in the Temple is told in I Macc. i.
20–24.

But the heroism of Judas the Maccabee and his famous
brothers would have availed nothing had the Syrian monarchy
remained united, as the following sketch of the Selucid kings,
their rivals, and those who usurped their crown, will clearly
show.

Antiochus Epiphanes died 164 B.C., leaving his son,
Antiochus V (Eupator), a mere child, under the guardianship
of Lysias.   This boy was put to death about 162 B.C. by his
cousin Demetrius, who had escaped from Rome and seized
the throne at Antioch (I Macc. vii. 1–3).

Demetrius I (Soter), 162–150 B.C., was the son of Seleucus
IV, and grandson of Antiochus the Great.   It is a popular
mistake to suppose that the later Seleucid kings were effemi-
nate Syrians who spent their time in Oriental luxury.   On the
contrary, including Epiphanes, they were brave and skilful
generals, and Demetrius was no exception.   But he had
incurred the enmity of the neighbouring kings and also of
Rome, who supported a supposed son of Epiphanes, known
as Alexander Balas, who arrived in Syria about 152 B.C.   The
two rivals began to bid for the support of the Asmonaeans, and
both recognised Jonathan, the brother of Judas, as High
Priest (I Macc. x. 21).

Alexander Balas (150–146 B.C.) was supported by and
afterwards opposed Ptolemy Philometor.   Both monarchs died
the same year.   Jonathan first helped Alexander against
his rival Demetrius and was rewarded for his services
(I Macc. x. 89).   The High Priest then went over to
Philometer (I Macc. xi.) and Alexander's rival, Demetrius II,
in the hope of getting possession of the *Acra* in Jerusalem.

Demetrius II (146–125 B.C.) had to quell a formidable
revolt in Antioch, and was helped by a contingent of Jews sent
to him by Jonathan.   A pretender to the throne now appeared
in a youthful son of Alexander Balas, known as Antiochus VI,
to whom Jonathan transferred his allegiance.   The new king
was upheld by a general called Diodotus, who murdered the
boy and reigned as Tryphon (142–139 B.C.).   This Tryphon
captured the High Priest Jonathan and put him to death.
Demetrius II in the meantime had attacked the King of
Parthia, and been taken prisoner.   Simon, now the only

surviving brother, had won the favour of Demetrius II, and in 143 B.C. became an independent prince (I Macc. xii. 41).

With Tryphon dead and Demetrius II in captivity, Syria now passed to a brother of Demetrius, Antiochus VII (140–128 B.C.), who had been brought up at Side, and is known as Sidetes. This very able prince soon showed the Jews that the Syrian power when in competent hands was irresistible. He laid siege to Jerusalem ; and having convinced the High Priest, John Hyrcanus, that he must submit, magnanimously left the city uninjured. He then made an expedition to Parthia and was killed in battle.

From the death of Sidetes to the abolition of the Syrian monarchy by Pompey (128–64 B.C.) the Seleucid record is merely one of rival kings and usurpers and a series of murders and intrigues, apparently inevitable in the story of a decaying Oriental dynasty. The Jewish priestly rulers had nothing to hinder their expansion in so disorganised a country as Palestine. Before and after the arrival of Pompey the Jewish princes were themselves engaged in intestine struggles, much resembling on a smaller scale those of the House of Seleucus.

APPENDIX D

Roman Rulers of Syria and Palestine

Of these, Merivale ('The History of the Romans under the Empire' (1866), vol. iv. chap. liv.), remarks: 'The history of the world presents us, perhaps, with no such a succession of able captains and administrators, as the long series of the governors of Syria.' The list given is that of A. W. Zumpt.

Q. Didius, 30–29 B.C.		
M. Messala Covinus, 29–28 B.C.		
M. Tullius Cicero, 28 B.C.	The son of the orator.	None of these are mentioned by Josephus.
A. Terentus Murena, 28–26 B.C.		
C. Sentius Saturninus, 26–23 B.C.		
M. Agrippa, 23–13 B.C.	Appointed, but left the government to his legates.	*Antiq.* xv. 10, *War*, i. 20. Herod the Great was one of Agrippa's legates.
C. Sentius Saturninus 9–6 B.C.	Was consul 19 B.C.	*Antiq.* xvi. 9. Frequently mentioned in *Antiq.* xvi–xvii and in *War*, i. He pronounced sentence on Herod's sons by Mariamne.
P. Quintilius Varus, 6–4 B.C.	Said by Vellius Paterculus to have entered the rich province of Syria as a poor man, and to have left it a poor province as a rich man. He was later utterly defeated by Arminius in Germany.	Varus condemned Antipater, the son of Herod, and after the King's death pacified the country, *Antiq.* xvii. 5, etc., *War*, i and ii.

P. Sulpicius Quirinius, 4–1 B.C.	(Assumed by some to have been twice in Syria.)	No mention of this in Josephus.
M. Lollius, 1 B.C.—A.D. 3		
C. Marcius Censorinus, A.D. 3–4		not mentioned by Josephus.
L. Volusius Saturninus, A.D. 4–6		
P. Sulpicius Quirinius, A.D. 6–11		This governorship is in the time of the deposition of Archelaus and the enrolment of his dominions. *Antiq.* xvii and xviii and *War*, ii.
Q. Caecilius Silvanus, A.D. 11–17		*Antiq.* xviii. 4, in connection with Parthian affairs.
L. Calpurnius Piso, A.D. 17–21	The colleague and enemy of Germanicus	No mention in Josephus.
T. Aelius Lamia, A.D. 21–32	Appointed, but not allowed by Tiberius to visit his province.	Not mentioned by Josephus.
L. Pomponius Flaccus, A.D. 32–35		*Antiq.* xviii. 6. Befriended Agrippa I in his days of poverty.
L. Vitellius A.D. 35–39	Father of the emperor. Tacitus says he was a good provincial administrator.	*Antiq.* xviii. 4. Deposed Pilate. Proclaimed Caligula and restored the high priestly vestments. Negotiated with Parthians.
P. Petronius, A.D. 39–42		Refused at his own risk to place the statue of Caligula in Temple, *Antiq.* xviii. 8, xix. 6 ; *War*, ii. 10.
C. Vibius Marsus, A.D. 42–45		*Antiq.* xix. 6 ff. Checked ambitions of Herod Agrippa I.

C. Cassius Longinus, A.D. 45–50		Satisfies the Jews, who were discontented with the procurator Fadus, *Antiq.* xx. 1.
C. Ummidius Quadratus, A.D. 50–61		Samaritans appealed to Quadratus. The procurator Cumanus was sent to Rome, *Antiq.* xx. 6 ; *War,* ii. 12.
Domitius Corbulo, A.D. 61–63	Nero's famous general	Not in Josephus.
Cestius Gallus, A.D. 63–66		Visits Jerusalem, suffers defeat at Bethhoron, *War,* passim.

APPENDIX E

HELPS TO THE STUDY OF JOSEPHUS

THE Greek manuscripts of Josephus are none of them earlier than the tenth century. The books ' Contra Apionem ' are only preserved in a single MS. supplemented by the Latin version of Cassiodorus (sixth century). There is a Latin version of the ' War,' wrongly attributed to St. Ambrose, but really the work of a converted Jew named Isaac, called, as a Christian, Hilarius or Gaudentius (fourth century). It is known as Hegesippus, a corruption of Josephus or Josippus. A Hebrew paraphrase of this is called Yosippon (see Thackeray, Loeb Library, vol. ii. introduction, pp. xxvii–xxix). The best printed text of Josephus is that of Benedictus Niese, 6 vols., Editio major, Berlin, 1887–89 ; minor, 1888–95.

There are several English translations, the standard one being that of William Whiston (1667–1752), a Cambridge mathematician, remarkable alike for his erudition and his eccentricity. He was deprived of his professorial chair, in which he had succeeded Sir Isaac Newton, for his peculiar views on the Trinity. His translation of Josephus appeared in 1737. Despite its ' cumbrous and crabbed style ' (Traill), it has long been the standard English version. It was revised by A. R. Shillito, 4 vols. (London, 1900–1903). The most useful translation of Josephus is in French : ' Œuvres complètes de Flavius Josephus,' 7 vols. (Paris, 1900–   ), *sous la direction de Théodore Reinach*, the notes to which are invaluable. The ' War,' ' Life,' and ' Contra Apionem ' have already appeared in the Loeb Series, and the volumes containing the ' Antiquities ' are eagerly expected. This translation is not likely to be superseded for many generations, and Dr. St. John Thackeray will soon give the world the important ' Josephus Lexicon,' which is a dictionary as well as a concordance; and is being published under the auspices of the Alexander Kohut Memorial Fund, by Paul Geuther, Paris. Dr. Thackeray has spent ten years in preparing this important work.

The ' War ' and the ' Life ' have been well translated by the Rev. Robert Traill, who lost his life ministering to his flock in Ireland during the famine of 1846–7 ('The Jewish War,' etc., London, 1868). The sketches of places and buildings in Palestine are most instructive.

The histories of the Jews by Milman and Graetz are easily accessible, and Mr. Norman Bentwich's book on Josephus is well worth study. Dr. Klausner in his ' Jesus of Nazareth ' (English translation by Canon Danby, the Macmillan Co., 1925), treats the historical parts of Josephus from the stand-point of a Zionist. Dr. Richard Laqueur gives a new view of Josephus as a writer in his ' Der jüdische Historiker Flavius Josephus ' (Giessen, 1920). Light is thrown on portions of the works of Josephus by :

Juster, J.	' Les Juives dans l'empire romain.'
Neubauer, A.	' La Géographie du Talmud.'
Niese, B.	' Kritik der Beiden Makkerbücher,' (Berlin, 1899).
Reinach, T.	' Textes relatifs au Judaïsme ' (Paris, 1925).
Mommsen	' Provinces of the Roman Empire ' (English translation, 1887).
Madden, F. W.	' Jewish Coins ' (London, 1864).
Willrich	' Juden und Griechen.'
Büchler	' Tobiaden und Oniaden ' (Wien, 1899).

For Chapter XVI, Krenkel, ' Josephus und Lukas' (Leip-zig, 1894), should be consulted. This writer endeavours to show by an immense mass of proof that Luke was indebted to Josephus. I am indebted to my pupil, Professor Fred D. Gealey, of Tokyo, Japan, for an admirable summary of this important, if tedious book.

' The History of the Jewish People in the time of Jesus Christ,' of E. Schürer, Edinburgh, 1890, is a perfect mine of information for the student of Josephus, and for a right understanding of traditional Rabbinic Judaism. Dr. G. F. Moore's ' Judaism ' (Harvard University Press, 1927) is equally indispensable. The reader is recommended to use E. R. Bevan's ' Jerusalem under the High Priests ' (London, 1924), and ' The House of Seleucus ' (London, 1902), as well as his ' Ptolemaic Dynasty ' (1927), an augmentation of the late Dr. Mahaffy's ' Empire of the Ptolemies.'

For the vexed question of Josephus' knowledge of Hebrew and of rabbinical theology one may, with profit, refer to Dr. Salomo Rappaport's ' Agada und Exegese bei Flavius Josephus,' in which he discusses the traditional use of Scripture in the earlier books of the ' Antiquities.' This has been published by the Alexander Kohut Memorial Foundation (Vienna, 1930). Dr. H. St. John Thackeray's ' Josephus, the Man and the Historian ' (Jewish Institute of Religion Press, 1929), is most valuable, especially where he comments on the Greek of Josephus and on his use of versions of Scripture in that language. The historian is very modest about his Greek, and quite the reverse about his acquirements as a Hebraist ; but the writer of this volume is equally suspicious of his modesty and his assumption of knowledge. Dr. Eisler's theories are to be found in his ' ΙΗΣΟΥΣ ΒΑΣΙΛΕΥΣ ' (Part I, Heidelberg, 1928) and elsewhere, and have been answered by Dr. Solomon Zeitlin, who courteously sent me a reprint of his article from the ' Jewish Quarterly Review,' vol. xx., No. i., and by Dr. Joshua Block. Solomon Reinach's ' Orpheus' (translated by Florence Simmons, New York, 1930), is important, especially pp. 238, 253. Dr. Leo Fuchs' ' Die Juden Aegyptens in Ptolemäischer und Römischer Zeitalter ' (Wien, 1924) should also be mentioned.

INDEX

CAESAR, Julius, 127
Caesarea, 133, 182
Caiaphas, App. A
Caligula (Gaius), xii, 151
Capharnaum, 191
Capharsalama, battle at, 107
Captivity, Prince of, 180
Carnaim, 104
Cassius, 127
Catullus, Governor of Cyrene, accuses Josephus, 225
Cendebeus, 115
Cestius Gallus, 5, 187
Chaldaean records, 21
Chaucer, 28
Cherubim, 237
Choerilus of Samos, 24
Christ (alleged mention of), 88, App. B
Christianity and Judaism contrasted, 68
Chuza, 146
Claudius, Emperor, xii, 152
Clearchus, 24
Cleopatra, wife of Euergetes, 96
Coele-Syria, 102
Coponius, 162
Crassus, 172
Cumanus, 166
Cuthaeans, 242
Cyrene, 225

DABARITTA, 10
Damascus, 122
Daniel, 242
David, 238
  tomb of, 115
Dedication of Temple, 103
Deliverance (Messianic), 84
Demetrius Soter, 106, App. C
Demon expelled, 239
Deuteronomy, 61
Diodorus Siculus, 253
Dionysius of Halicarnassus, 247
Dius, 23
Domitia, 18
Domitian, 18
Drusilla, 167

ECCLESIASTICUS, book of, 120
Edomites, 116
Education, Jewish, 31
Egypt, Jews under Ptolemies, 06
Egyptian, the, 272
Egyptian records, 22
Eleasa, battle at, 107
Eleazar and Izates, 82
Eleazar, High Priest, 55
Eleazar the Maccabee, 112
Elephantine, temple at, 58
Eliashib, 48
Elijah, 240
Elisha, 195
Empire (Roman), xiv, 154
Endor, witch of, 238
Epaphroditus, 18
Ephron, 104
Essenes, 75 *et passim*
Eusebius, church historian, 88
Eutychus, 150
Exodus, book of, 60
Ezekiel, 40
Ezra, 48

FADUS, 165
Felix, 166
Festus, 168
Flaccus Avilius, 151
Flaccus *legatus*, 149
Formalism, 71

GALILEE, 190
Gamala, siege of, 194
Gamaliel—ignored by Josephus, 226
Genesis, 234
George Syncellus, 23
Gerizim, Temple on, 50
Gessius Florus, 169
Gezer, 113
Gilead, 105
Glaphyra, 144
Gorgias, 102
Gospels, 69
Grammarian (meaning of), 27
Gratus, Valerius, 162
Greek hostility to Jews, 19

HECATAEUS of Abdera, 24
Hecataeus of Miletus, 24
Helena, Queen, 81
Hermippus, 24
Herod the Great, xiv
  temple of, 43
  career of, 129 *et passim*
Herod the Tetrarch, 144
Herodias, 145
Herodotus, 20, 95
Hieroglyphics, Josephus ignorant of, 24
Hezekiah, robber chief, 91
High Priests, 47, App. A
Hiram, 23
Homer, 20
Hyrcanus, son of Joseph, 98
Hyrcanus, John, 114

IDUMAEANS, 201
India, 171
Irenaeus, orator, 142
Isaac, 234
Isaiah, 242
Izates, 81

JACOB, son of Judas of Galilee, 91
Jaddua, High Priest, 50
James, brother of the Christ, 169
Jamnia, 113
Jason, 103
Jazer, 104
Jeremiah, 242
Jericho, 195
Jerome, St., 254
Jesus, the Christ, 88
Jesus, son of Sapphias, 10
Jesus, brother of the High Priest, 50
Jesus or Jason, 52
Jewish history, 226
Jewish observance practised by Gentiles, 32
Jews all agreed on religion, 31
Johanan ben Zakkai ignored by Josephus, 226
John Hyrcanus, 115
John the publican, 182
John of Gischala, 9, 201
Jehoiada, High Priest, 48
Jonathan, High Priest, 107
Joppa, 113, 193
Jordan, 191
Joseph, son of Tobias, 51, 96
Josephus as an historian, xiii
  neglected by Jews, xii
  his *Life*, 3
  War, 7
  Antiquities, 246
  Apion, 3
  writes for Gentiles, 66
  visits Rome, 6
  pedigree, 5
  education, 5
  Galilee, 8
  dream of, 12
  privileges from Rome, 18
  religion of, 33
  describes the Temple, 42
  on tradition, 63
  compared with Philo, 244
  his speeches, 16, 209
  and St. Luke, 259
Josiah, 39
Jotapata, siege of, 14
Judaea, 95
Judaism saved by its students, 70
Judas, an Essene, 79

Judas, son of Hezekiah, 91
Judas of Galilee, 91
Judas the Maccabee, 102 *et passim*
Judas the Gaulonite, 91
Justus of Tiberias, 9

KLAUSNER, Dr., 119
Kennett, Prof., 55

LAQUEUR, R., 3
Law, Jewish, 58 *et passim*
Legalism, 68
Legati, 156 *et passim*
Leontopolis, temple at, 58, 224
Lights, feast of, 103
Livy, 253
Loisy, M., 272
Lugudunum, 148
Luke, St., 56
Lysanias, 265
Lysias, Syrian general, 102

MACCABEES, 101 *et passim*
Maccabees, books of, xiv, 106
Magnesia, battle of, 109
Mahaffy, late Dr., 172
Manaem, 79
Manasseh, High Priest, 51
Manetho, 22
Mariamne, wife of Herod, 131
Marsus, 159
Masada, 224
Maspha, 104
Massacres and reprisals, 184
Mattathias, 101
Menahem, son of Judas of Galilee, 91
Menander of Ephesus, 23
Menelaus, 103
Mercenaries, 115
Messiah, 84 *et passim*
Middoth, 41
Mithradates, 122
Modin, 100
Moore, Dr. G. F., 83
Moses, 23, 30, 235
Mutilation of ears, 130

NABOPOLASSAR, 24
Nahardea, 175
Narbata, 183
Nebuchadrezzar, 242
Nehemiah, 48, 95
Nero, 195
New Testament, 259 *passim*